GARFIELD
DONUT DISTURB

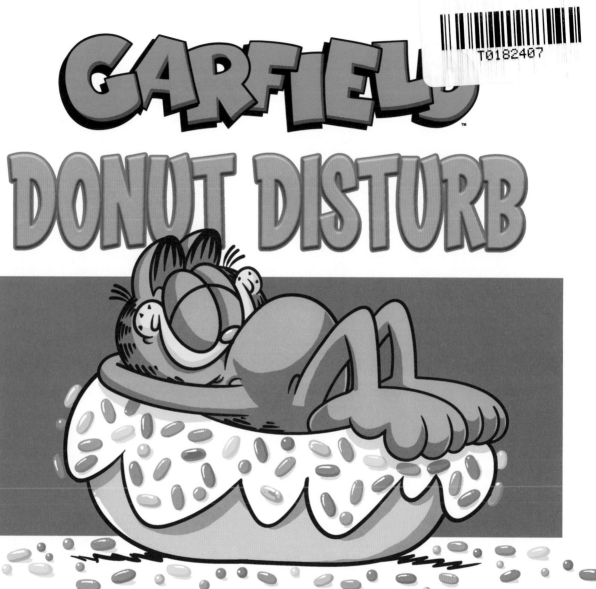

BY JIM DAVIS

Random House Worlds ● New York

A Random House Worlds Trade Paperback Original

Based on the Garfield® characters created by Jim Davis

Published in the United States by Random House Worlds, an imprint of Random House,
a division of Penguin Random House LLC, New York.

All of the comics in this work have been previously published.

ISBN 978-0-593-87333-5
Ebook ISBN 978-0-593-87334-2

Printed in China on acid-free paper

randomhousebooks.com

T#1247678

9 8 7 6 5 4 3 2 1

nickelodeon

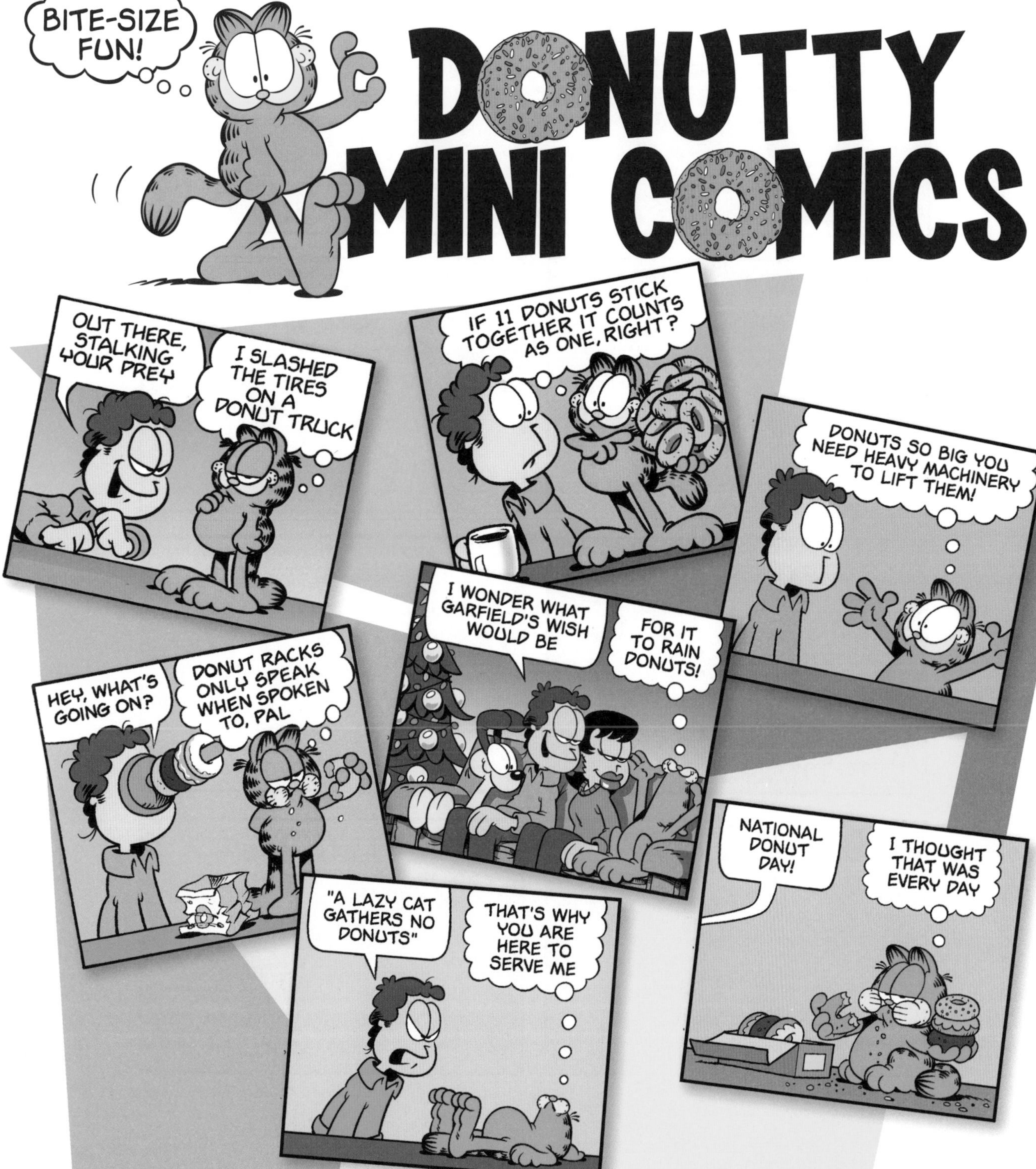
BITE-SIZE FUN!
DONUTTY MINI COMICS
OUT THERE, STALKING YOUR PREY
I SLASHED THE TIRES ON A DONUT TRUCK
IF 11 DONUTS STICK TOGETHER IT COUNTS AS ONE, RIGHT?
DONUTS SO BIG YOU NEED HEAVY MACHINERY TO LIFT THEM!
HEY, WHAT'S GOING ON?
DONUT RACKS ONLY SPEAK WHEN SPOKEN TO, PAL
I WONDER WHAT GARFIELD'S WISH WOULD BE
FOR IT TO RAIN DONUTS!
"A LAZY CAT GATHERS NO DONUTS"
THAT'S WHY YOU ARE HERE TO SERVE ME
NATIONAL DONUT DAY!
I THOUGHT THAT WAS EVERY DAY

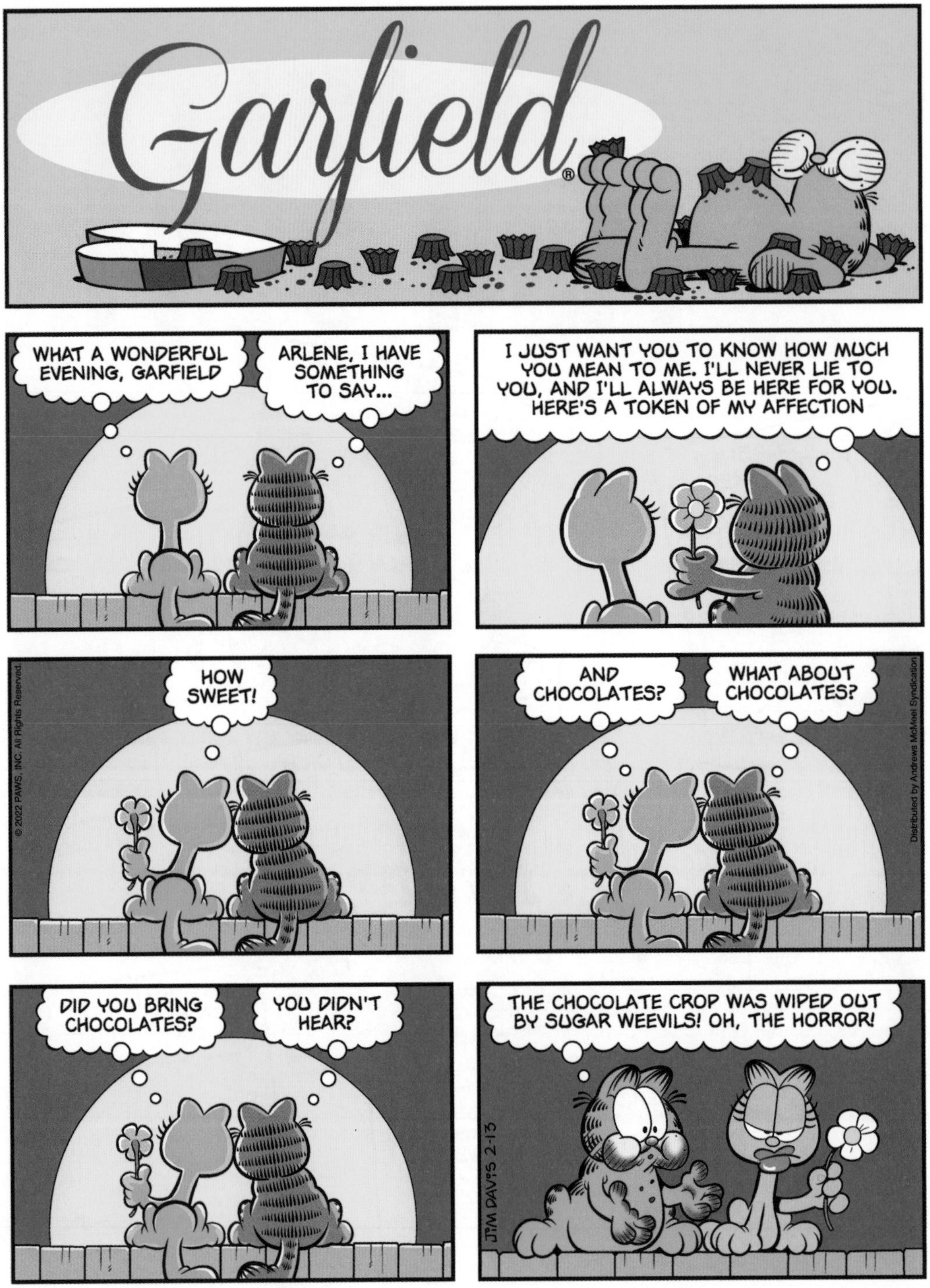

Garfield®
WHAT A WONDERFUL EVENING, GARFIELD
ARLENE, I HAVE SOMETHING TO SAY...
I JUST WANT YOU TO KNOW HOW MUCH YOU MEAN TO ME. I'LL NEVER LIE TO YOU, AND I'LL ALWAYS BE HERE FOR YOU. HERE'S A TOKEN OF MY AFFECTION
HOW SWEET!
AND CHOCOLATES?
WHAT ABOUT CHOCOLATES?
DID YOU BRING CHOCOLATES?
YOU DIDN'T HEAR?
THE CHOCOLATE CROP WAS WIPED OUT BY SUGAR WEEVILS! OH, THE HORROR!
JIM DAVIS 2-13

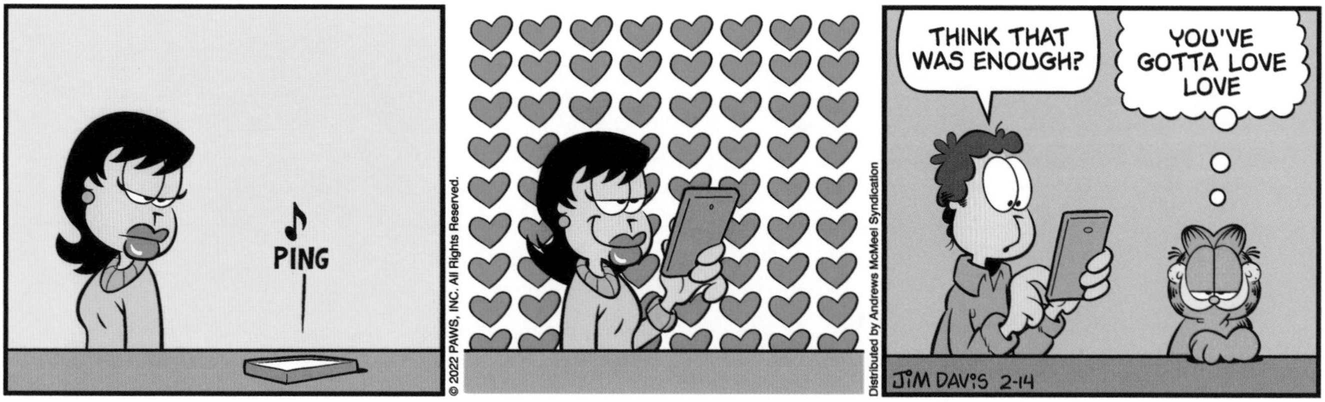
PING
© 2022 PAWS, INC. All Rights Reserved.
Distributed by Andrews McMeel Syndication
THINK THAT WAS ENOUGH?
YOU'VE GOTTA LOVE LOVE
JIM DAVIS 2-14

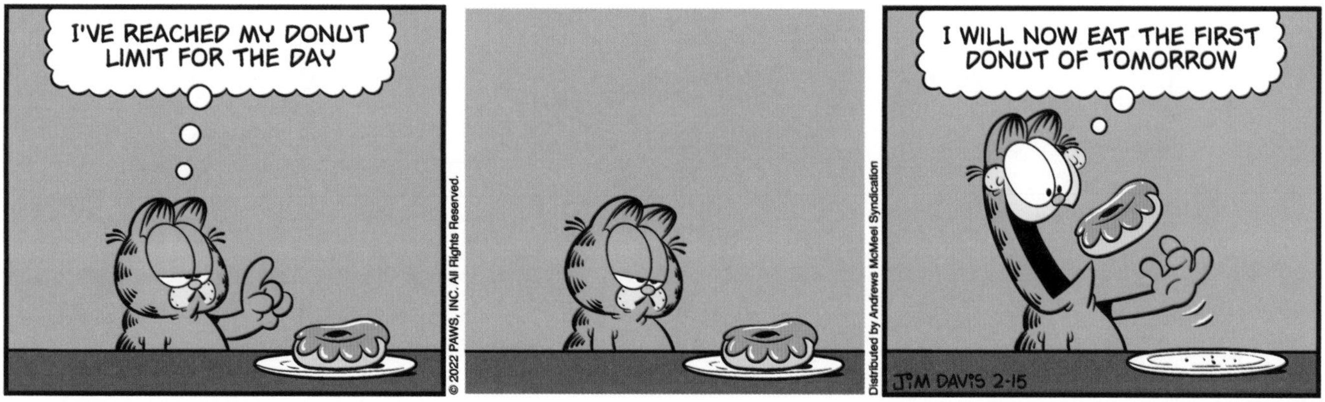
I'VE REACHED MY DONUT LIMIT FOR THE DAY
© 2022 PAWS, INC. All Rights Reserved.
Distributed by Andrews McMeel Syndication
I WILL NOW EAT THE FIRST DONUT OF TOMORROW
JIM DAVIS 2-15

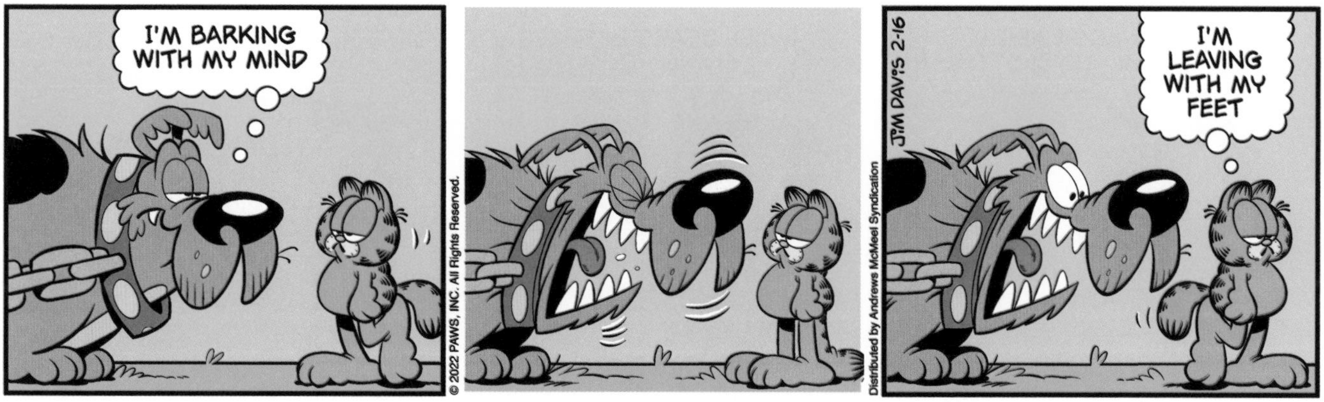
I'M BARKING WITH MY MIND
© 2022 PAWS, INC. All Rights Reserved.
JIM DAVIS 2-16
Distributed by Andrews McMeel Syndication
I'M LEAVING WITH MY FEET

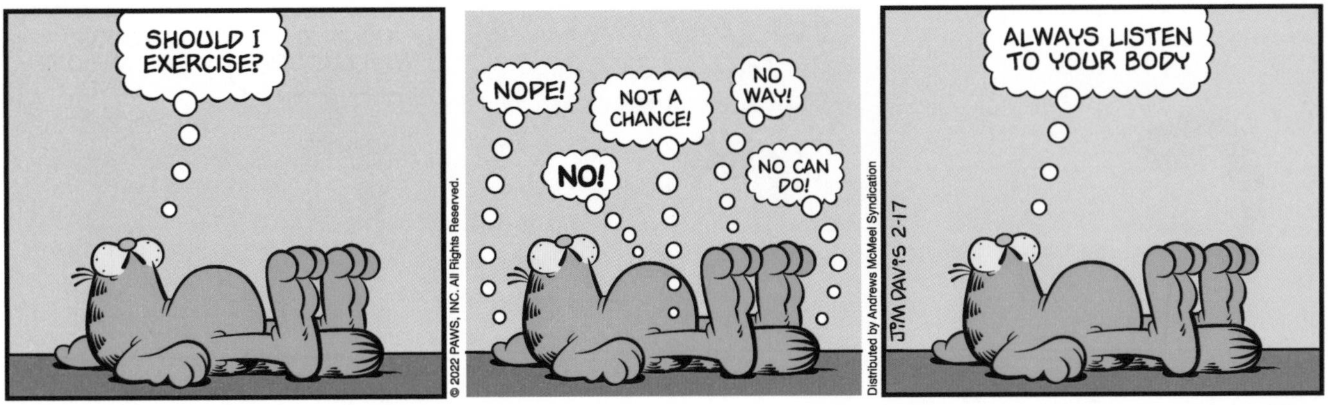
SHOULD I EXERCISE?
NOPE!
NO!
NOT A CHANCE!
NO WAY!
NO CAN DO!
ALWAYS LISTEN TO YOUR BODY
© 2022 PAWS, INC. All Rights Reserved.
Distributed by Andrews McMeel Syndication
JIM DAVIS 2-17

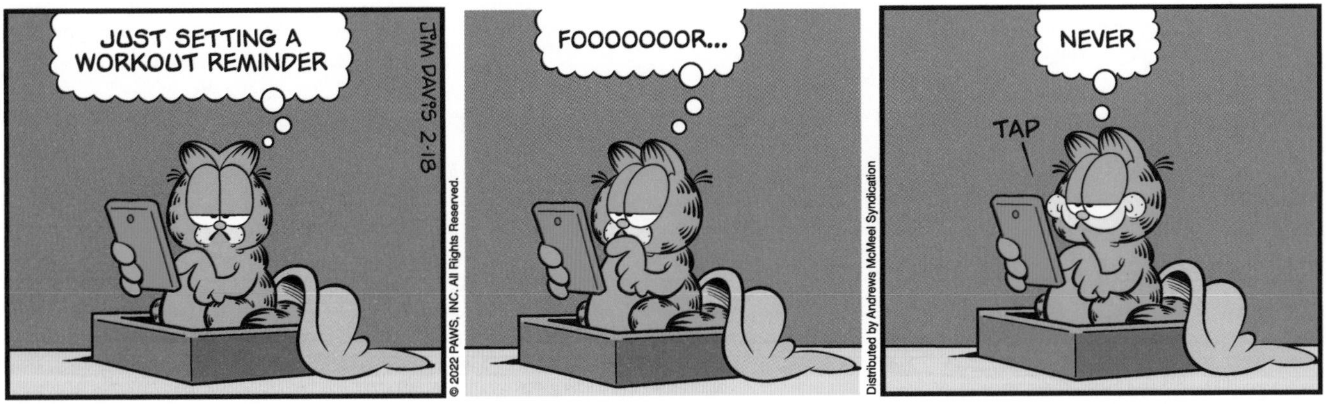
JUST SETTING A WORKOUT REMINDER
FOOOOOOOR...
TAP
NEVER
JIM DAVIS 2-18
© 2022 PAWS, INC. All Rights Reserved.
Distributed by Andrews McMeel Syndication

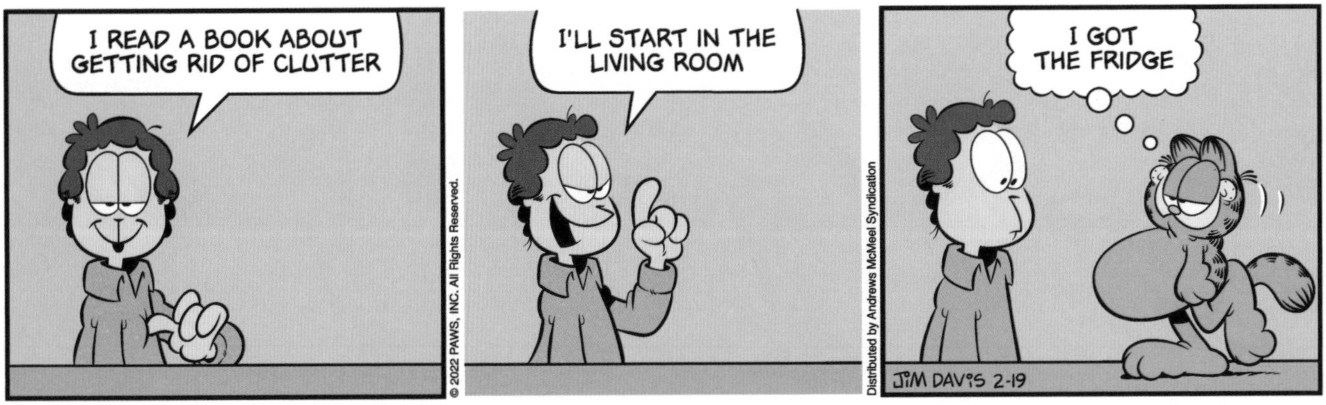
I READ A BOOK ABOUT GETTING RID OF CLUTTER
I'LL START IN THE LIVING ROOM
I GOT THE FRIDGE
© 2022 PAWS, INC. All Rights Reserved.
Distributed by Andrews McMeel Syndication
JIM DAVIS 2-19

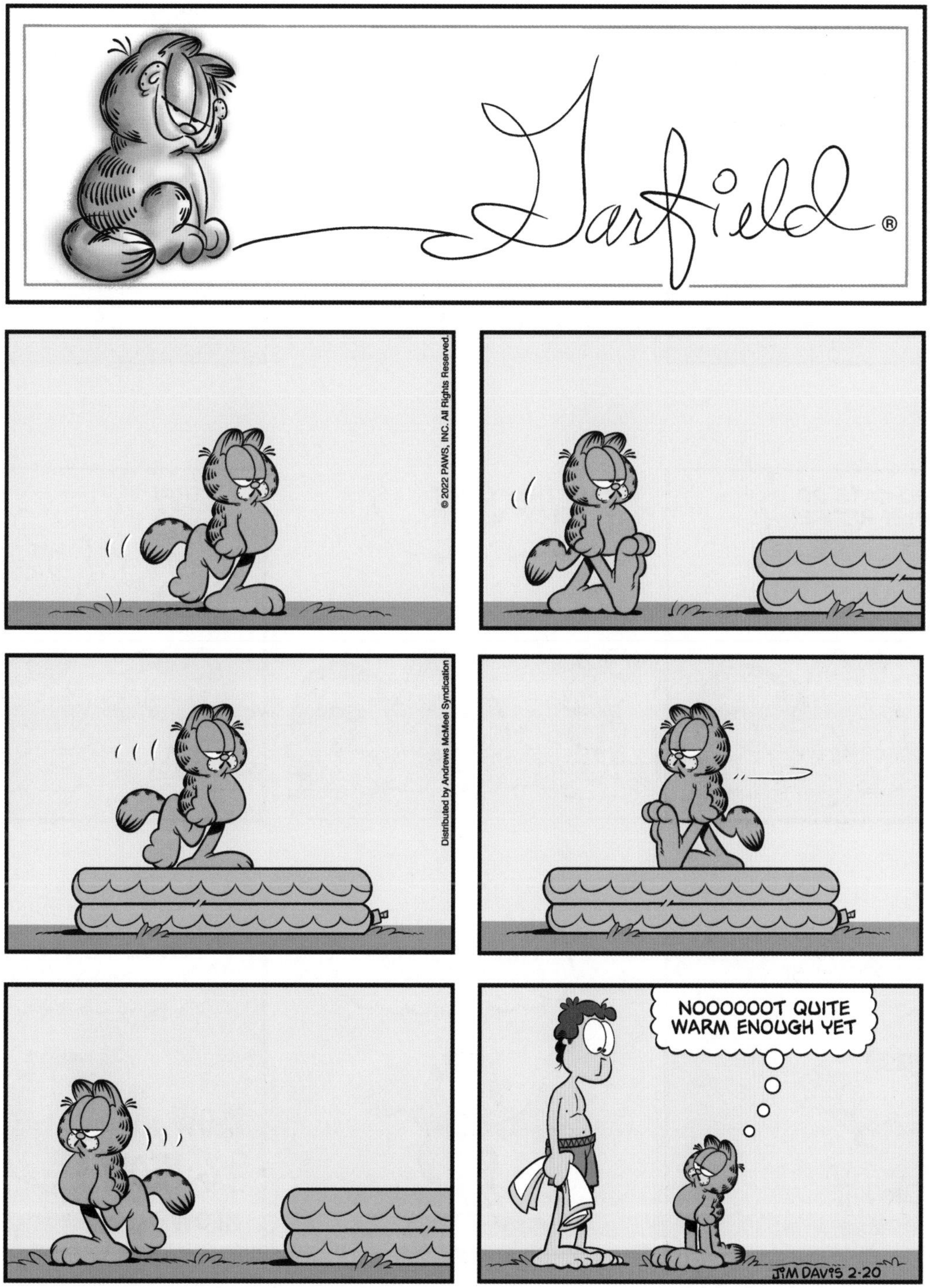
Garfield®
© 2022 PAWS, INC. All Rights Reserved.
Distributed by Andrews McMeel Syndication
NOOOOOOT QUITE WARM ENOUGH YET
JIM DAVIS 2-20

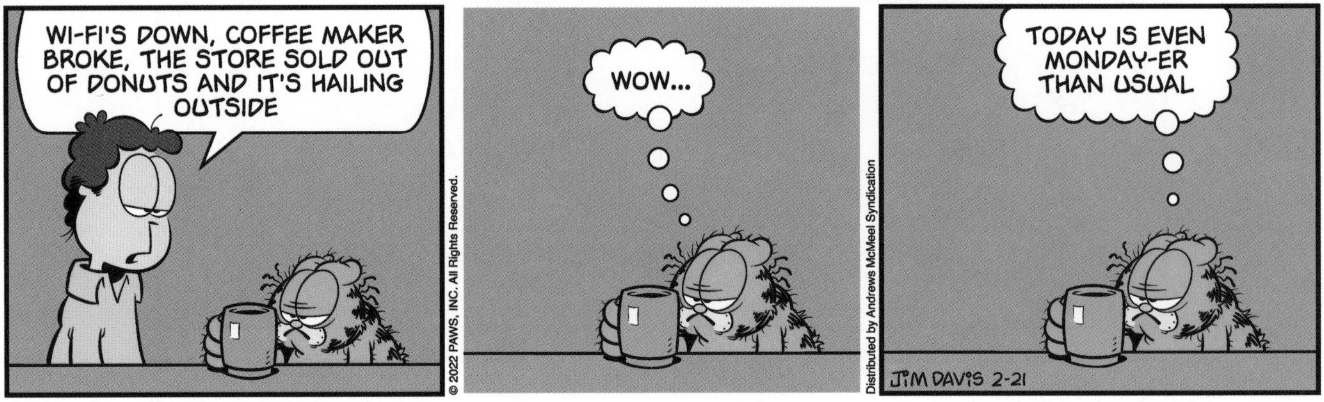
WI-FI'S DOWN, COFFEE MAKER BROKE, THE STORE SOLD OUT OF DONUTS AND IT'S HAILING OUTSIDE
WOW...
TODAY IS EVEN MONDAY-ER THAN USUAL
© 2022 PAWS, INC. All Rights Reserved.
Distributed by Andrews McMeel Syndication
JIM DAVIS 2-21

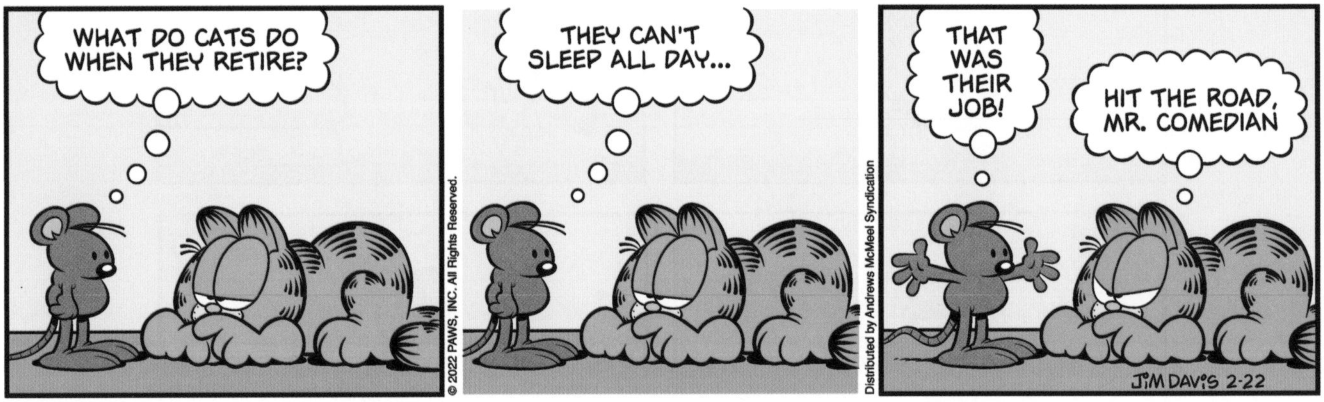
WHAT DO CATS DO WHEN THEY RETIRE?
THEY CAN'T SLEEP ALL DAY...
THAT WAS THEIR JOB!
HIT THE ROAD, MR. COMEDIAN
© 2022 PAWS, INC. All Rights Reserved.
Distributed by Andrews McMeel Syndication
JIM DAVIS 2-22

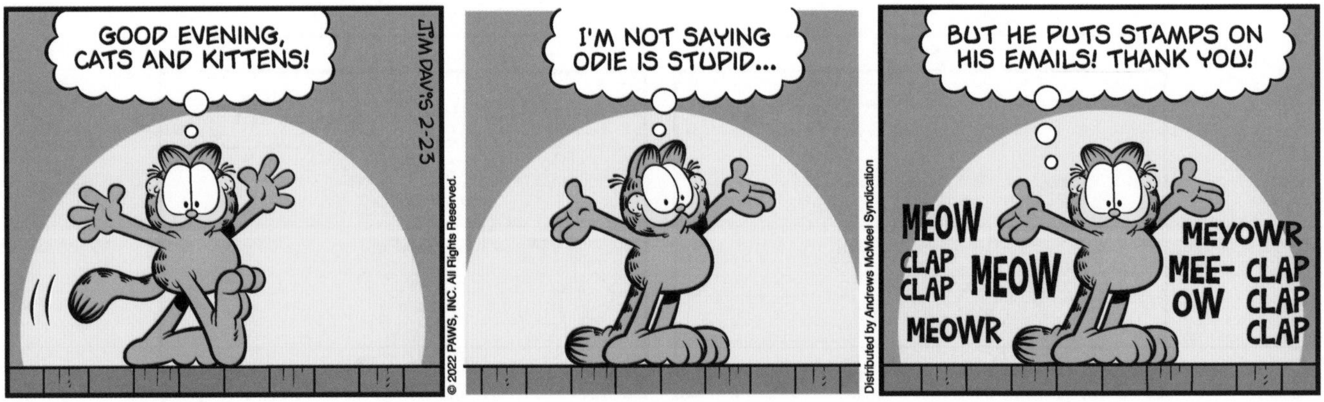
GOOD EVENING, CATS AND KITTENS!
JIM DAVIS 2-23
I'M NOT SAYING ODIE IS STUPID...
BUT HE PUTS STAMPS ON HIS EMAILS! THANK YOU!
MEOW
CLAP CLAP
MEOW
MEOWR
MEYOWR
MEE-OW
CLAP CLAP CLAP
© 2022 PAWS, INC. All Rights Reserved.
Distributed by Andrews McMeel Syndication

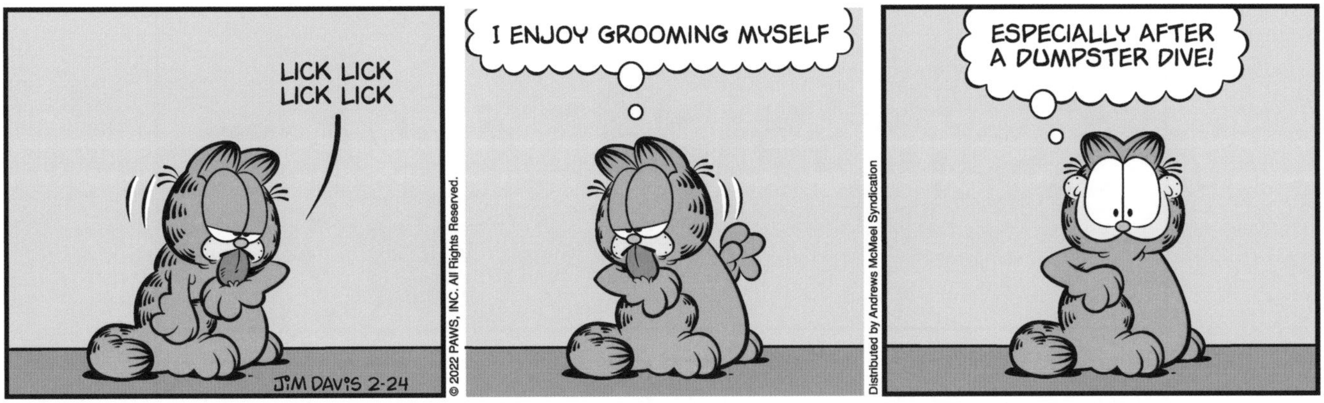
LICK LICK
LICK LICK
JIM DAVIS 2-24
© 2022 PAWS, INC. All Rights Reserved.
I ENJOY GROOMING MYSELF
Distributed by Andrews McMeel Syndication
ESPECIALLY AFTER A DUMPSTER DIVE!

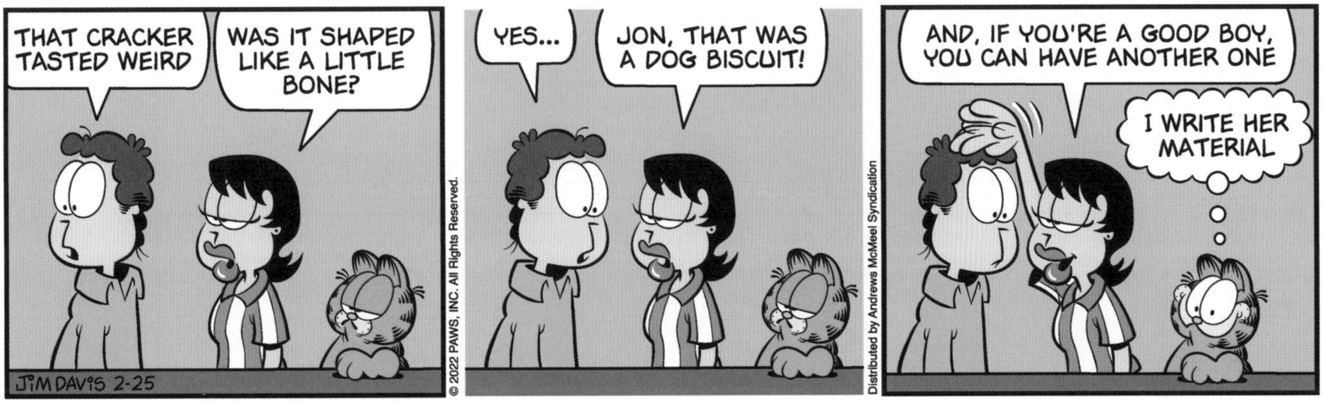
THAT CRACKER TASTED WEIRD
WAS IT SHAPED LIKE A LITTLE BONE?
JIM DAVIS 2-25
© 2022 PAWS, INC. All Rights Reserved.
YES...
JON, THAT WAS A DOG BISCUIT!
Distributed by Andrews McMeel Syndication
AND, IF YOU'RE A GOOD BOY, YOU CAN HAVE ANOTHER ONE
I WRITE HER MATERIAL

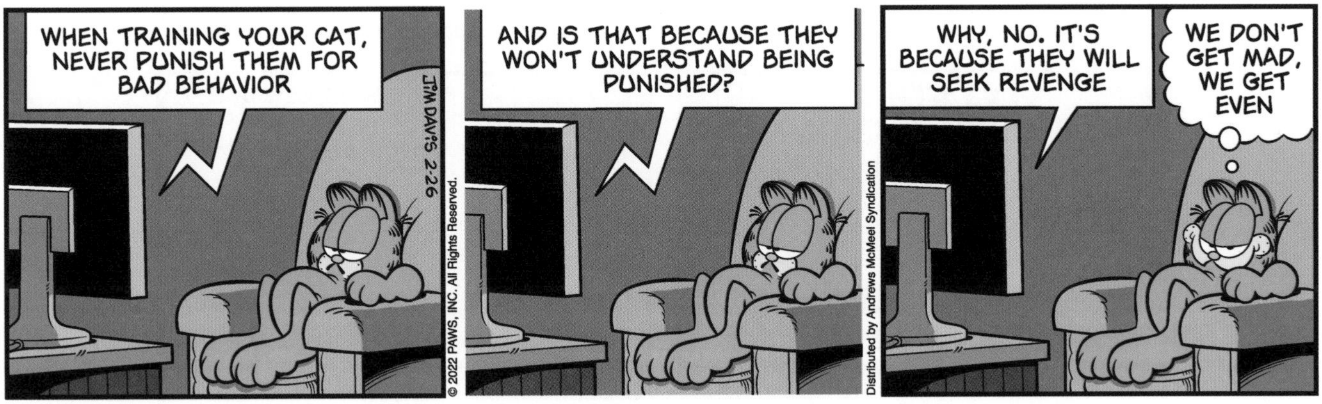
WHEN TRAINING YOUR CAT, NEVER PUNISH THEM FOR BAD BEHAVIOR
JIM DAVIS 2-26
© 2022 PAWS, INC. All Rights Reserved.
AND IS THAT BECAUSE THEY WON'T UNDERSTAND BEING PUNISHED?
Distributed by Andrews McMeel Syndication
WHY, NO. IT'S BECAUSE THEY WILL SEEK REVENGE
WE DON'T GET MAD, WE GET EVEN

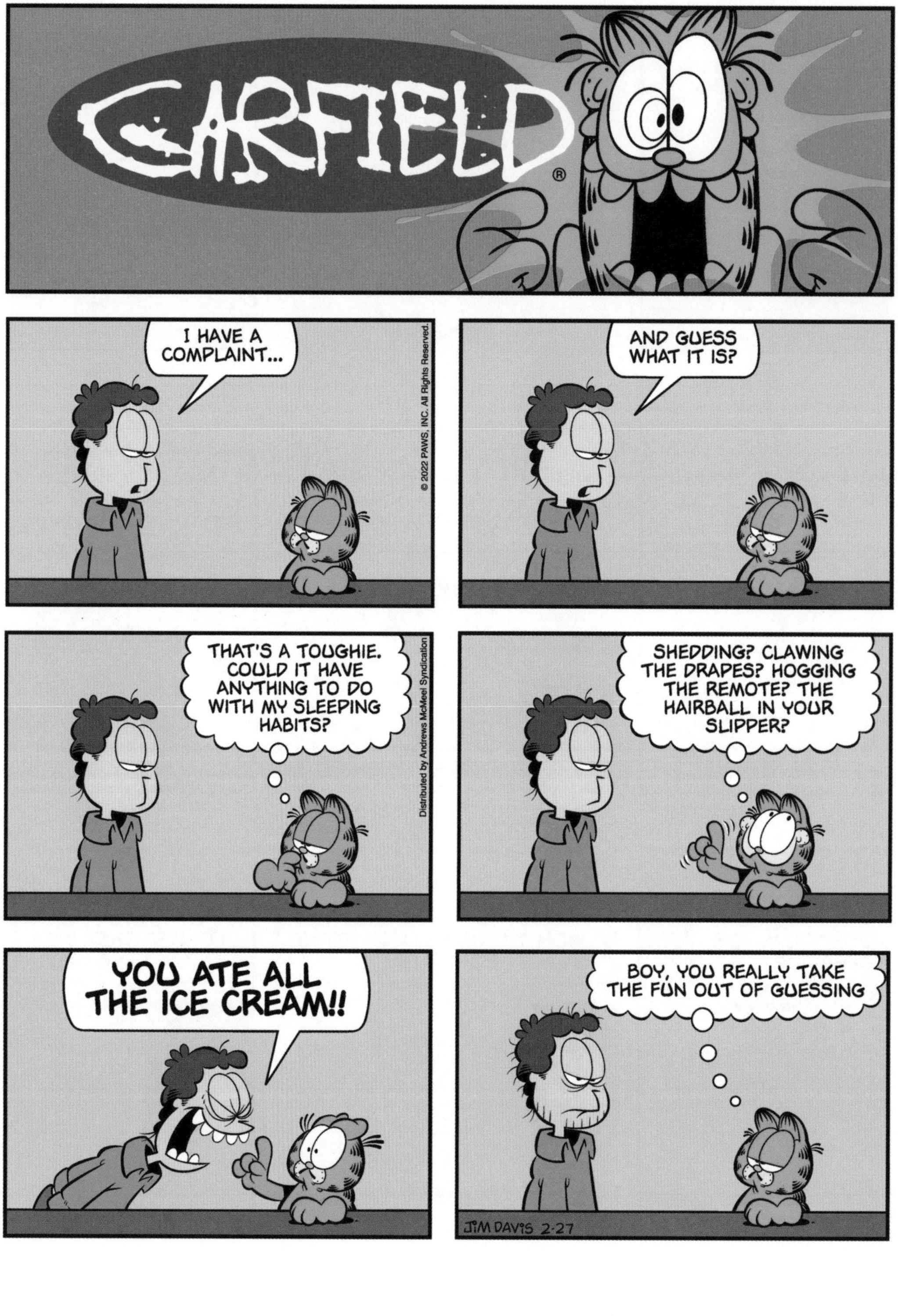
GARFIELD®
I HAVE A COMPLAINT...
© 2022 PAWS, INC. All Rights Reserved.
AND GUESS WHAT IT IS?
THAT'S A TOUGHIE. COULD IT HAVE ANYTHING TO DO WITH MY SLEEPING HABITS?
Distributed by Andrews McMeel Syndication
SHEDDING? CLAWING THE DRAPES? HOGGING THE REMOTE? THE HAIRBALL IN YOUR SLIPPER?
YOU ATE ALL THE ICE CREAM!!
BOY, YOU REALLY TAKE THE FUN OUT OF GUESSING
JIM DAVIS 2-27

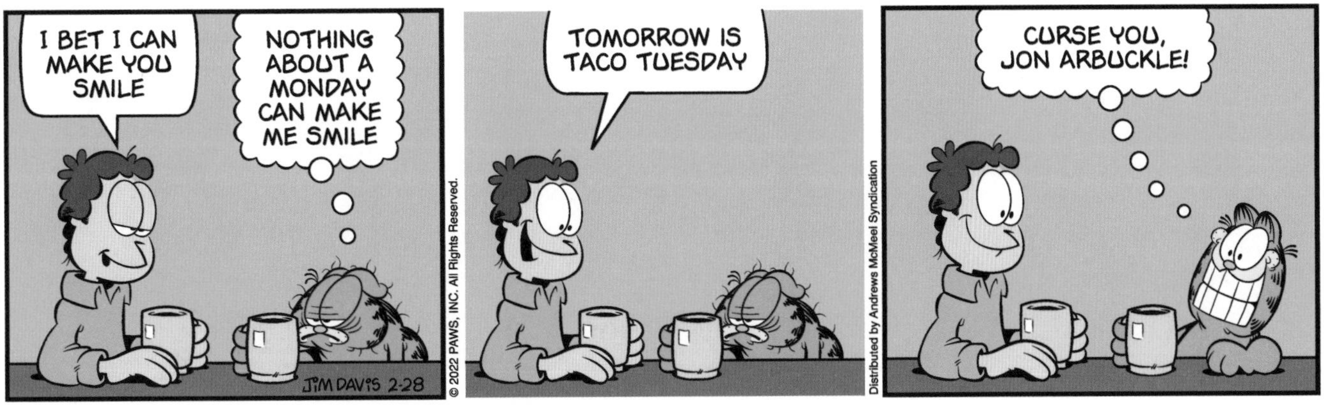
I BET I CAN MAKE YOU SMILE
NOTHING ABOUT A MONDAY CAN MAKE ME SMILE
JIM DAVIS 2-28
© 2022 PAWS, INC. All Rights Reserved.
TOMORROW IS TACO TUESDAY
Distributed by Andrews McMeel Syndication
CURSE YOU, JON ARBUCKLE!

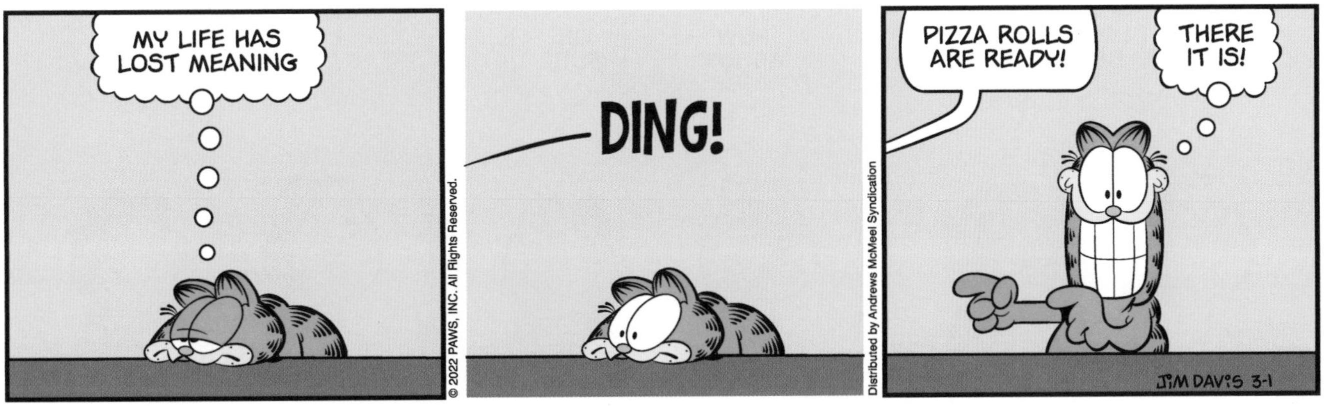
MY LIFE HAS LOST MEANING
© 2022 PAWS, INC. All Rights Reserved.
DING!
Distributed by Andrews McMeel Syndication
PIZZA ROLLS ARE READY!
THERE IT IS!
JIM DAVIS 3-1

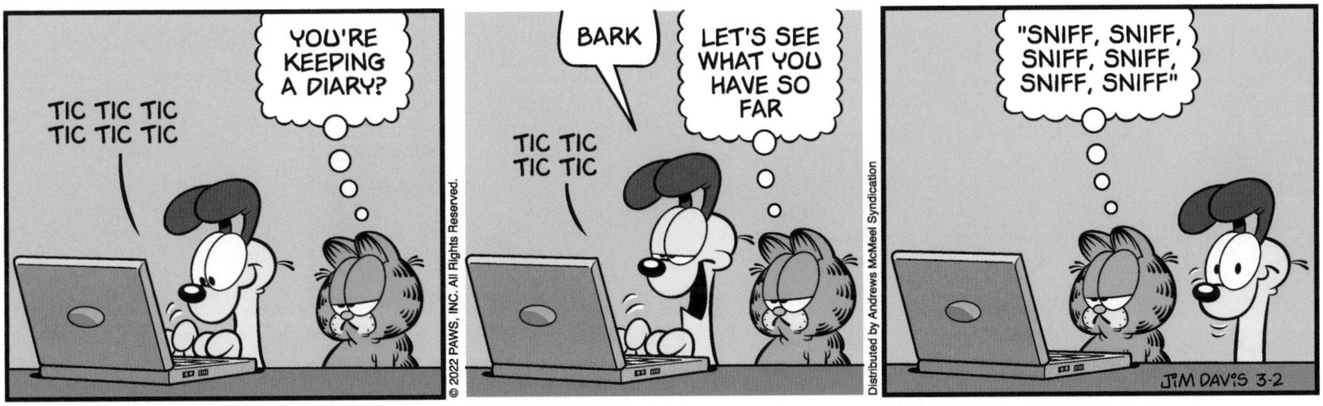
TIC TIC TIC TIC TIC TIC
YOU'RE KEEPING A DIARY?
© 2022 PAWS, INC. All Rights Reserved.
BARK
LET'S SEE WHAT YOU HAVE SO FAR
TIC TIC TIC TIC
Distributed by Andrews McMeel Syndication
"SNIFF, SNIFF, SNIFF, SNIFF, SNIFF, SNIFF"
JIM DAVIS 3-2

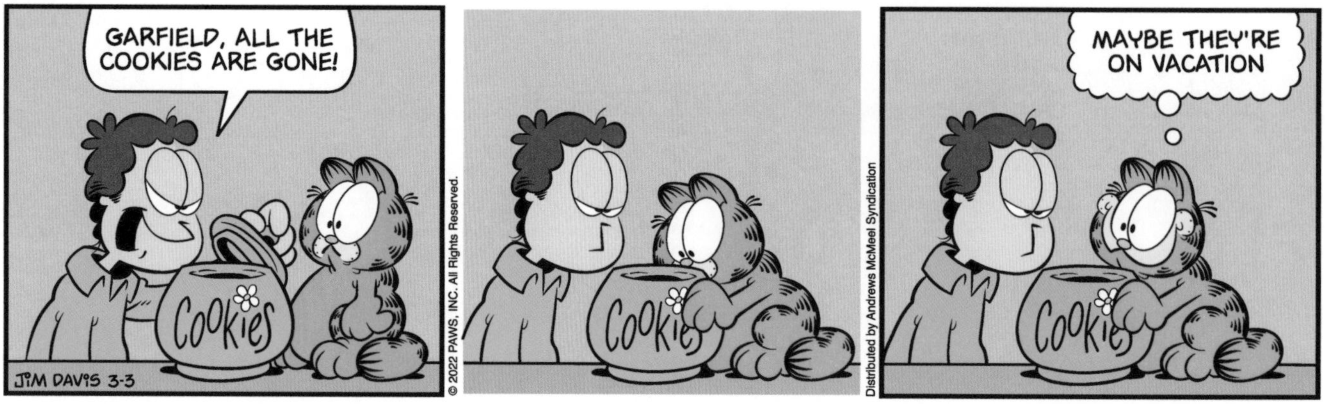
GARFIELD, ALL THE COOKIES ARE GONE!
JIM DAVIS 3-3
COOKIES
© 2022 PAWS, INC. All Rights Reserved.
MAYBE THEY'RE ON VACATION
Distributed by Andrews McMeel Syndication

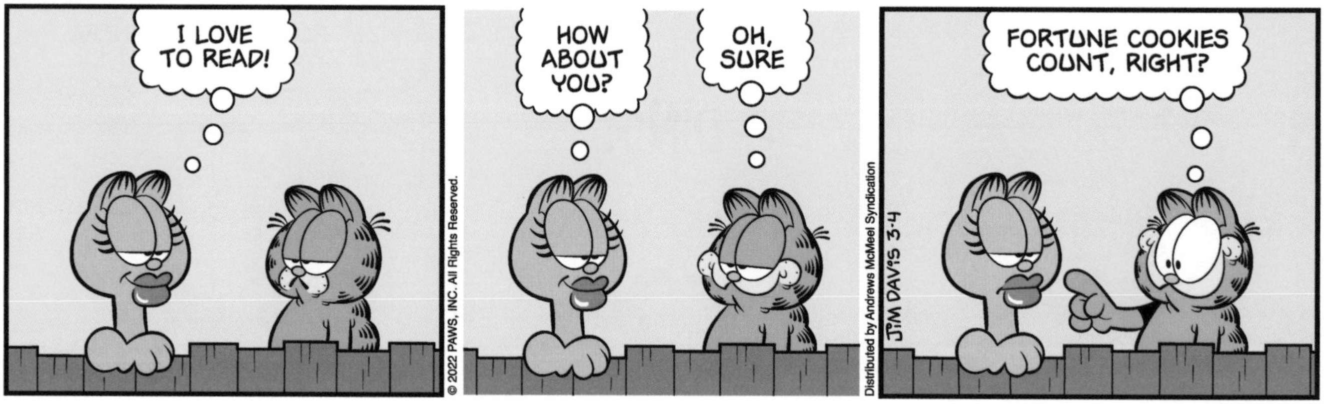
I LOVE TO READ!
© 2022 PAWS, INC. All Rights Reserved.
HOW ABOUT YOU?
OH, SURE
Distributed by Andrews McMeel Syndication
JIM DAVIS 3-4
FORTUNE COOKIES COUNT, RIGHT?

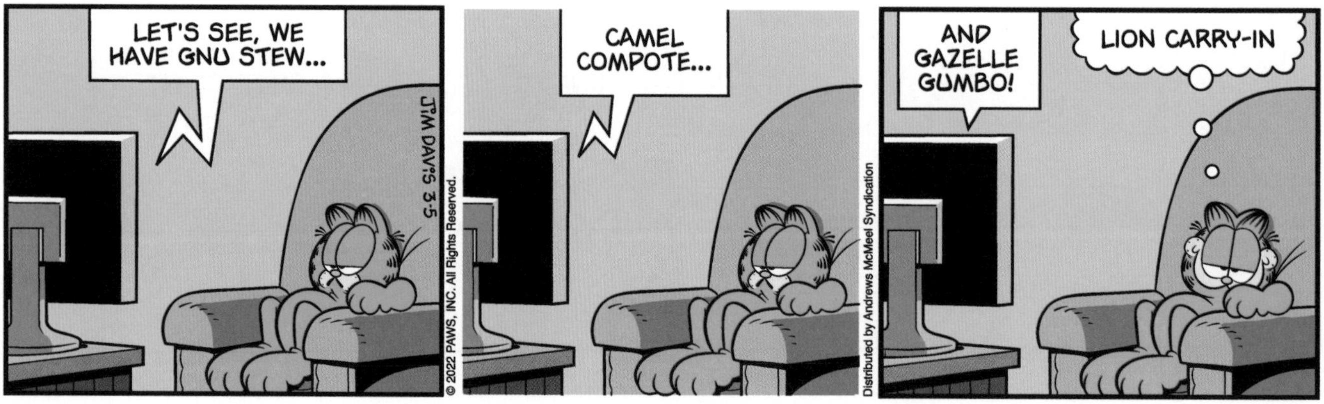
LET'S SEE, WE HAVE GNU STEW...
JIM DAVIS 3-5
© 2022 PAWS, INC. All Rights Reserved.
CAMEL COMPOTE...
Distributed by Andrews McMeel Syndication
AND GAZELLE GUMBO!
LION CARRY-IN

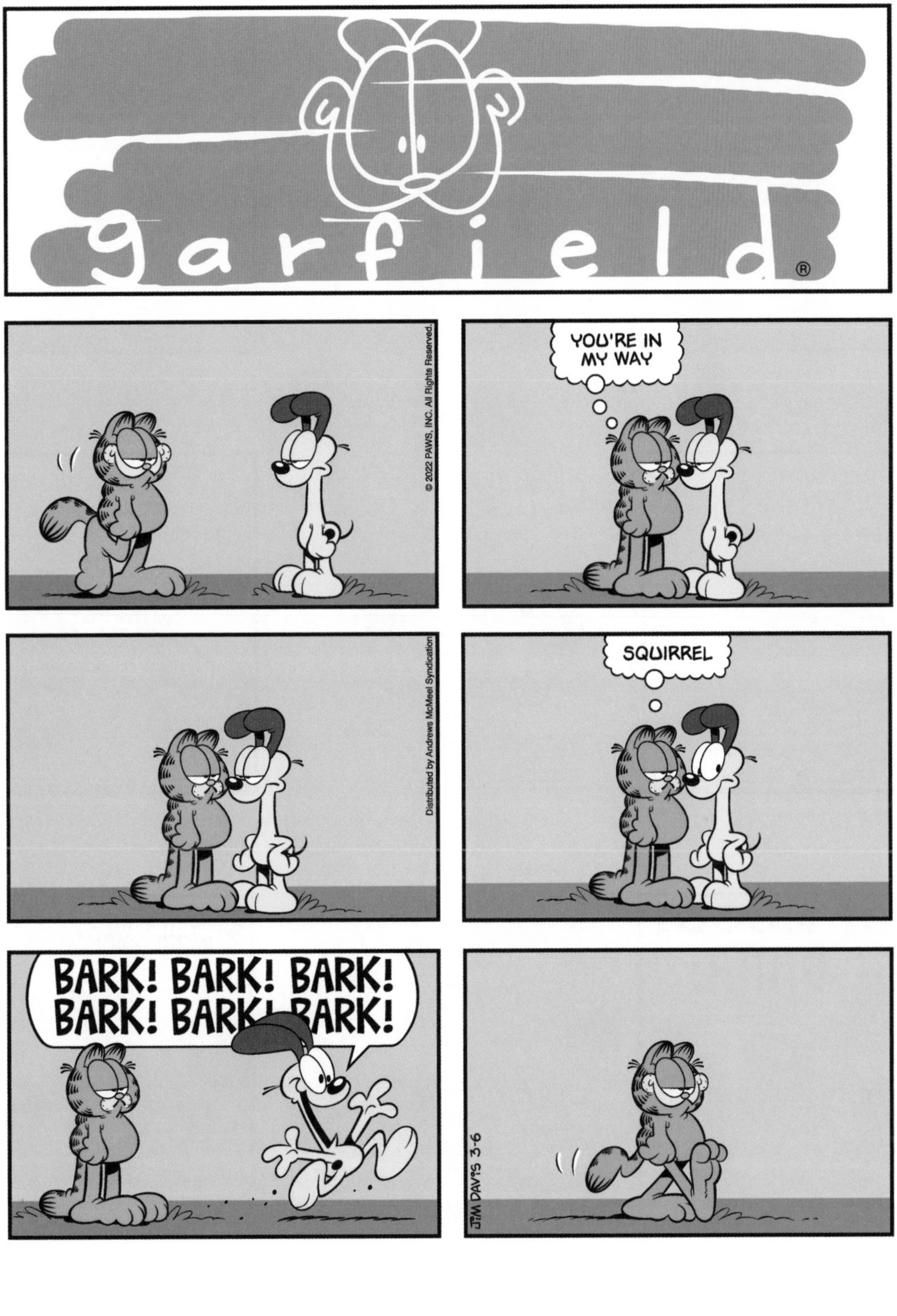
garfield®
© 2022 PAWS, INC. All Rights Reserved.
YOU'RE IN MY WAY
Distributed by Andrews McMeel Syndication
SQUIRREL
BARK! BARK! BARK!
BARK! BARK! BARK!
JIM DAVIS 3-6

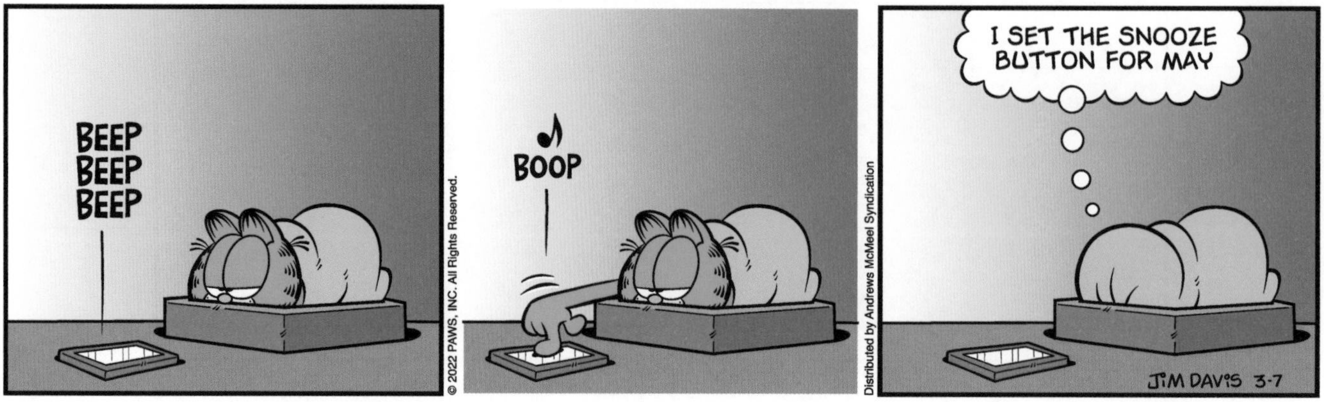
BEEP
BEEP
BEEP
BOOP
© 2022 PAWS, INC. All Rights Reserved.
I SET THE SNOOZE BUTTON FOR MAY
Distributed by Andrews McMeel Syndication
JIM DAVIS 3-7

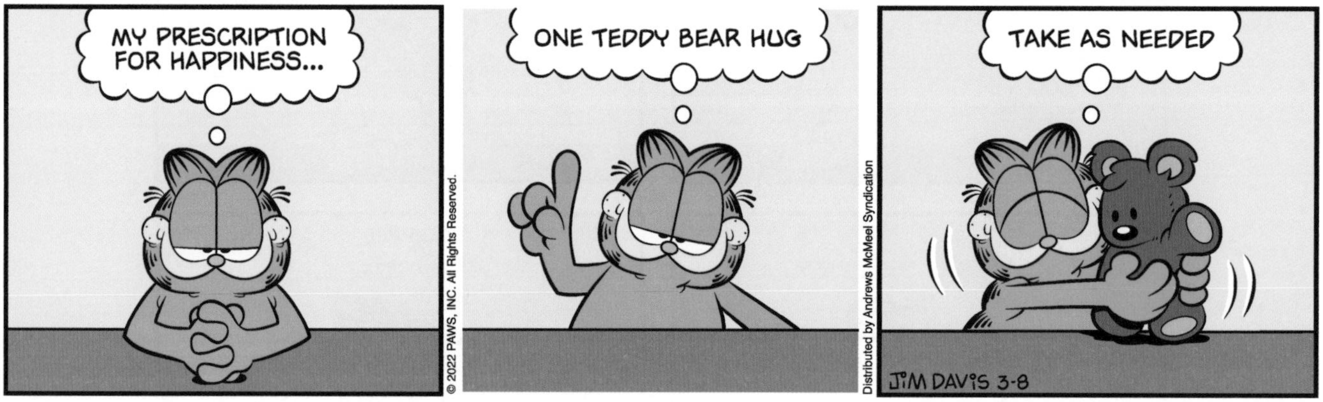
MY PRESCRIPTION FOR HAPPINESS...
© 2022 PAWS, INC. All Rights Reserved.
ONE TEDDY BEAR HUG
TAKE AS NEEDED
Distributed by Andrews McMeel Syndication
JIM DAVIS 3-8

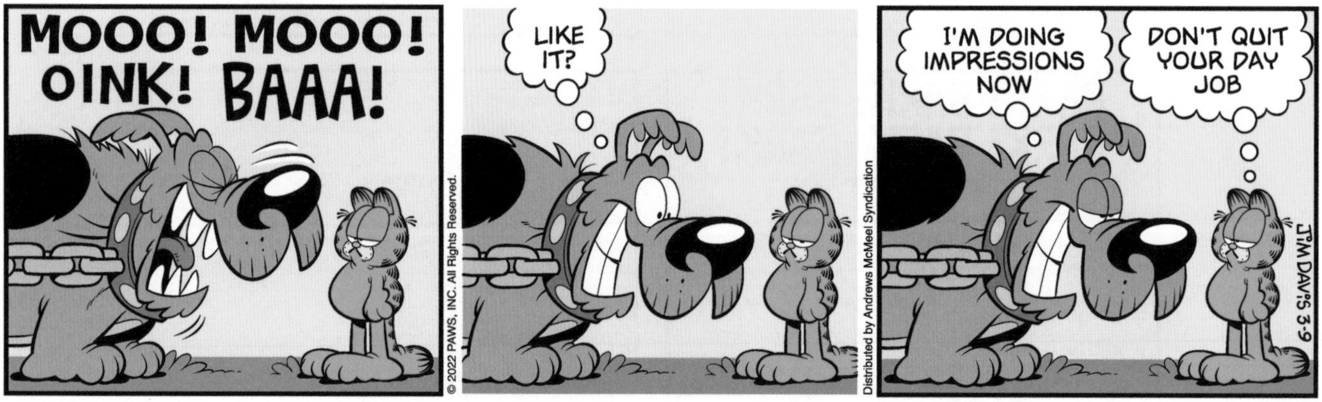
MOOO! MOOO!
OINK! BAAA!
© 2022 PAWS, INC. All Rights Reserved.
LIKE IT?
I'M DOING IMPRESSIONS NOW
DON'T QUIT YOUR DAY JOB
Distributed by Andrews McMeel Syndication
JIM DAVIS 3-9

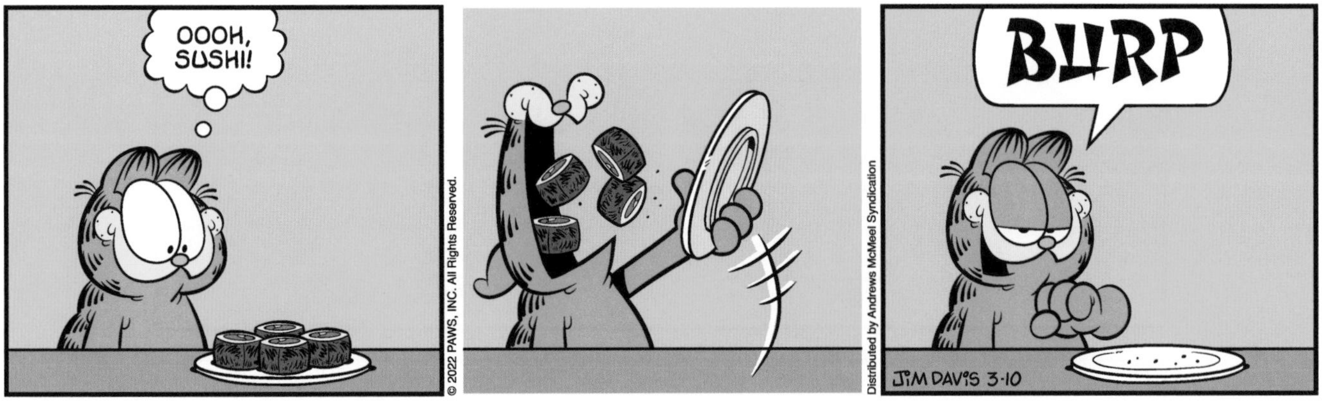
OOOH, SUSHI!
BURP
© 2022 PAWS, INC. All Rights Reserved.
Distributed by Andrews McMeel Syndication
JIM DAVIS 3-10

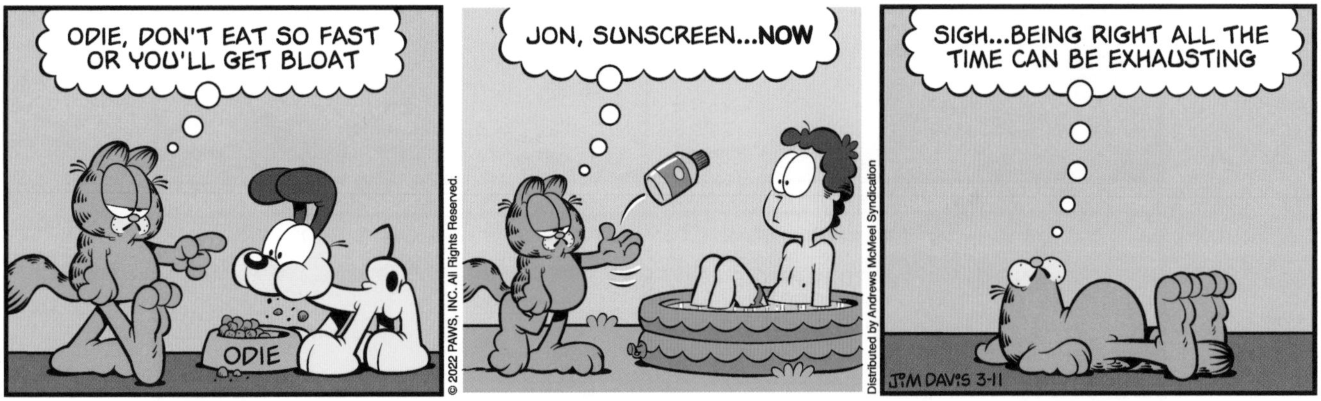
ODIE, DON'T EAT SO FAST OR YOU'LL GET BLOAT
ODIE
JON, SUNSCREEN...**NOW**
SIGH...BEING RIGHT ALL THE TIME CAN BE EXHAUSTING
© 2022 PAWS, INC. All Rights Reserved.
Distributed by Andrews McMeel Syndication
JIM DAVIS 3-11

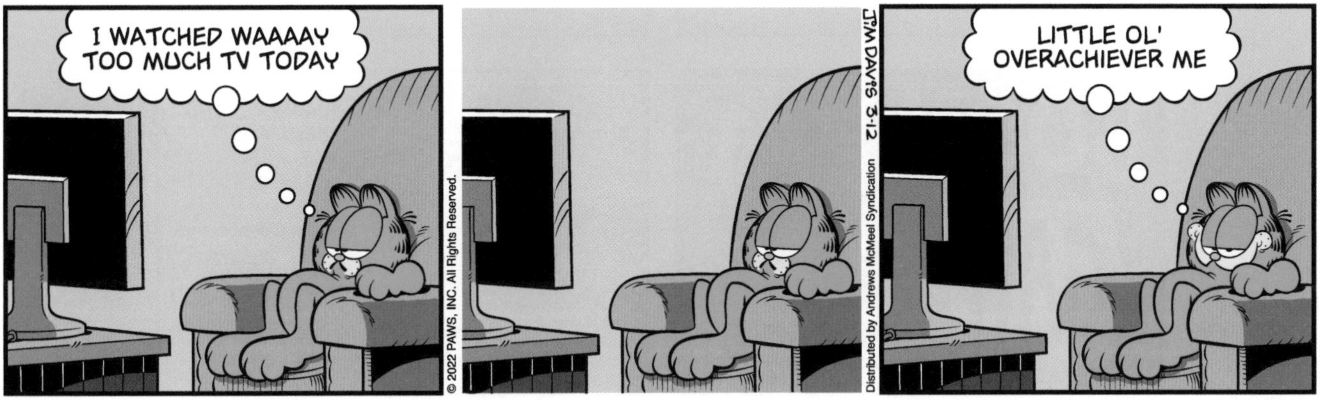
I WATCHED WAAAAY TOO MUCH TV TODAY
LITTLE OL' OVERACHIEVER ME
© 2022 PAWS, INC. All Rights Reserved.
Distributed by Andrews McMeel Syndication
JIM DAVIS 3-12

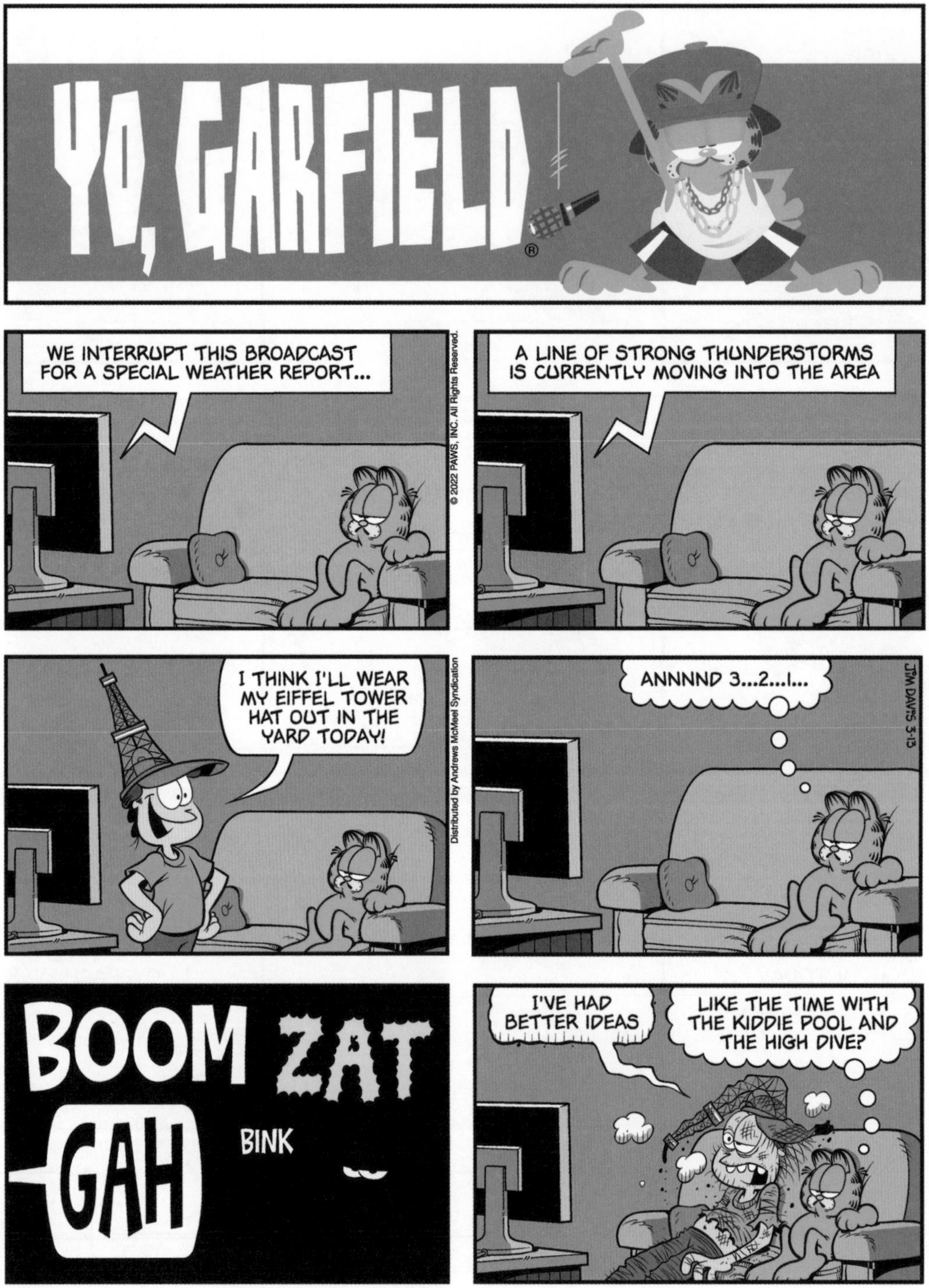
YO, GARFIELD
WE INTERRUPT THIS BROADCAST FOR A SPECIAL WEATHER REPORT...
A LINE OF STRONG THUNDERSTORMS IS CURRENTLY MOVING INTO THE AREA
I THINK I'LL WEAR MY EIFFEL TOWER HAT OUT IN THE YARD TODAY!
ANNNND 3...2...1...
BOOM
ZAT
GAH
BINK
I'VE HAD BETTER IDEAS
LIKE THE TIME WITH THE KIDDIE POOL AND THE HIGH DIVE?
© 2022 PAWS, INC. All Rights Reserved.
Distributed by Andrews McMeel Syndication
JiM DAVIS 3-13

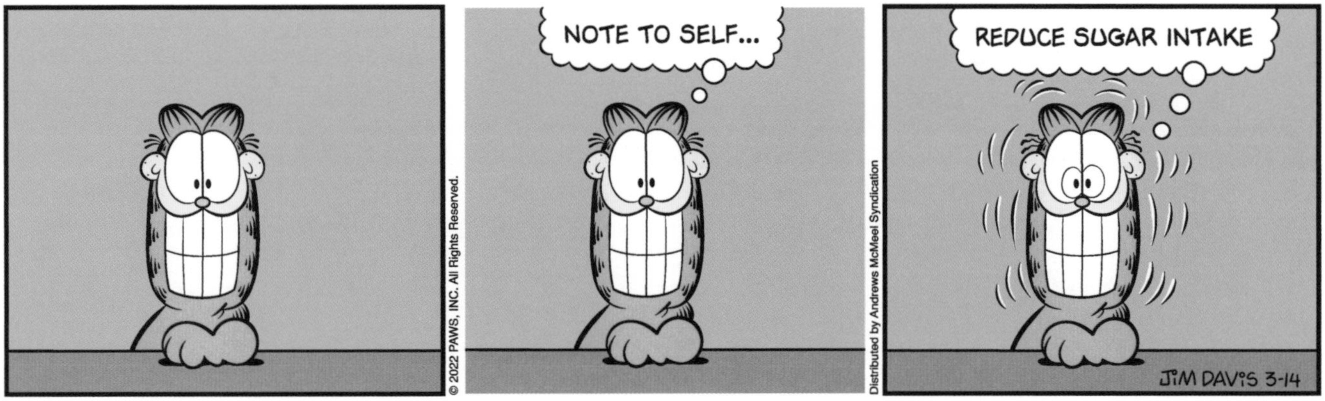
NOTE TO SELF...
REDUCE SUGAR INTAKE
JIM DAVIS 3-14
© 2022 PAWS, INC. All Rights Reserved.
Distributed by Andrews McMeel Syndication

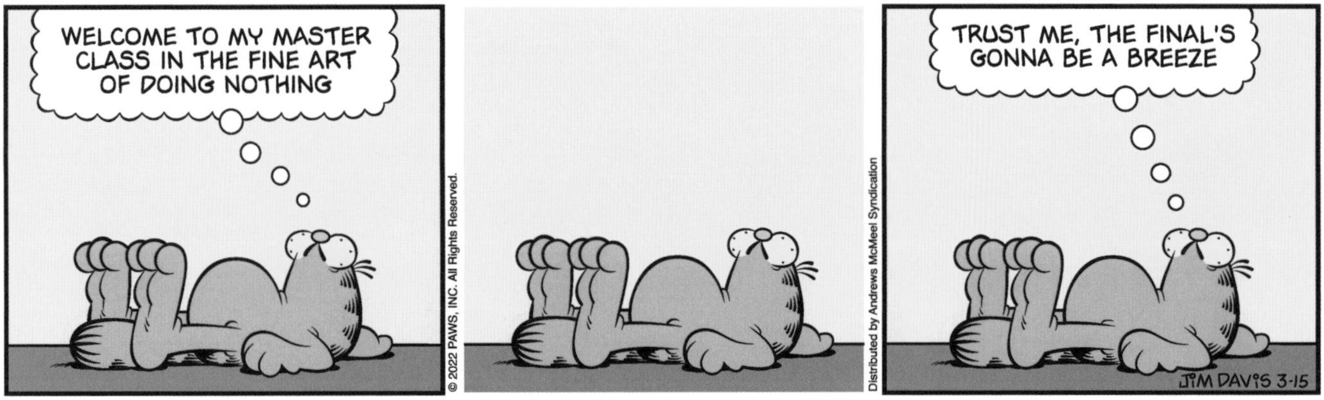
WELCOME TO MY MASTER CLASS IN THE FINE ART OF DOING NOTHING
TRUST ME, THE FINAL'S GONNA BE A BREEZE
JIM DAVIS 3-15
© 2022 PAWS, INC. All Rights Reserved.
Distributed by Andrews McMeel Syndication

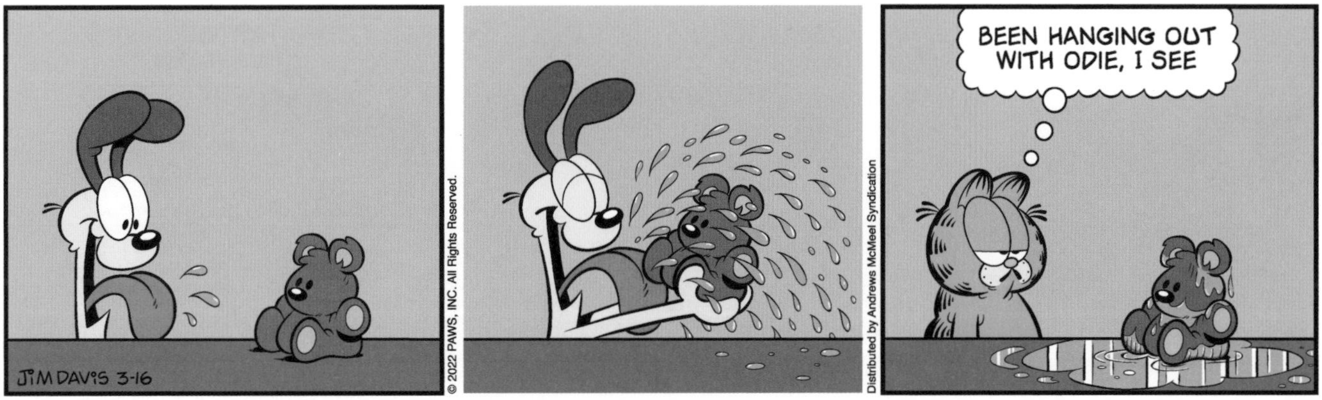
JIM DAVIS 3-16
BEEN HANGING OUT WITH ODIE, I SEE
© 2022 PAWS, INC. All Rights Reserved.
Distributed by Andrews McMeel Syndication

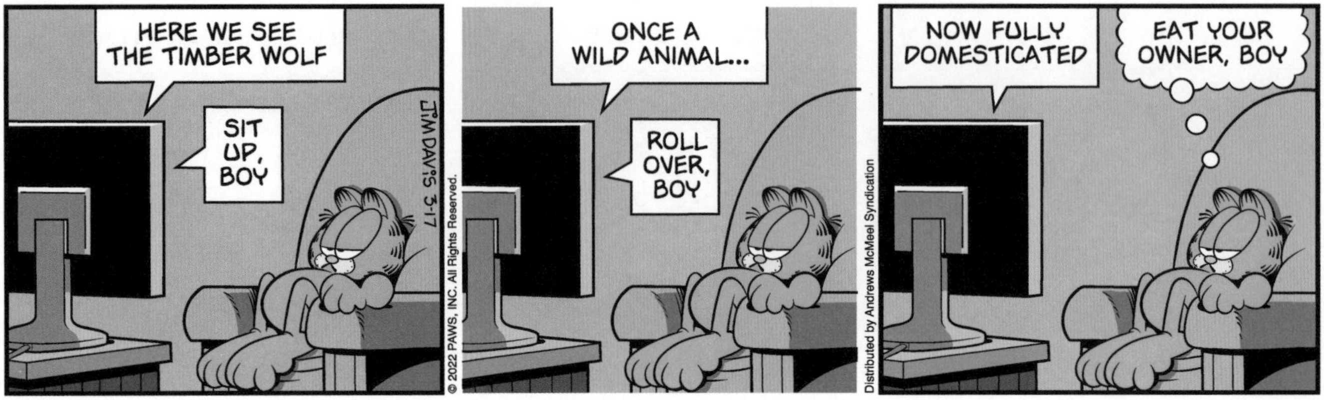
HERE WE SEE THE TIMBER WOLF
SIT UP, BOY
JIM DAVIS 3-17
© 2022 PAWS, INC. All Rights Reserved.
ONCE A WILD ANIMAL...
ROLL OVER, BOY
Distributed by Andrews McMeel Syndication
NOW FULLY DOMESTICATED
EAT YOUR OWNER, BOY

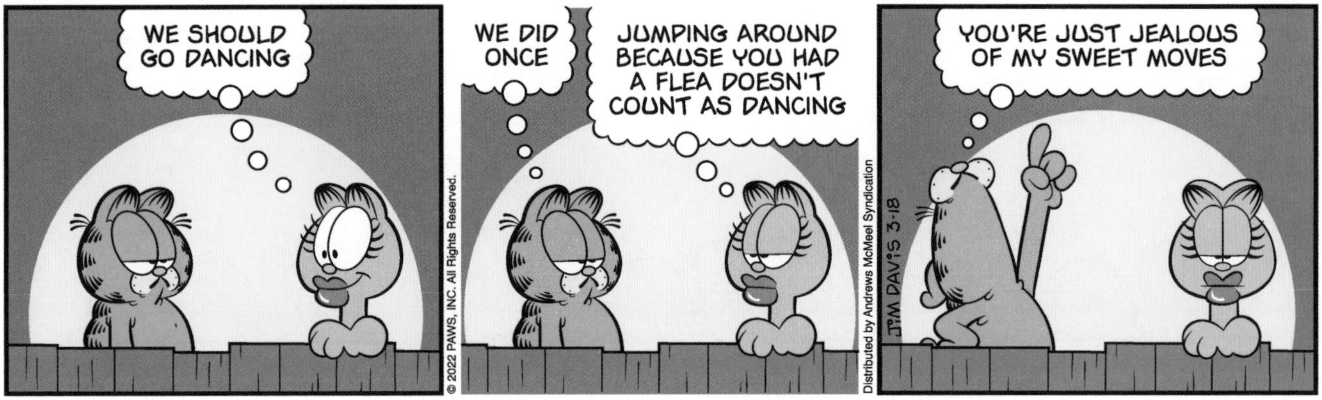
WE SHOULD GO DANCING
© 2022 PAWS, INC. All Rights Reserved.
WE DID ONCE
JUMPING AROUND BECAUSE YOU HAD A FLEA DOESN'T COUNT AS DANCING
Distributed by Andrews McMeel Syndication
JIM DAVIS 3-18
YOU'RE JUST JEALOUS OF MY SWEET MOVES

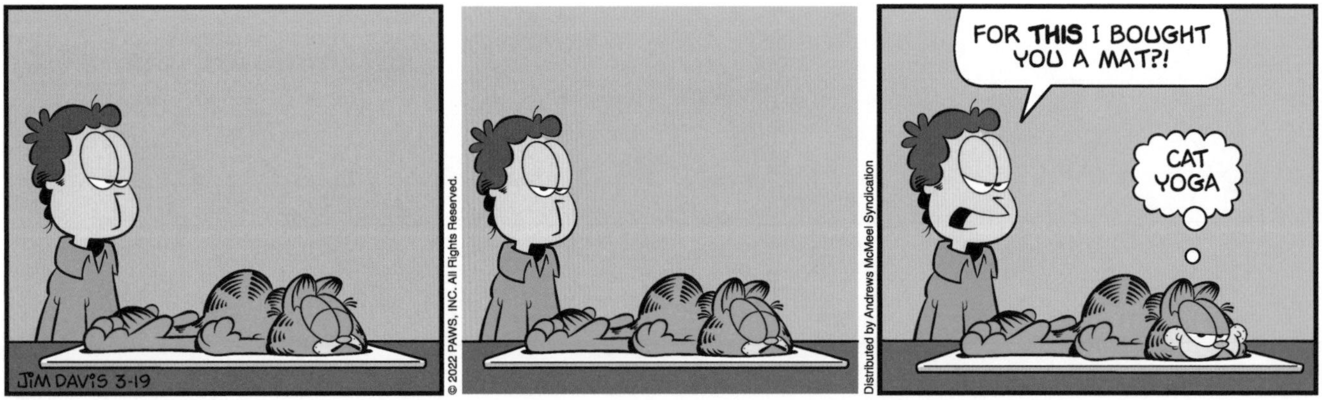
JIM DAVIS 3-19
© 2022 PAWS, INC. All Rights Reserved.
Distributed by Andrews McMeel Syndication
FOR **THIS** I BOUGHT YOU A MAT?!
CAT YOGA

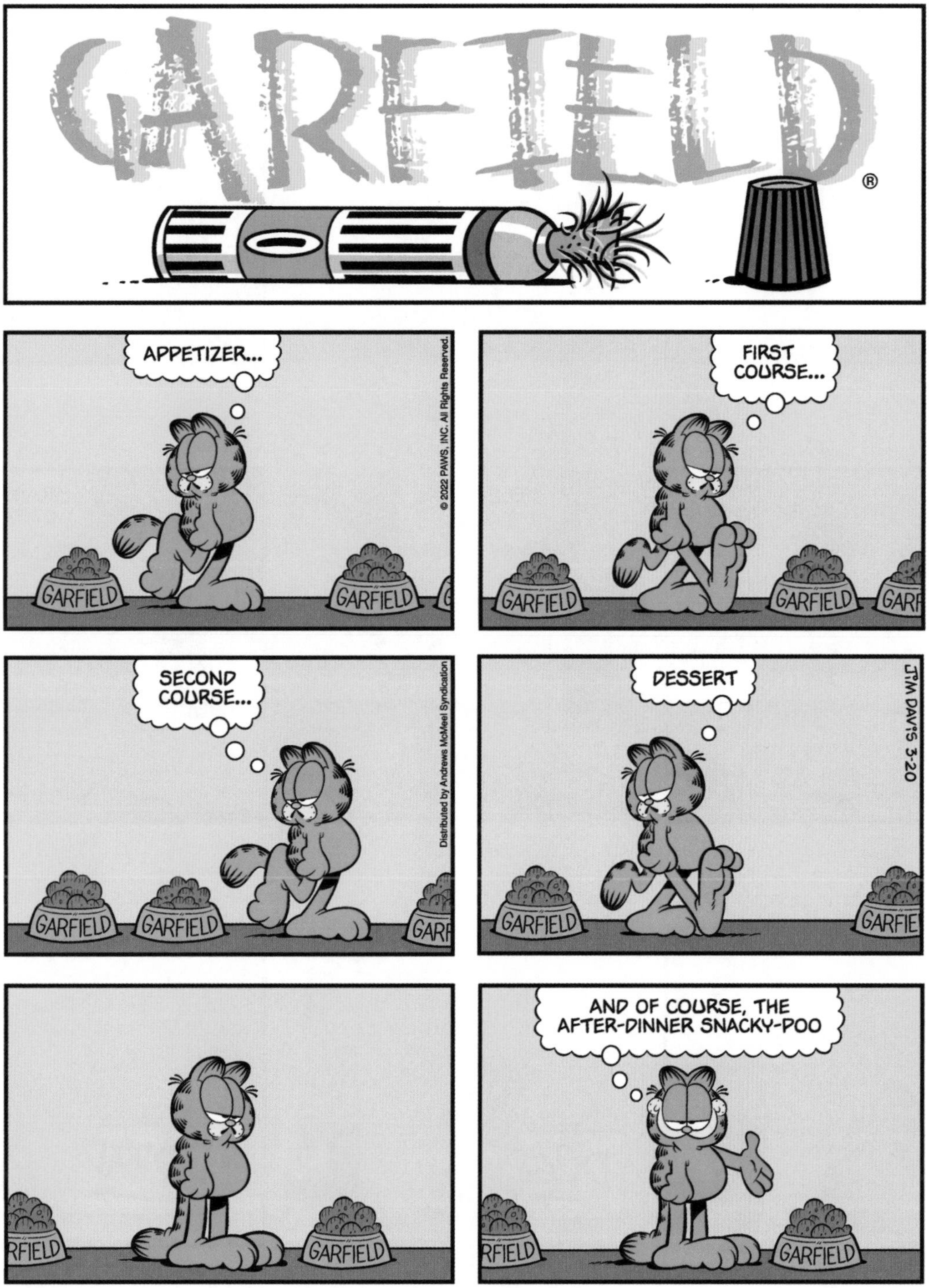
GARFIELD
APPETIZER...
© 2022 PAWS, INC. All Rights Reserved.
GARFIELD
GARFIELD
FIRST COURSE...
GARFIELD
GARFIELD
SECOND COURSE...
Distributed by Andrews McMeel Syndication
GARFIELD
GARFIELD
DESSERT
JIM DAVIS 3-20
GARFIELD
GARFIELD
AND OF COURSE, THE AFTER-DINNER SNACKY-POO
GARFIELD

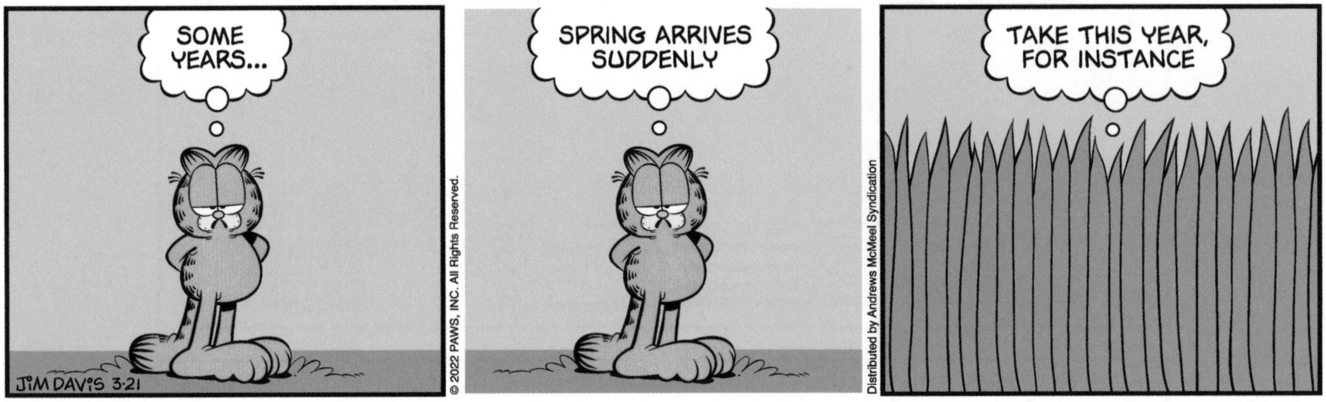
JIM DAVIS 3-21
SOME YEARS...
SPRING ARRIVES SUDDENLY
TAKE THIS YEAR, FOR INSTANCE
© 2022 PAWS, INC. All Rights Reserved.
Distributed by Andrews McMeel Syndication

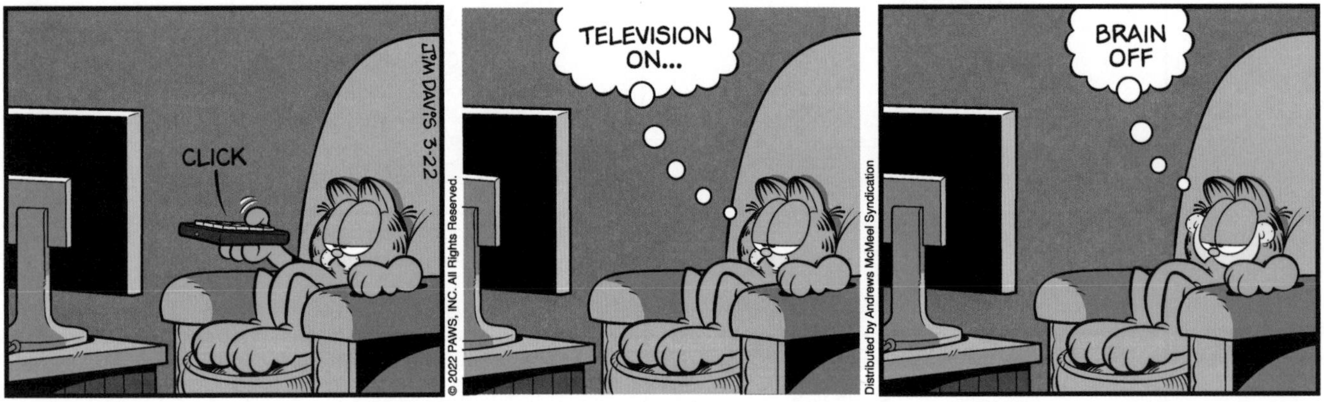
JIM DAVIS 3-22
CLICK
TELEVISION ON...
BRAIN OFF
© 2022 PAWS, INC. All Rights Reserved.
Distributed by Andrews McMeel Syndication

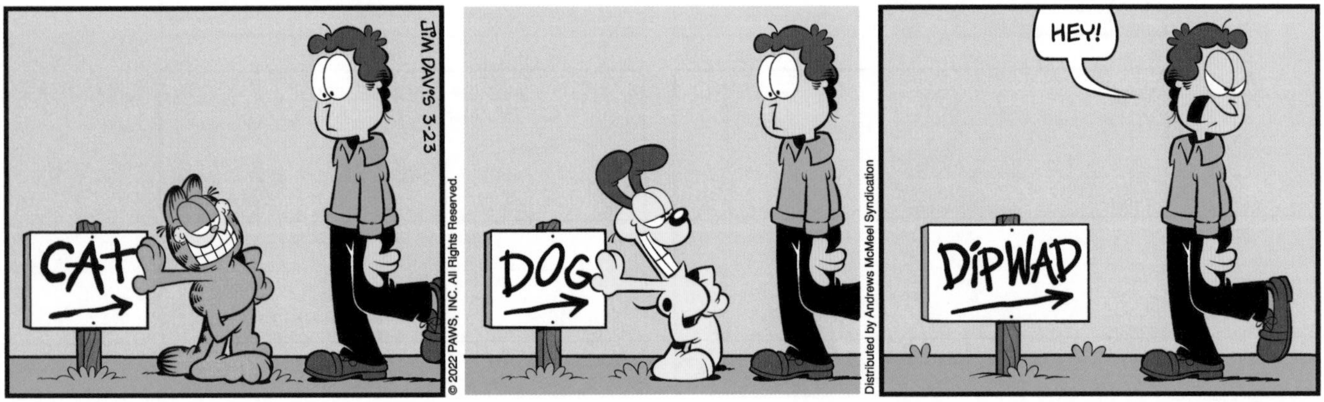
JIM DAVIS 3-23
CAT
DOG
HEY!
DIPWAD
© 2022 PAWS, INC. All Rights Reserved.
Distributed by Andrews McMeel Syndication

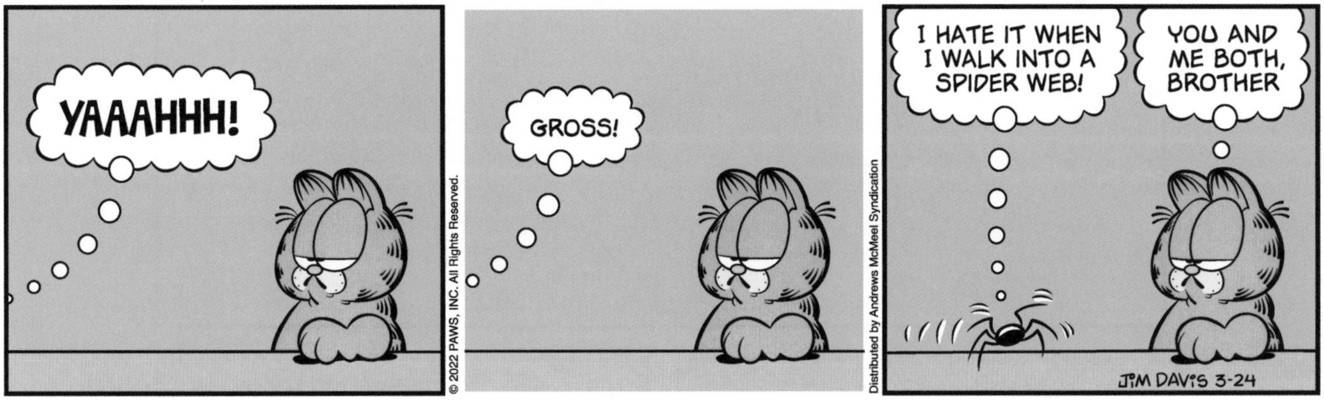
YAAAHHH!
GROSS!
I HATE IT WHEN I WALK INTO A SPIDER WEB!
YOU AND ME BOTH, BROTHER
© 2022 PAWS, INC. All Rights Reserved.
Distributed by Andrews McMeel Syndication
JIM DAVIS 3-24

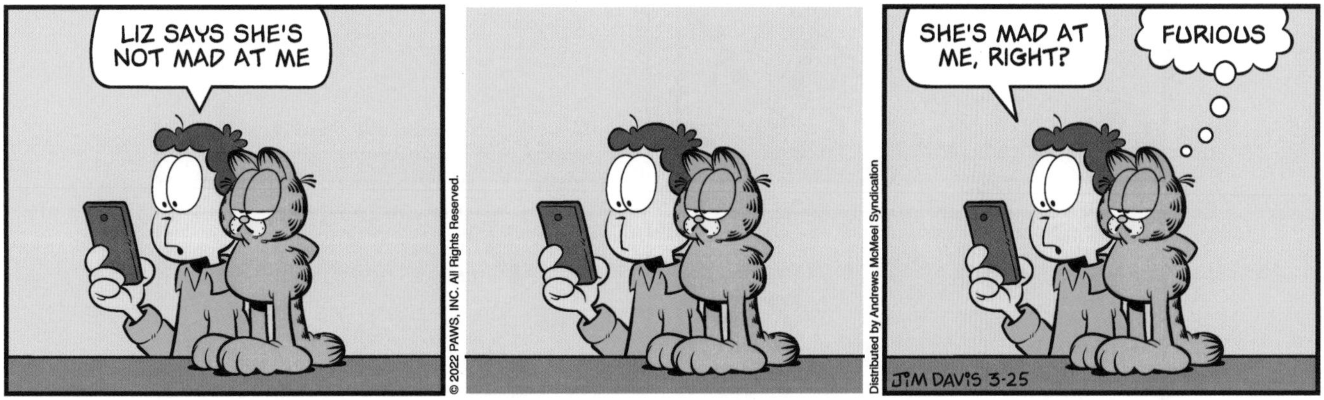
LIZ SAYS SHE'S NOT MAD AT ME
SHE'S MAD AT ME, RIGHT?
FURIOUS
© 2022 PAWS, INC. All Rights Reserved.
Distributed by Andrews McMeel Syndication
JIM DAVIS 3-25

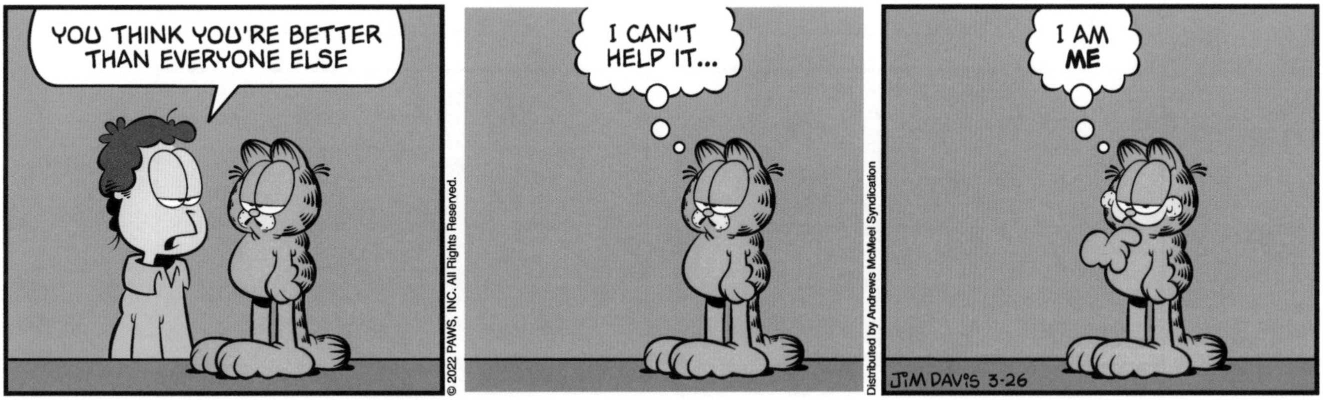
YOU THINK YOU'RE BETTER THAN EVERYONE ELSE
I CAN'T HELP IT...
I AM **ME**
© 2022 PAWS, INC. All Rights Reserved.
Distributed by Andrews McMeel Syndication
JIM DAVIS 3-26

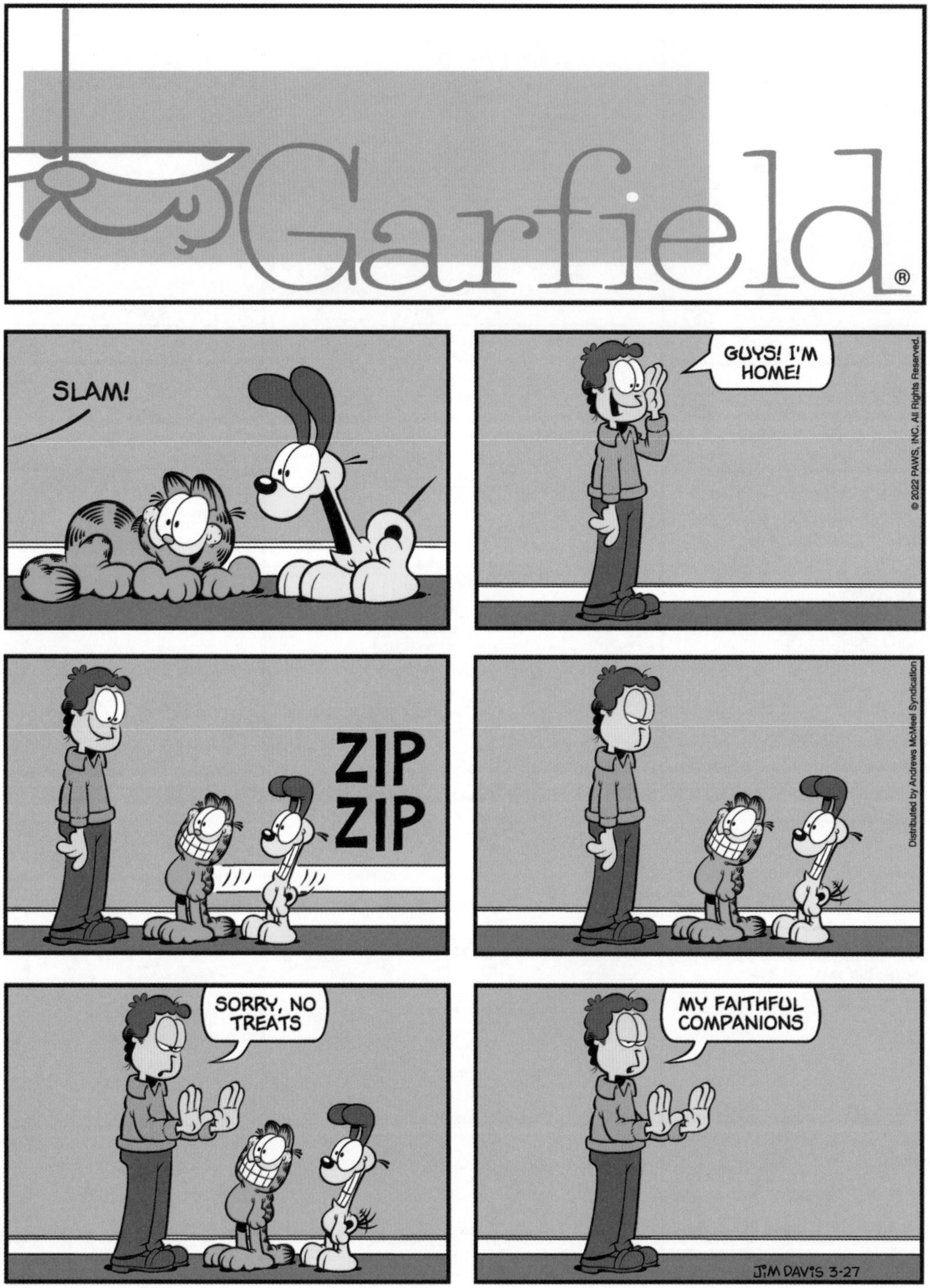
Garfield®
SLAM!
GUYS! I'M HOME!
© 2022 PAWS, INC. All Rights Reserved.
ZIP ZIP
Distributed by Andrews McMeel Syndication
SORRY, NO TREATS
MY FAITHFUL COMPANIONS
JIM DAVIS 3-27

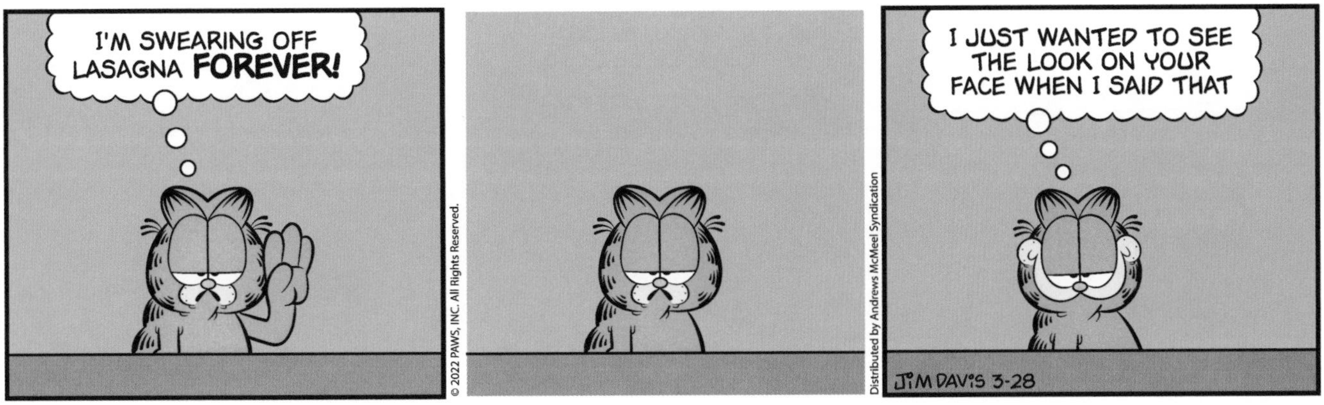
I'M SWEARING OFF LASAGNA **FOREVER!**
I JUST WANTED TO SEE THE LOOK ON YOUR FACE WHEN I SAID THAT
© 2022 PAWS, INC. All Rights Reserved.
Distributed by Andrews McMeel Syndication
JIM DAVIS 3-28

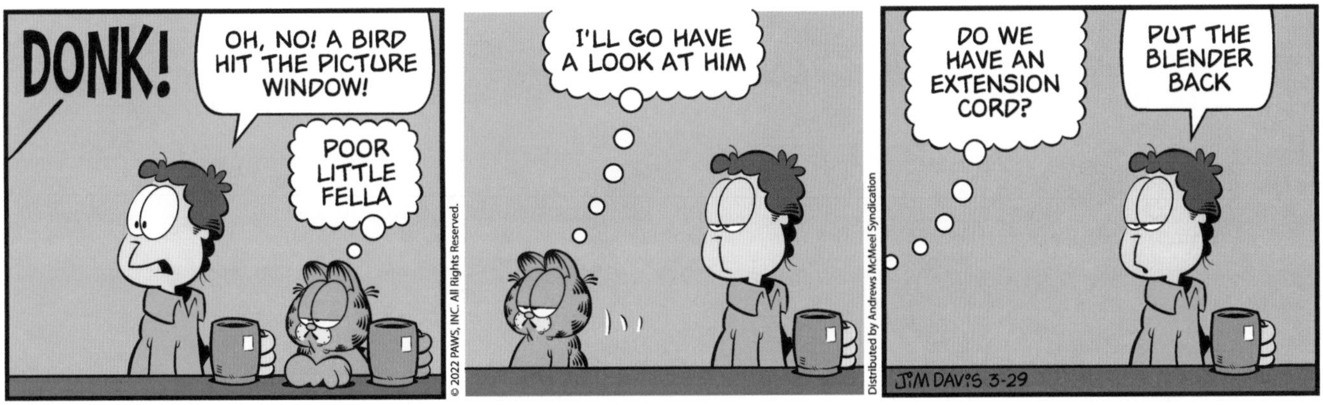
DONK!
OH, NO! A BIRD HIT THE PICTURE WINDOW!
POOR LITTLE FELLA
I'LL GO HAVE A LOOK AT HIM
DO WE HAVE AN EXTENSION CORD?
PUT THE BLENDER BACK
© 2022 PAWS, INC. All Rights Reserved.
Distributed by Andrews McMeel Syndication
JIM DAVIS 3-29

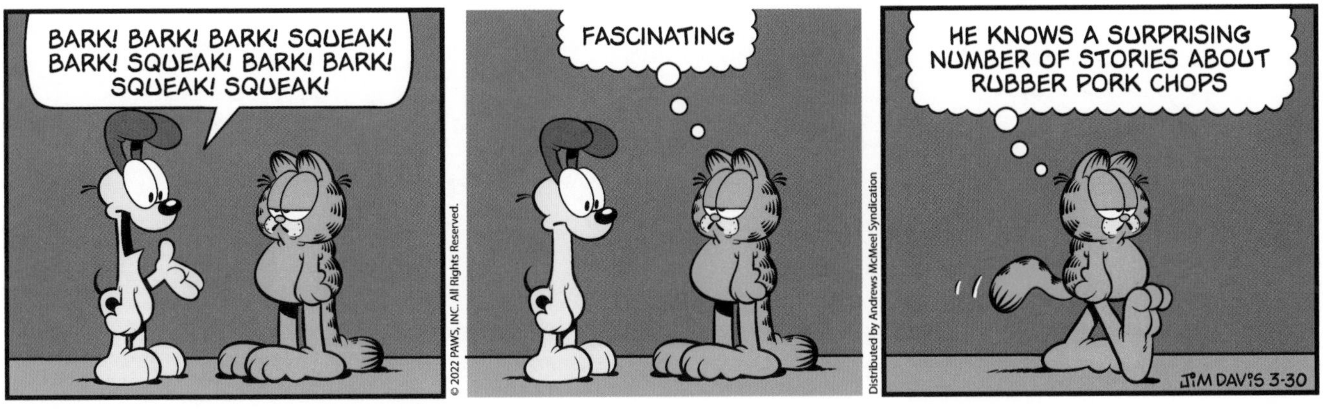
BARK! BARK! BARK! SQUEAK! BARK! SQUEAK! BARK! BARK! SQUEAK! SQUEAK!
FASCINATING
HE KNOWS A SURPRISING NUMBER OF STORIES ABOUT RUBBER PORK CHOPS
© 2022 PAWS, INC. All Rights Reserved.
Distributed by Andrews McMeel Syndication
JIM DAVIS 3-30

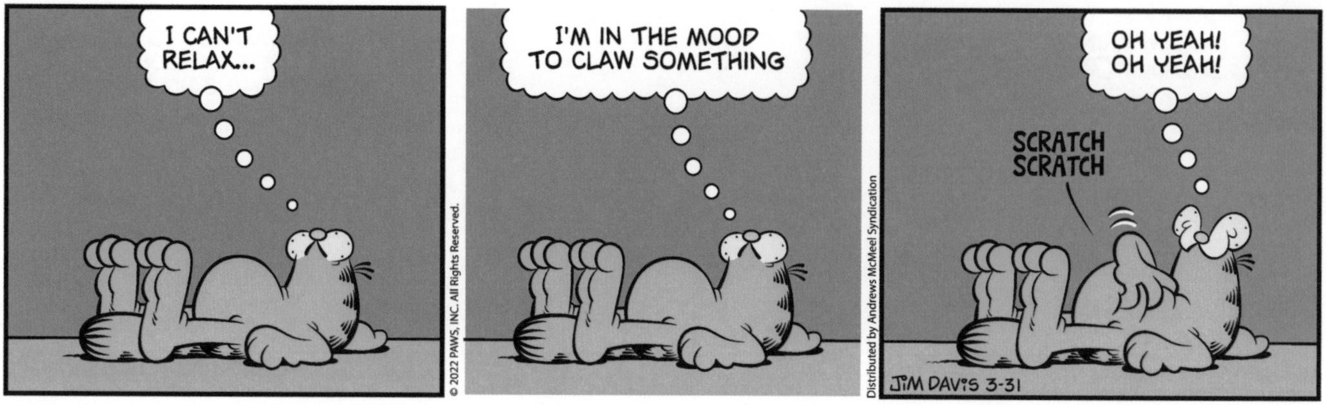
I CAN'T RELAX...
I'M IN THE MOOD TO CLAW SOMETHING
SCRATCH SCRATCH
OH YEAH! OH YEAH!
© 2022 PAWS, INC. All Rights Reserved.
Distributed by Andrews McMeel Syndication
JIM DAVIS 3-31

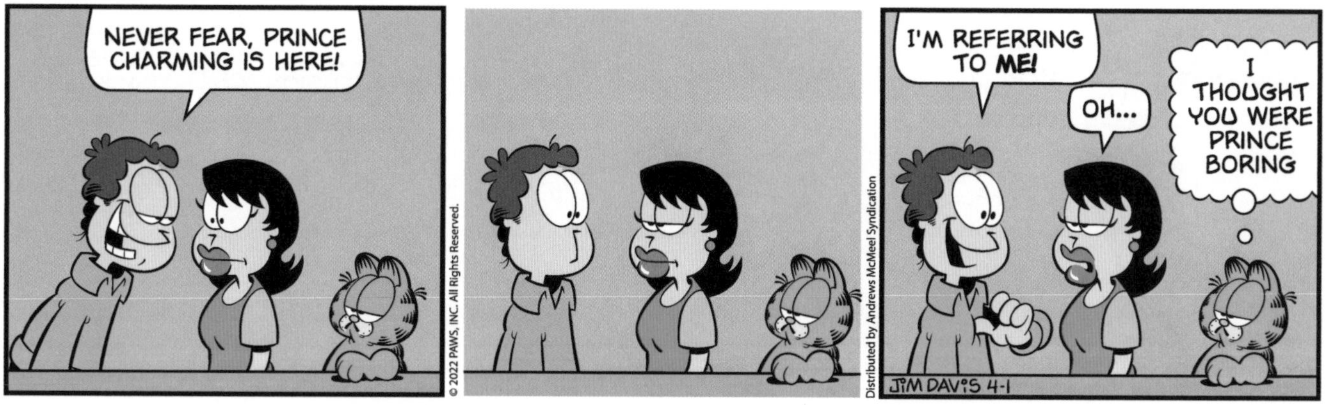
NEVER FEAR, PRINCE CHARMING IS HERE!
I'M REFERRING TO ME!
OH...
I THOUGHT YOU WERE PRINCE BORING
© 2022 PAWS, INC. All Rights Reserved.
Distributed by Andrews McMeel Syndication
JIM DAVIS 4-1

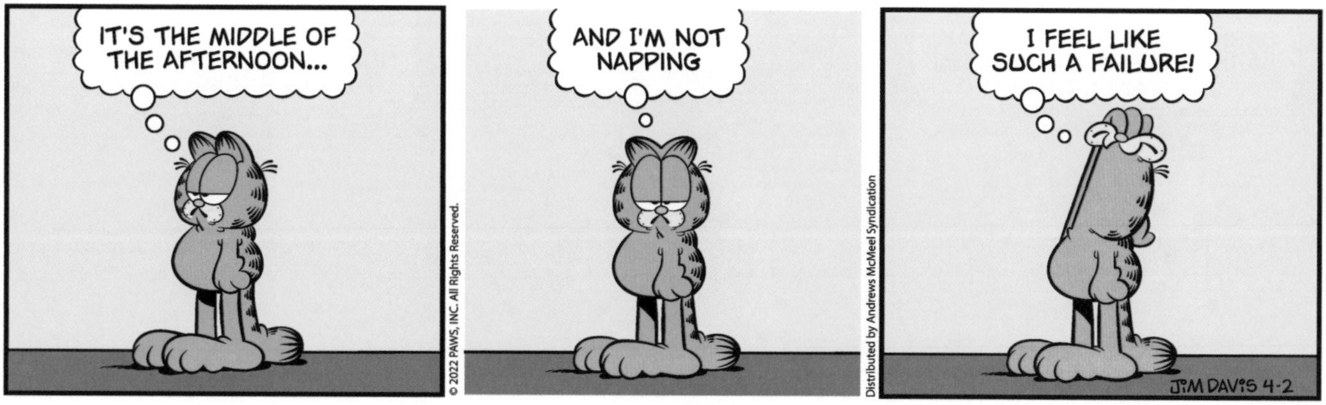
IT'S THE MIDDLE OF THE AFTERNOON...
AND I'M NOT NAPPING
I FEEL LIKE SUCH A FAILURE!
© 2022 PAWS, INC. All Rights Reserved.
Distributed by Andrews McMeel Syndication
JIM DAVIS 4-2

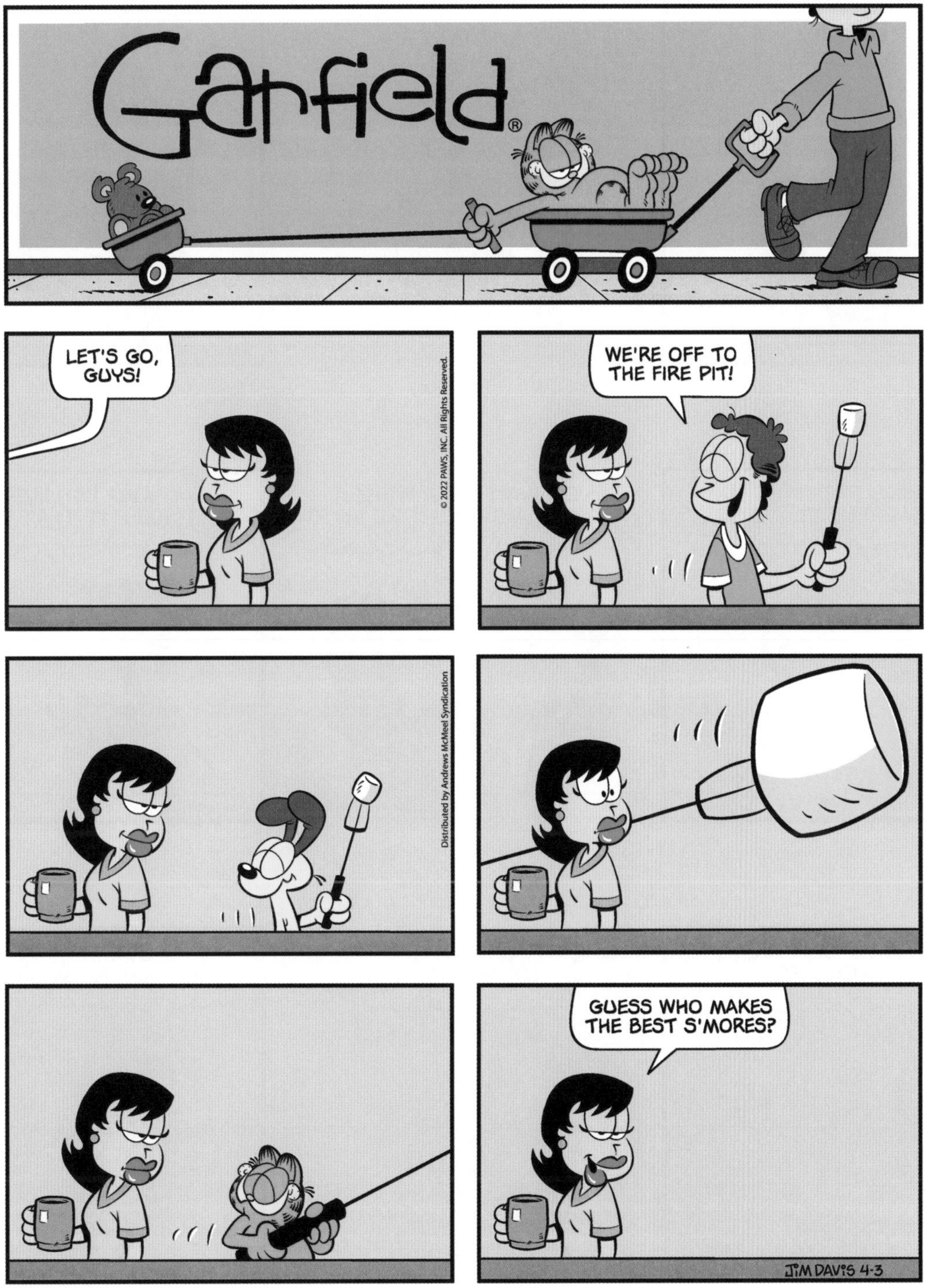

Garfield®
LET'S GO, GUYS!
© 2022 PAWS, INC. All Rights Reserved.
WE'RE OFF TO THE FIRE PIT!
Distributed by Andrews McMeel Syndication
GUESS WHO MAKES THE BEST S'MORES?
JIM DAVIS 4-3

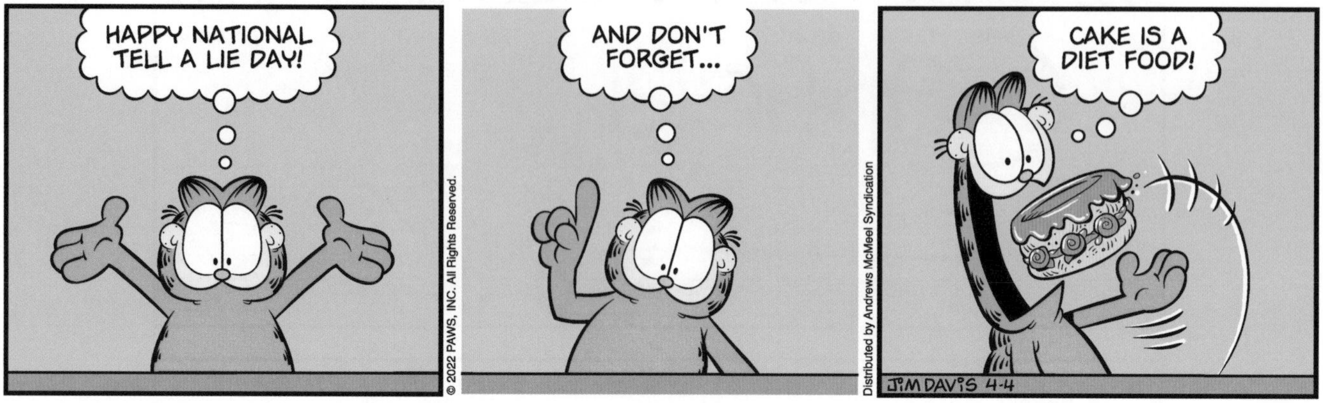
HAPPY NATIONAL TELL A LIE DAY!
AND DON'T FORGET...
CAKE IS A DIET FOOD!
© 2022 PAWS, INC. All Rights Reserved.
Distributed by Andrews McMeel Syndication
JIM DAVIS 4-4

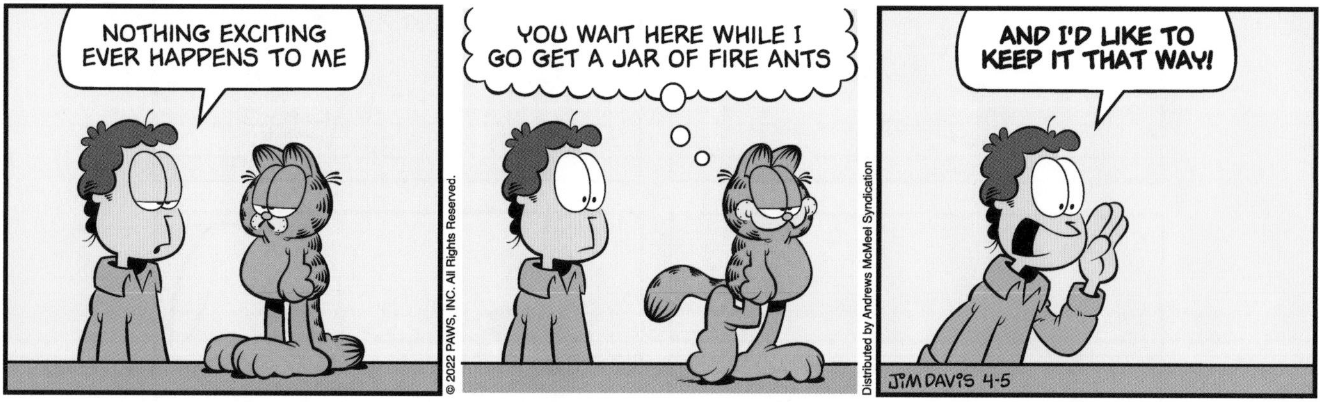
NOTHING EXCITING EVER HAPPENS TO ME
YOU WAIT HERE WHILE I GO GET A JAR OF FIRE ANTS
AND I'D LIKE TO KEEP IT THAT WAY!
© 2022 PAWS, INC. All Rights Reserved.
Distributed by Andrews McMeel Syndication
JIM DAVIS 4-5

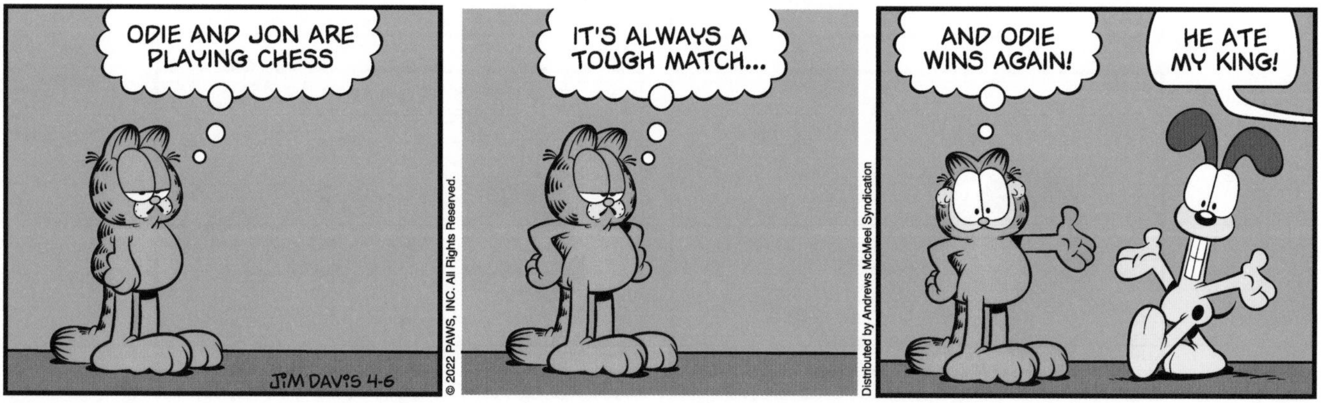
ODIE AND JON ARE PLAYING CHESS
IT'S ALWAYS A TOUGH MATCH...
AND ODIE WINS AGAIN!
HE ATE MY KING!
© 2022 PAWS, INC. All Rights Reserved.
Distributed by Andrews McMeel Syndication
JIM DAVIS 4-6

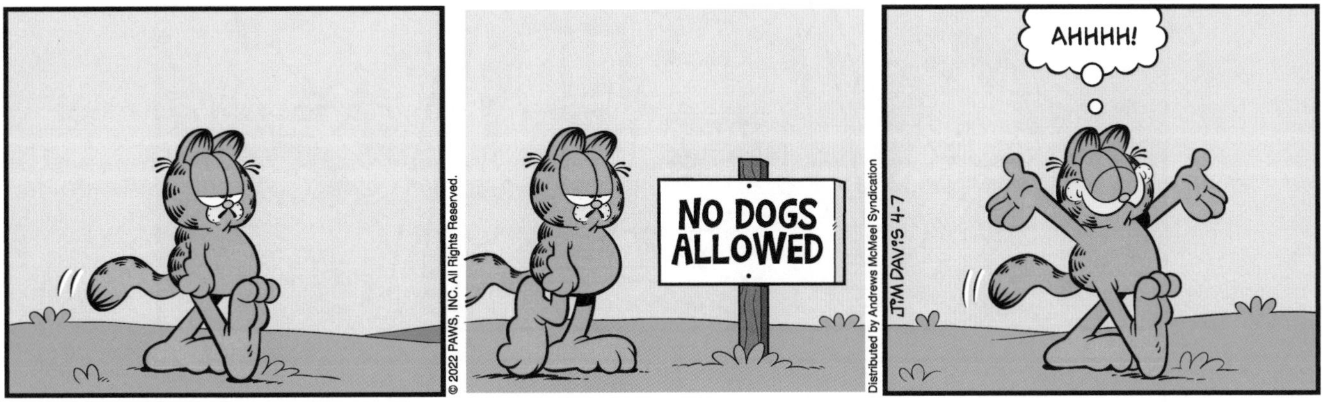
© 2022 PAWS, INC. All Rights Reserved.
NO DOGS ALLOWED
Distributed by Andrews McMeel Syndication
JIM DAVIS 4-7
AHHHH!

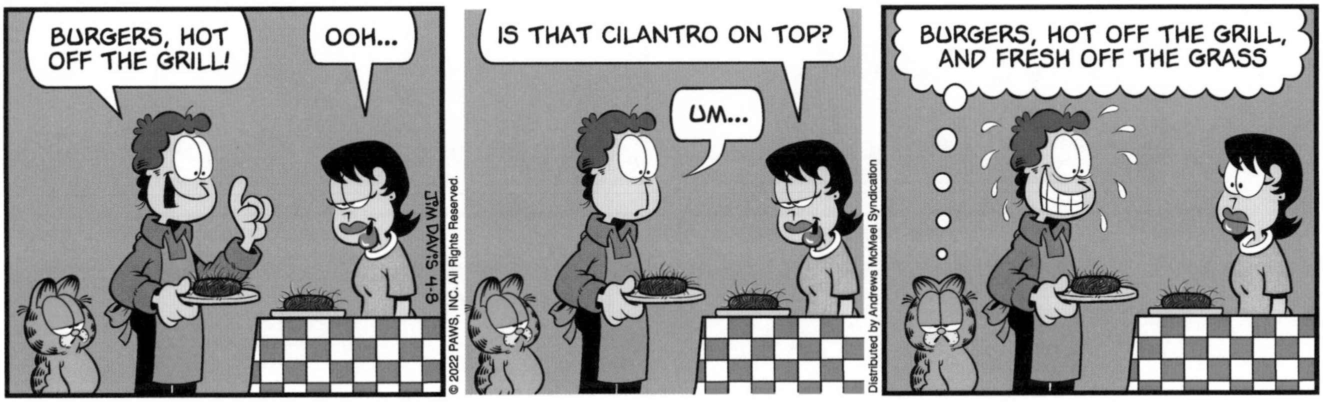
BURGERS, HOT OFF THE GRILL!
OOH...
JIM DAVIS 4-8
© 2022 PAWS, INC. All Rights Reserved.
IS THAT CILANTRO ON TOP?
UM...
Distributed by Andrews McMeel Syndication
BURGERS, HOT OFF THE GRILL, AND FRESH OFF THE GRASS

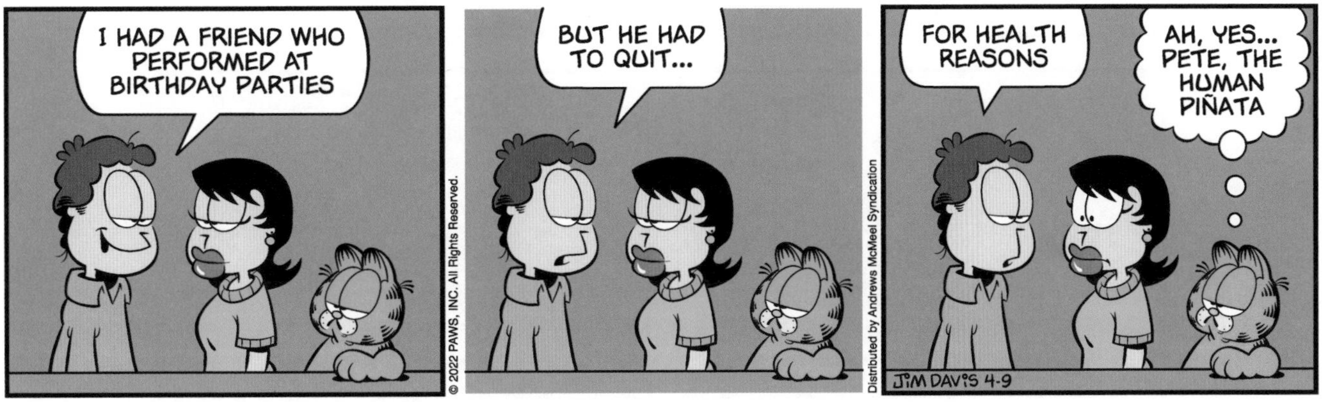
I HAD A FRIEND WHO PERFORMED AT BIRTHDAY PARTIES
© 2022 PAWS, INC. All Rights Reserved.
BUT HE HAD TO QUIT...
Distributed by Andrews McMeel Syndication
FOR HEALTH REASONS
AH, YES... PETE, THE HUMAN PIÑATA
JIM DAVIS 4-9

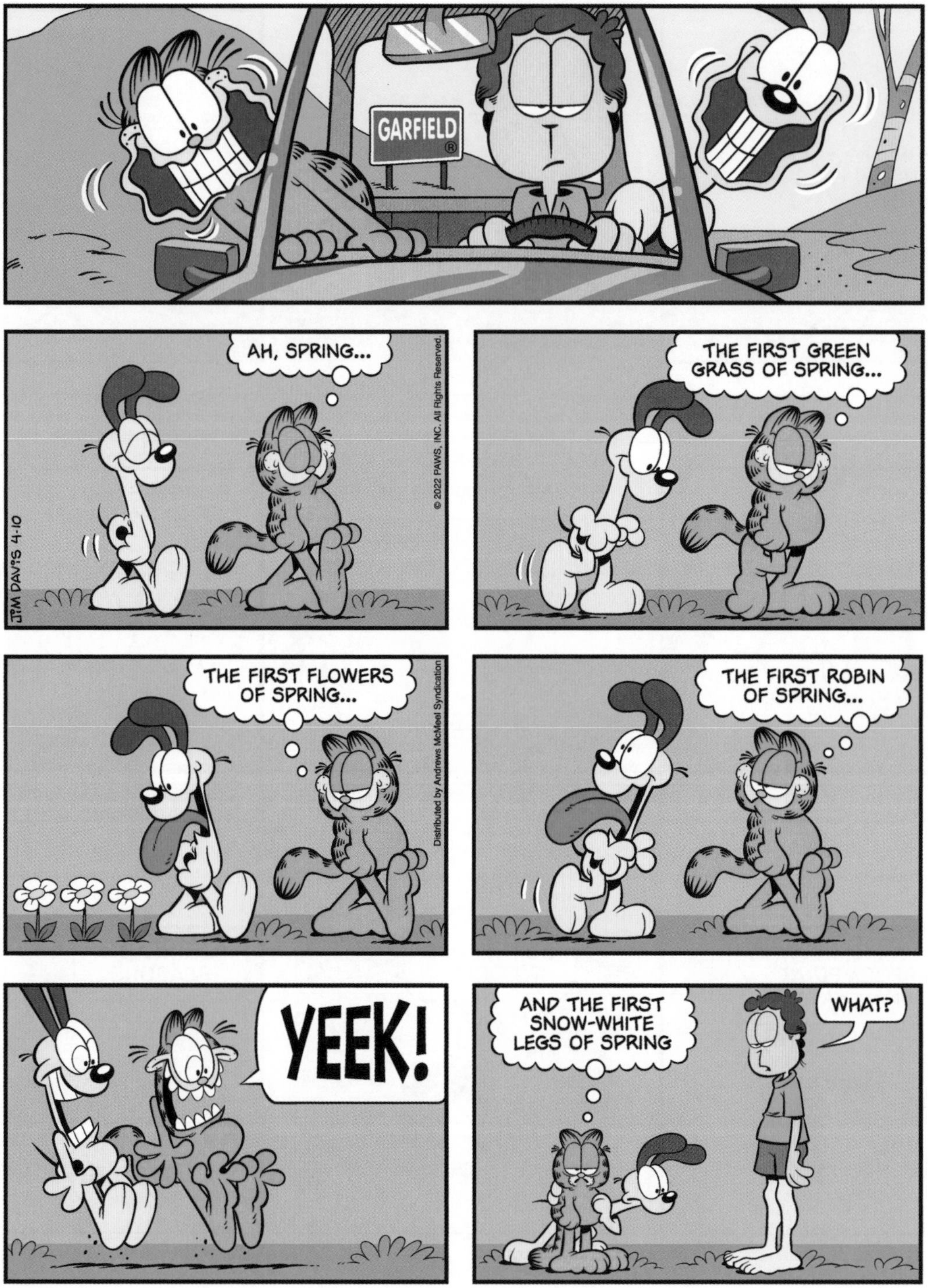
GARFIELD®
JIM DAVIS 4-10
AH, SPRING...
© 2022 PAWS, INC. All Rights Reserved.
THE FIRST GREEN GRASS OF SPRING...
THE FIRST FLOWERS OF SPRING...
Distributed by Andrews McMeel Syndication
THE FIRST ROBIN OF SPRING...
YEEK!
AND THE FIRST SNOW-WHITE LEGS OF SPRING
WHAT?

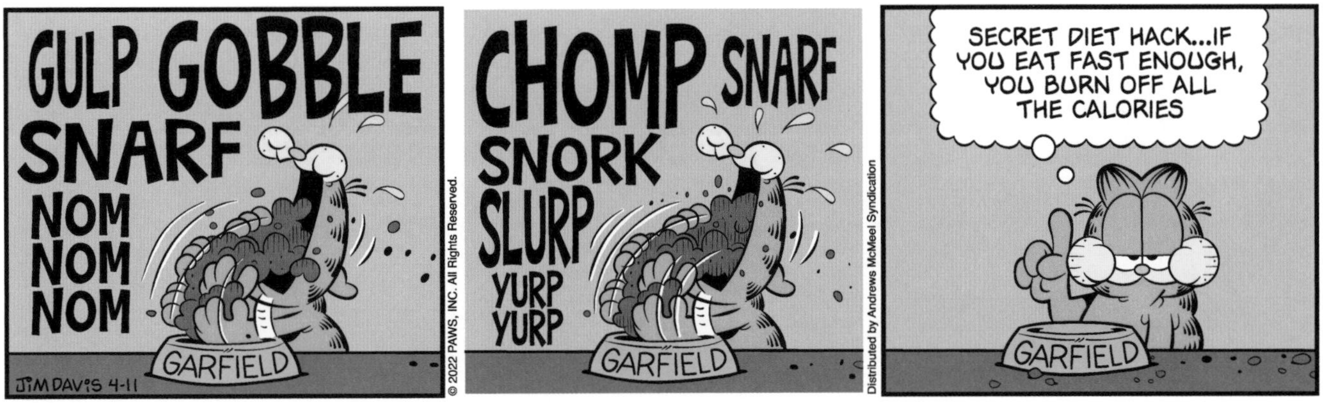
GULP GOBBLE
SNARF
NOM NOM NOM
GARFIELD
JIM DAVIS 4-11
© 2022 PAWS, INC. All Rights Reserved.
CHOMP SNARF
SNORK
SLURP
YURP YURP
GARFIELD
Distributed by Andrews McMeel Syndication
SECRET DIET HACK...IF YOU EAT FAST ENOUGH, YOU BURN OFF ALL THE CALORIES
GARFIELD

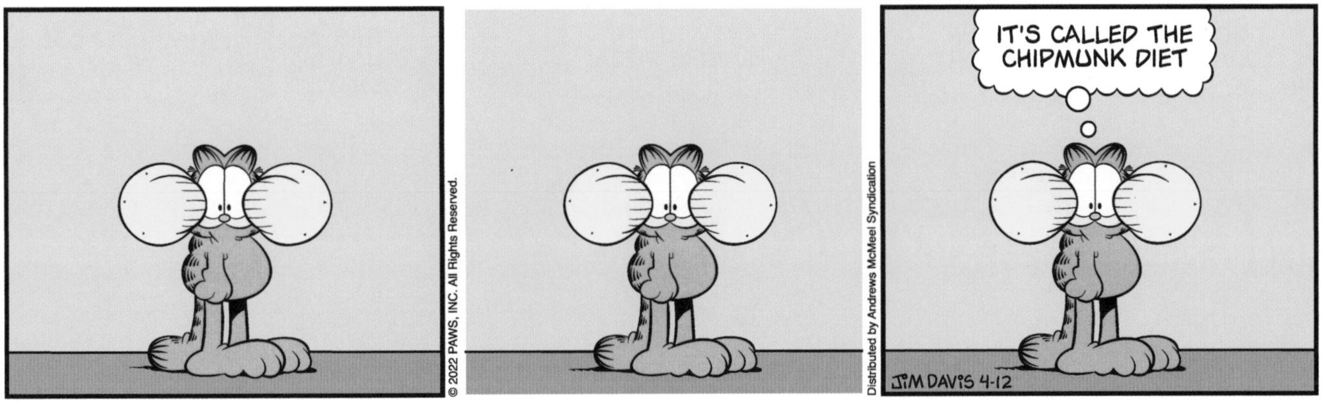
© 2022 PAWS, INC. All Rights Reserved.
Distributed by Andrews McMeel Syndication
IT'S CALLED THE CHIPMUNK DIET
JIM DAVIS 4-12

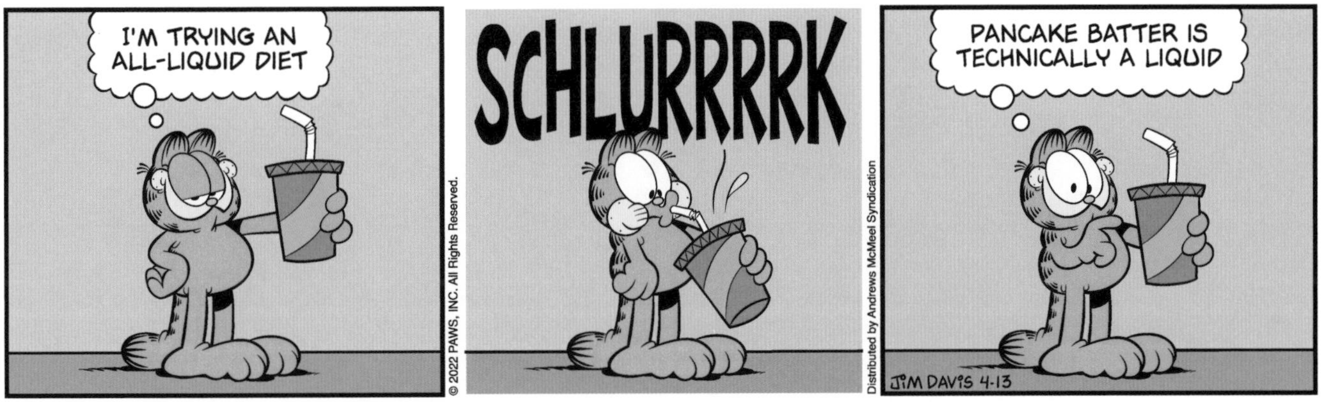
I'M TRYING AN ALL-LIQUID DIET
© 2022 PAWS, INC. All Rights Reserved.
SCHLURRRRK
Distributed by Andrews McMeel Syndication
PANCAKE BATTER IS TECHNICALLY A LIQUID
JIM DAVIS 4-13

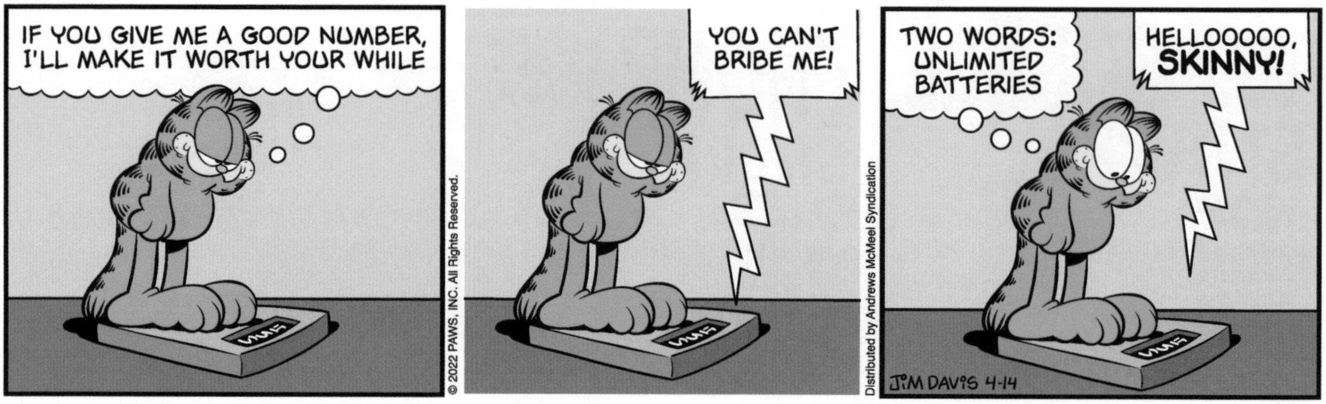
IF YOU GIVE ME A GOOD NUMBER, I'LL MAKE IT WORTH YOUR WHILE
YOU CAN'T BRIBE ME!
TWO WORDS: UNLIMITED BATTERIES
HELLOOOOO, **SKINNY!**
JIM DAVIS 4-14
© 2022 PAWS, INC. All Rights Reserved.
Distributed by Andrews McMeel Syndication

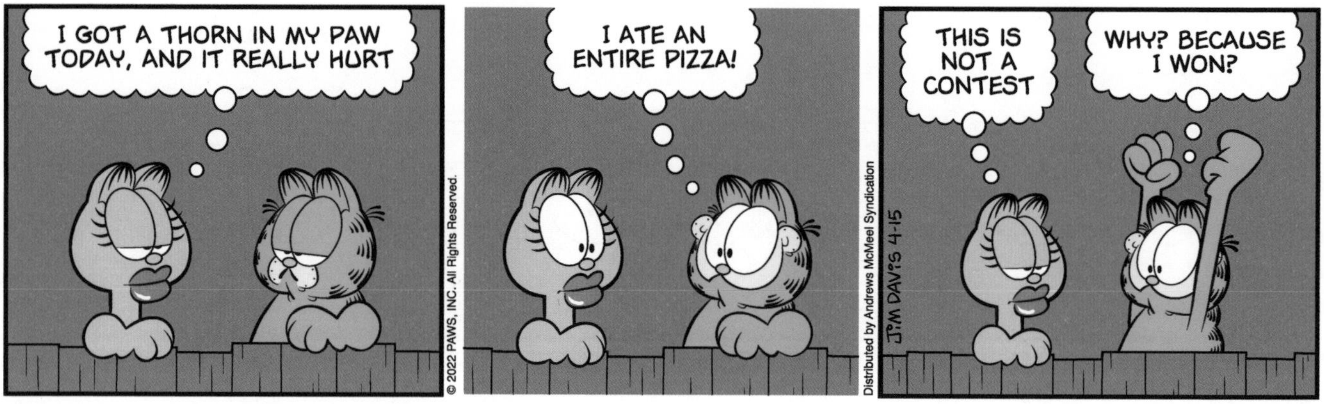
I GOT A THORN IN MY PAW TODAY, AND IT REALLY HURT
I ATE AN ENTIRE PIZZA!
THIS IS NOT A CONTEST
WHY? BECAUSE I WON?
JIM DAVIS 4-15
© 2022 PAWS, INC. All Rights Reserved.
Distributed by Andrews McMeel Syndication

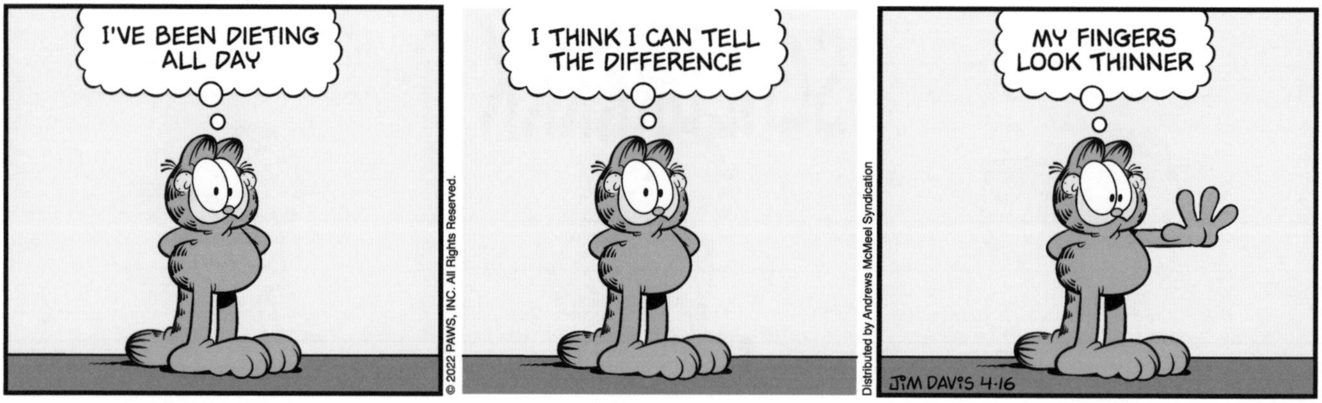
I'VE BEEN DIETING ALL DAY
I THINK I CAN TELL THE DIFFERENCE
MY FINGERS LOOK THINNER
JIM DAVIS 4-16
© 2022 PAWS, INC. All Rights Reserved.
Distributed by Andrews McMeel Syndication

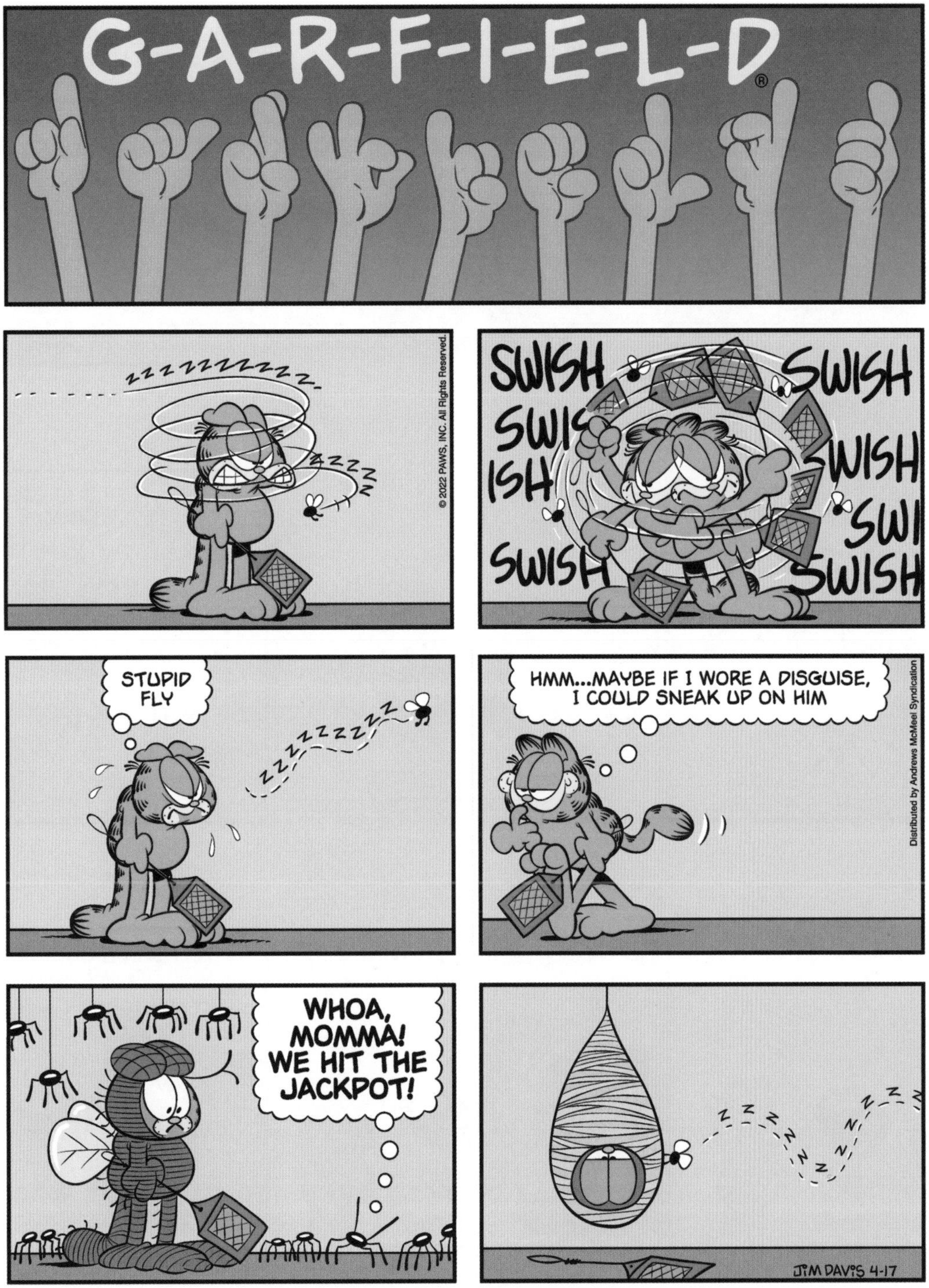

G-A-R-F-I-E-L-D®
© 2022 PAWS, INC. All Rights Reserved.
SWISH
SWISH
SWISH
SWISH
SWISH
SWISH
STUPID FLY
HMM...MAYBE IF I WORE A DISGUISE, I COULD SNEAK UP ON HIM
Distributed by Andrews McMeel Syndication
WHOA, MOMMA! WE HIT THE JACKPOT!
JIM DAVIS 4-17

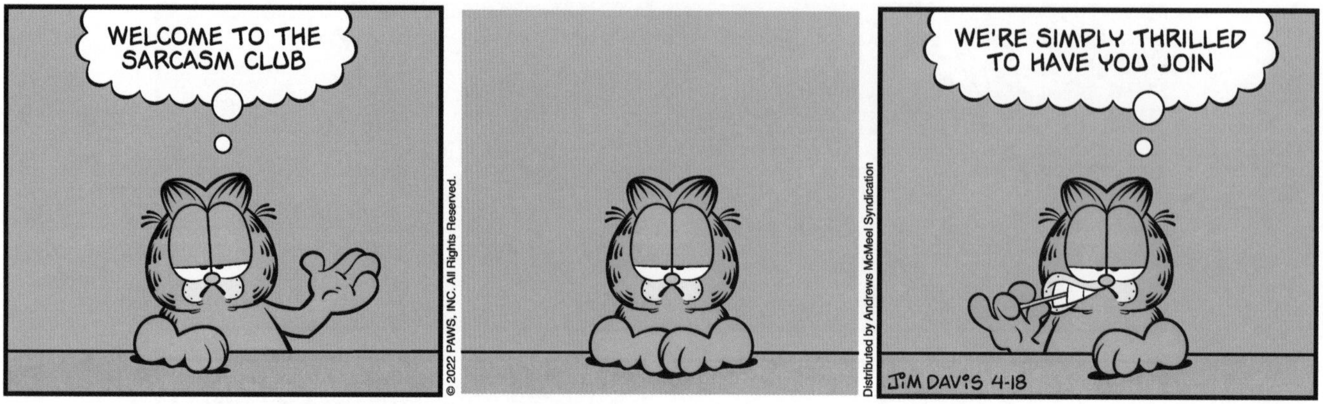
WELCOME TO THE SARCASM CLUB
WE'RE SIMPLY THRILLED TO HAVE YOU JOIN
© 2022 PAWS, INC. All Rights Reserved.
Distributed by Andrews McMeel Syndication
JIM DAVIS 4-18

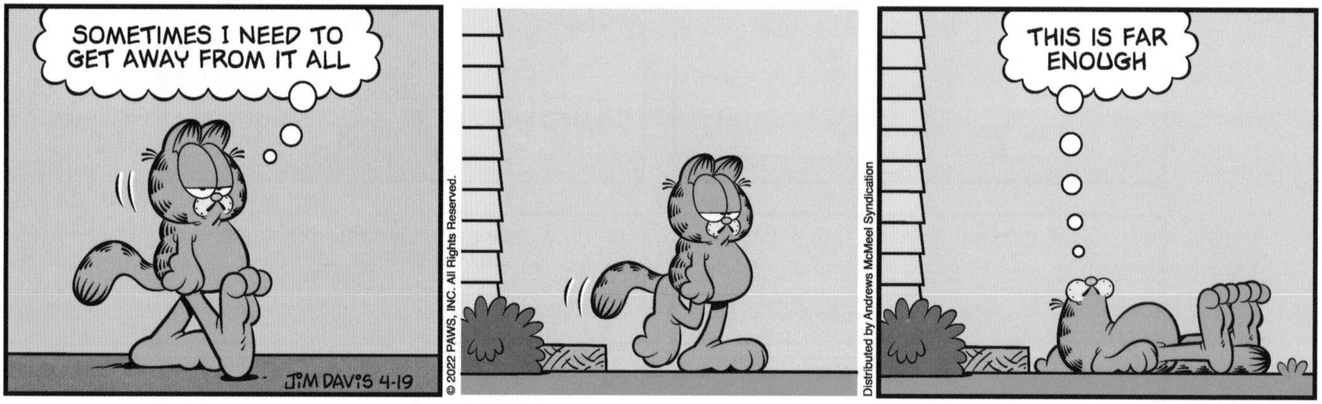
SOMETIMES I NEED TO GET AWAY FROM IT ALL
JIM DAVIS 4-19
THIS IS FAR ENOUGH
© 2022 PAWS, INC. All Rights Reserved.
Distributed by Andrews McMeel Syndication

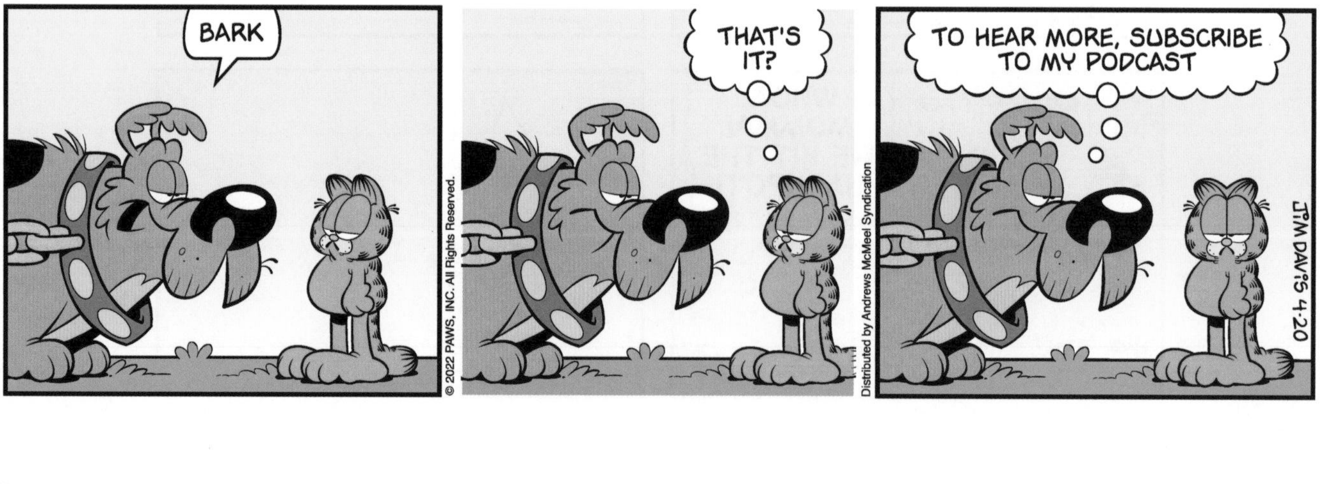
BARK
THAT'S IT?
TO HEAR MORE, SUBSCRIBE TO MY PODCAST
© 2022 PAWS, INC. All Rights Reserved.
Distributed by Andrews McMeel Syndication
JIM DAVIS 4-20

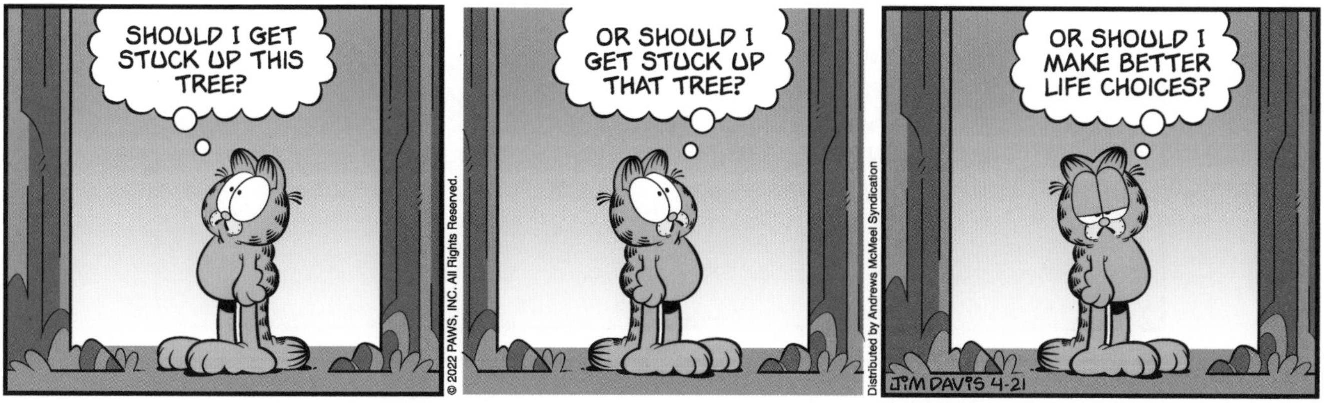
SHOULD I GET STUCK UP THIS TREE?
OR SHOULD I GET STUCK UP THAT TREE?
OR SHOULD I MAKE BETTER LIFE CHOICES?
JIM DAVIS 4-21

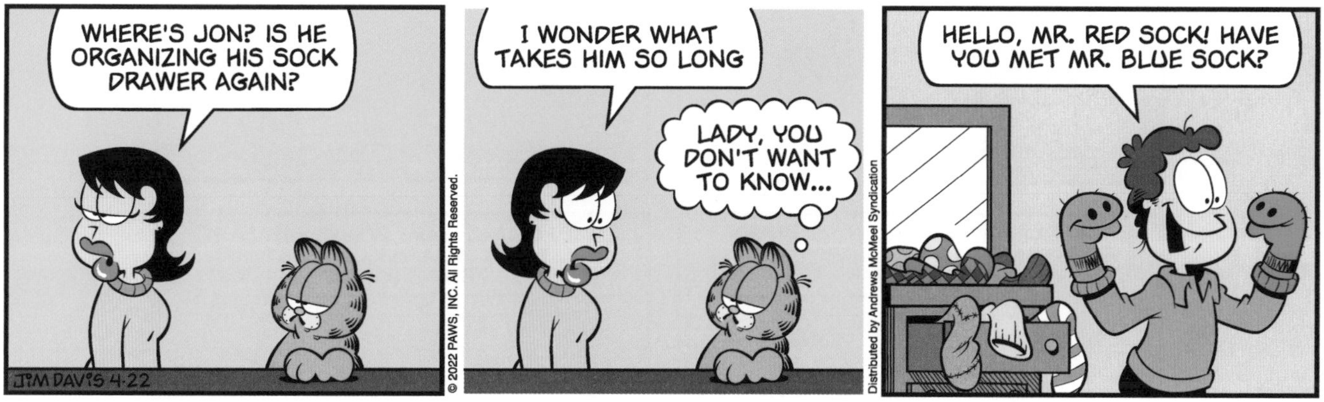
WHERE'S JON? IS HE ORGANIZING HIS SOCK DRAWER AGAIN?
JIM DAVIS 4-22
I WONDER WHAT TAKES HIM SO LONG
LADY, YOU DON'T WANT TO KNOW...
HELLO, MR. RED SOCK! HAVE YOU MET MR. BLUE SOCK?

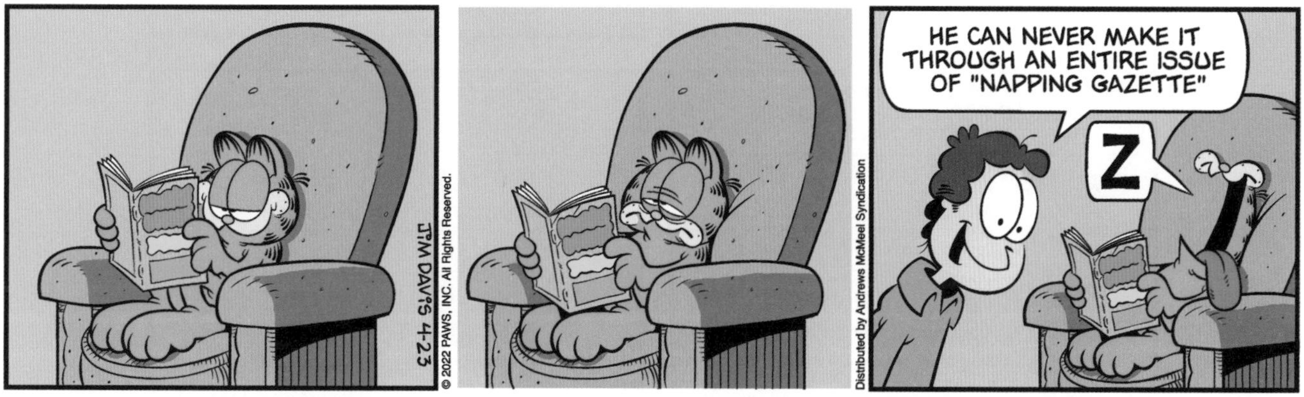
JIM DAVIS 4-23
HE CAN NEVER MAKE IT THROUGH AN ENTIRE ISSUE OF "NAPPING GAZETTE"
Z

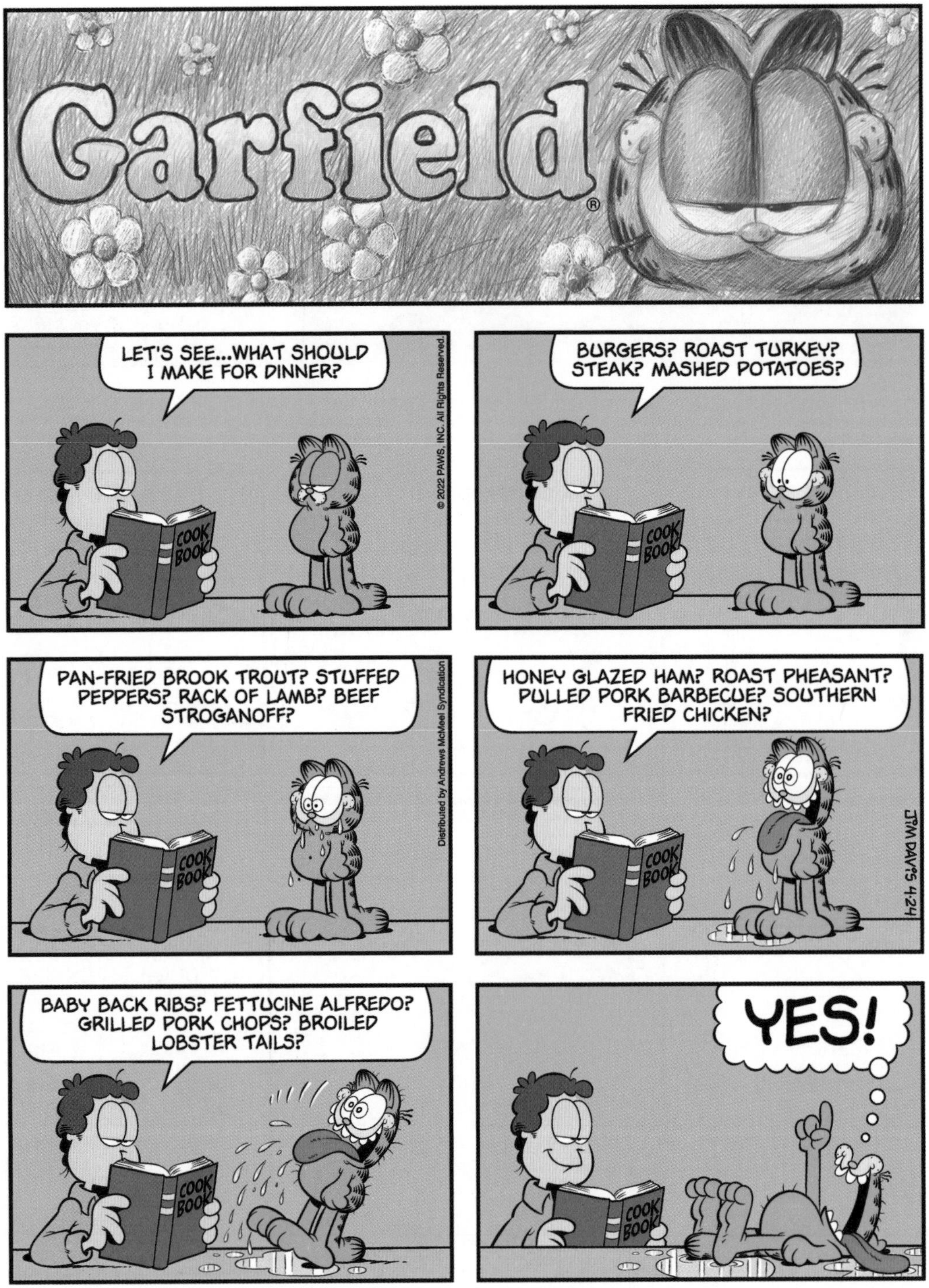
Garfield®
LET'S SEE...WHAT SHOULD I MAKE FOR DINNER?
© 2022 PAWS, INC. All Rights Reserved.
COOK BOOK
BURGERS? ROAST TURKEY? STEAK? MASHED POTATOES?
PAN-FRIED BROOK TROUT? STUFFED PEPPERS? RACK OF LAMB? BEEF STROGANOFF?
Distributed by Andrews McMeel Syndication
HONEY GLAZED HAM? ROAST PHEASANT? PULLED PORK BARBECUE? SOUTHERN FRIED CHICKEN?
JIM DAVIS 4-24
BABY BACK RIBS? FETTUCINE ALFREDO? GRILLED PORK CHOPS? BROILED LOBSTER TAILS?
YES!

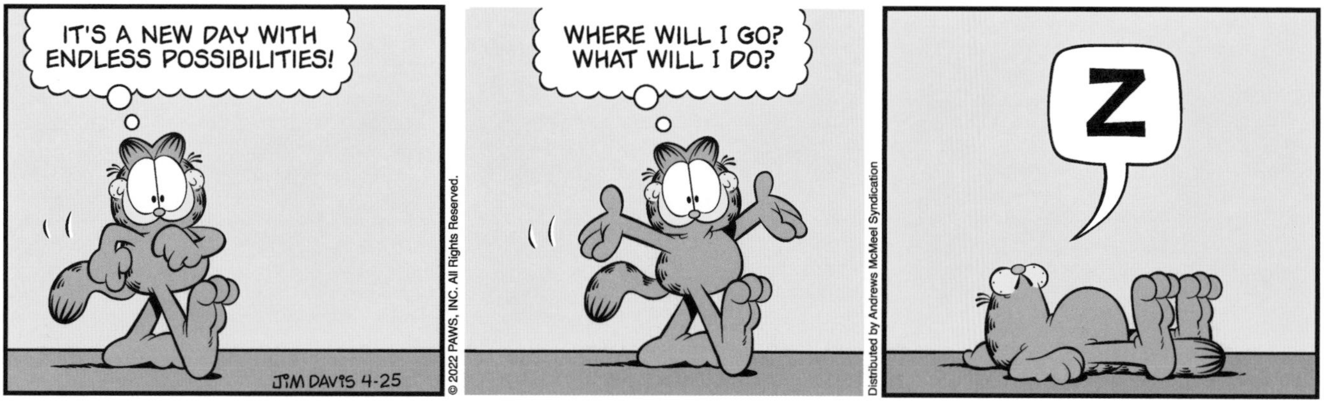
IT'S A NEW DAY WITH ENDLESS POSSIBILITIES!
JIM DAVIS 4-25
© 2022 PAWS, INC. All Rights Reserved.
WHERE WILL I GO? WHAT WILL I DO?
Distributed by Andrews McMeel Syndication
Z

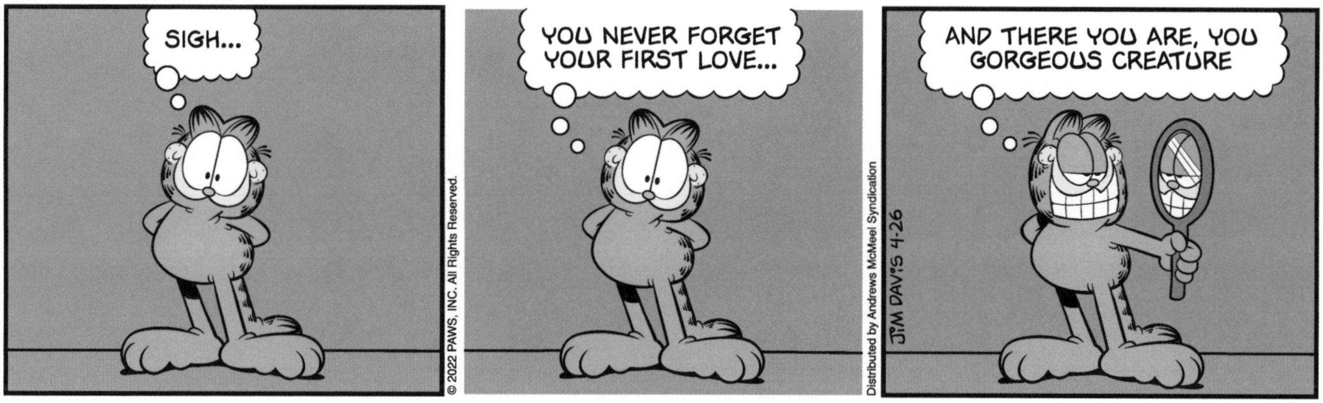
SIGH...
© 2022 PAWS, INC. All Rights Reserved.
YOU NEVER FORGET YOUR FIRST LOVE...
Distributed by Andrews McMeel Syndication
JIM DAVIS 4-26
AND THERE YOU ARE, YOU GORGEOUS CREATURE

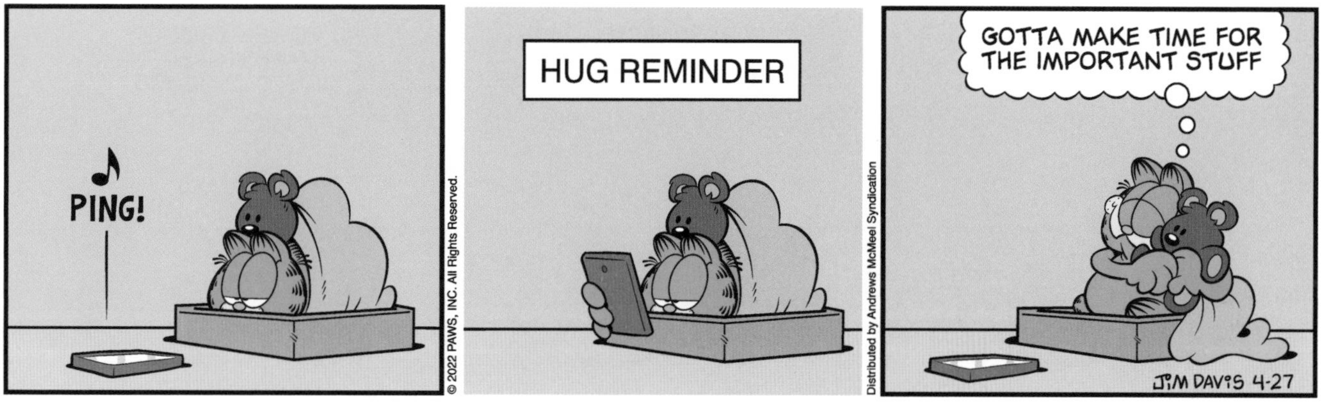
PING!
© 2022 PAWS, INC. All Rights Reserved.
HUG REMINDER
Distributed by Andrews McMeel Syndication
GOTTA MAKE TIME FOR THE IMPORTANT STUFF
JIM DAVIS 4-27

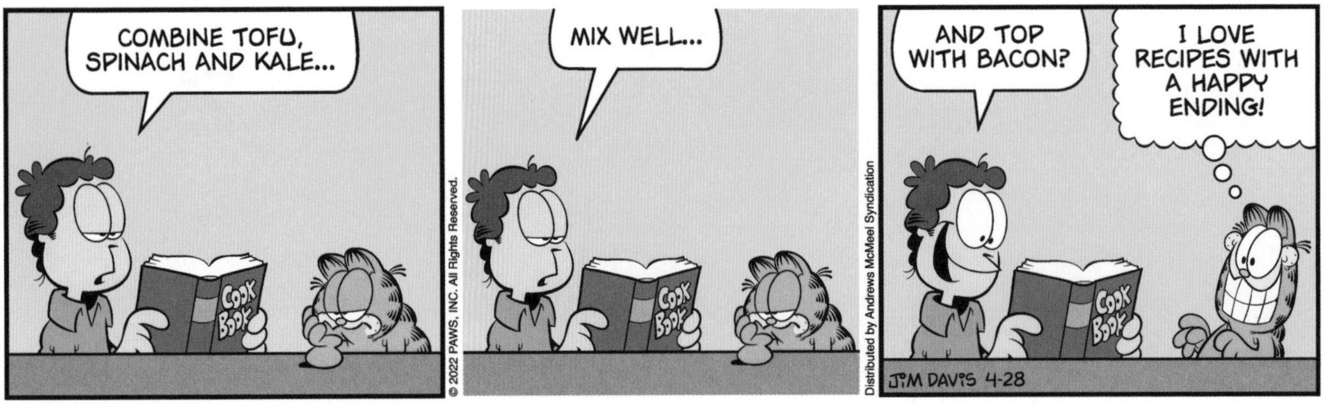
COMBINE TOFU, SPINACH AND KALE...
MIX WELL...
AND TOP WITH BACON?
I LOVE RECIPES WITH A HAPPY ENDING!
COOK BOOK
© 2022 PAWS, INC. All Rights Reserved.
Distributed by Andrews McMeel Syndication
JIM DAVIS 4-28

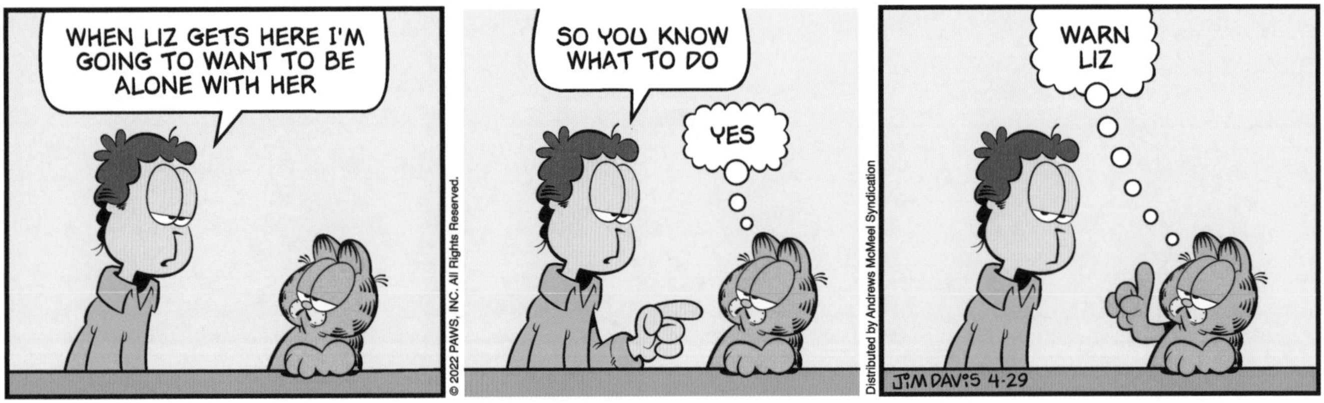
WHEN LIZ GETS HERE I'M GOING TO WANT TO BE ALONE WITH HER
SO YOU KNOW WHAT TO DO
YES
WARN LIZ
© 2022 PAWS, INC. All Rights Reserved.
Distributed by Andrews McMeel Syndication
JIM DAVIS 4-29

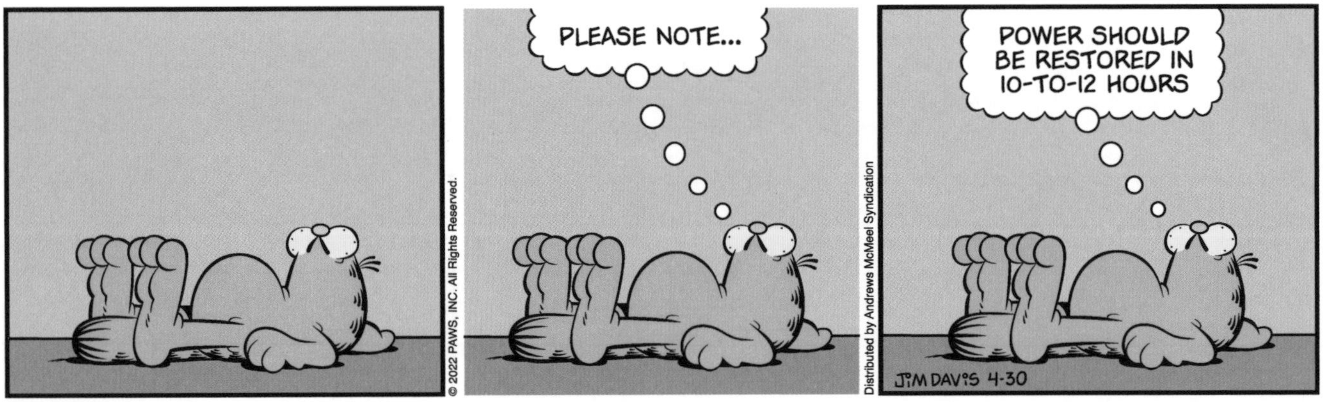
PLEASE NOTE...
POWER SHOULD BE RESTORED IN 10-TO-12 HOURS
© 2022 PAWS, INC. All Rights Reserved.
Distributed by Andrews McMeel Syndication
JIM DAVIS 4-30

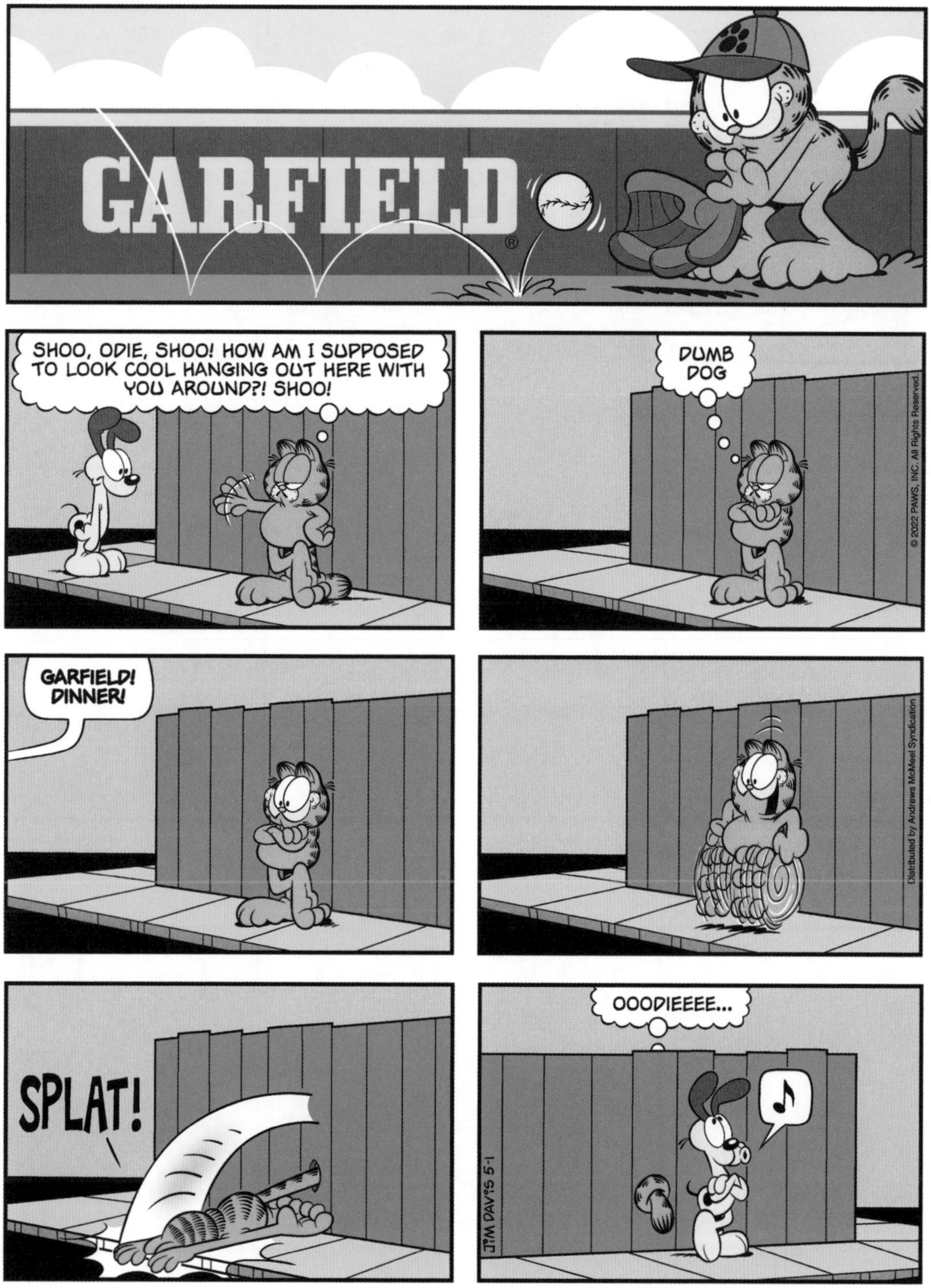
GARFIELD®
SHOO, ODIE, SHOO! HOW AM I SUPPOSED TO LOOK COOL HANGING OUT HERE WITH YOU AROUND?! SHOO!
DUMB DOG
© 2022 PAWS, INC. All Rights Reserved.
GARFIELD! DINNER!
Distributed by Andrews McMeel Syndication
SPLAT!
JPM DAVIS 5-1
OOODIEEEE...
♪

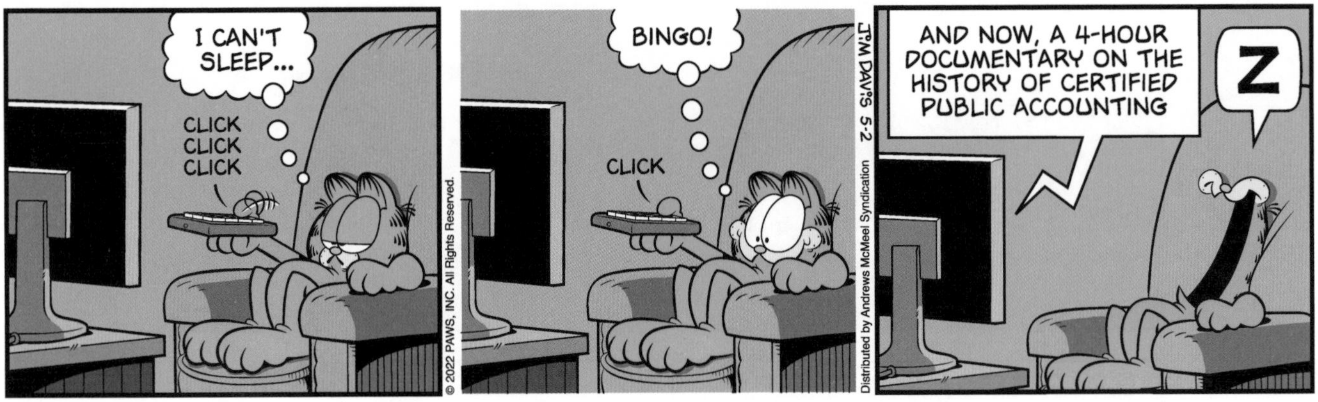
I CAN'T SLEEP...
CLICK CLICK CLICK
BINGO!
CLICK
AND NOW, A 4-HOUR DOCUMENTARY ON THE HISTORY OF CERTIFIED PUBLIC ACCOUNTING
Z
JIM DAVIS 5-2
© 2022 PAWS, INC. All Rights Reserved.
Distributed by Andrews McMeel Syndication

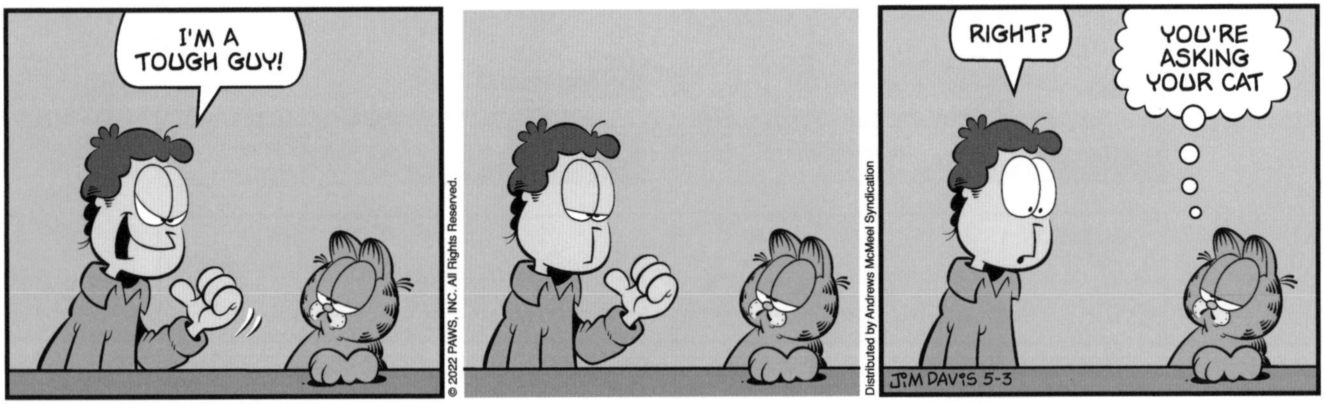
I'M A TOUGH GUY!
RIGHT?
YOU'RE ASKING YOUR CAT
JIM DAVIS 5-3
© 2022 PAWS, INC. All Rights Reserved.
Distributed by Andrews McMeel Syndication

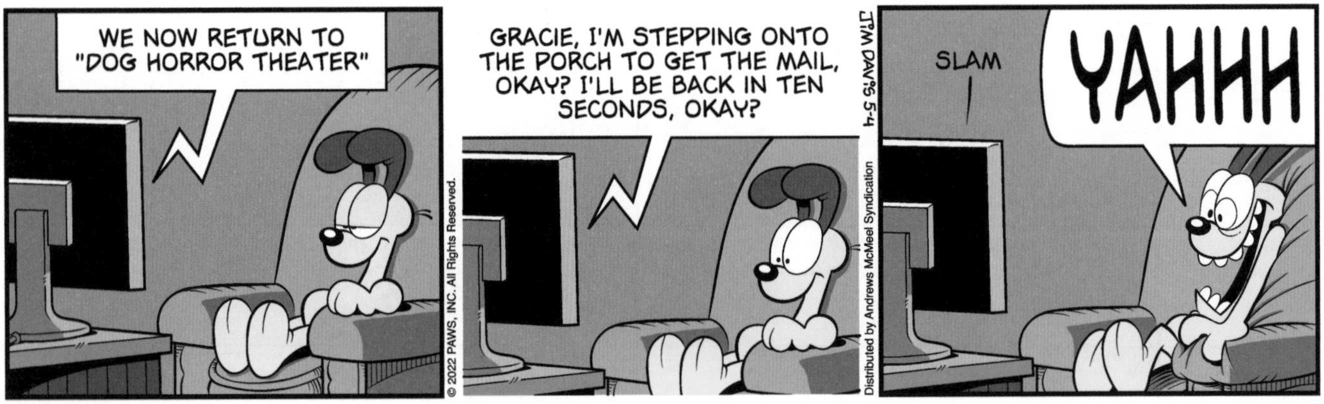
WE NOW RETURN TO "DOG HORROR THEATER"
GRACIE, I'M STEPPING ONTO THE PORCH TO GET THE MAIL, OKAY? I'LL BE BACK IN TEN SECONDS, OKAY?
SLAM
YAHHH
JIM DAVIS 5-4
© 2022 PAWS, INC. All Rights Reserved.
Distributed by Andrews McMeel Syndication

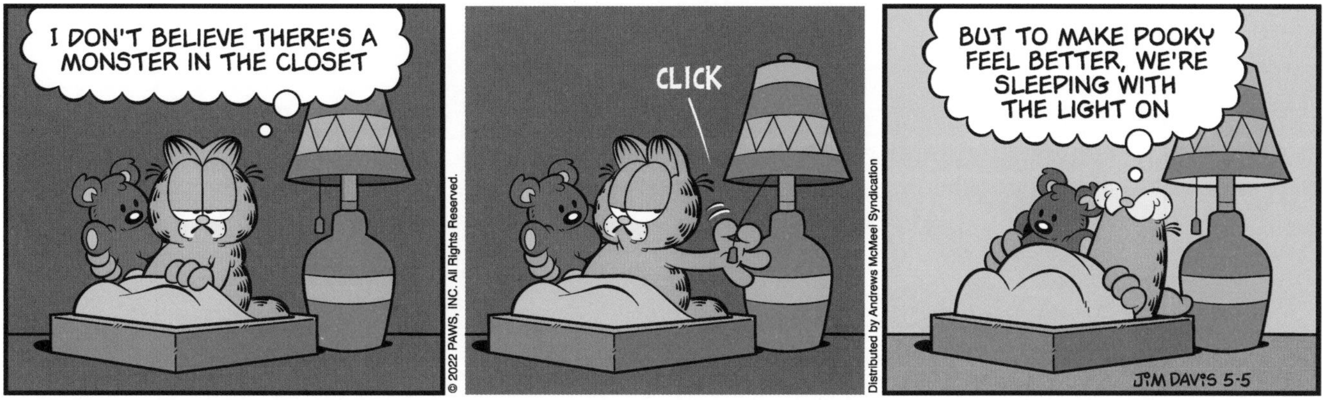
I DON'T BELIEVE THERE'S A MONSTER IN THE CLOSET
© 2022 PAWS, INC. All Rights Reserved.
CLICK
Distributed by Andrews McMeel Syndication
BUT TO MAKE POOKY FEEL BETTER, WE'RE SLEEPING WITH THE LIGHT ON
JIM DAVIS 5-5

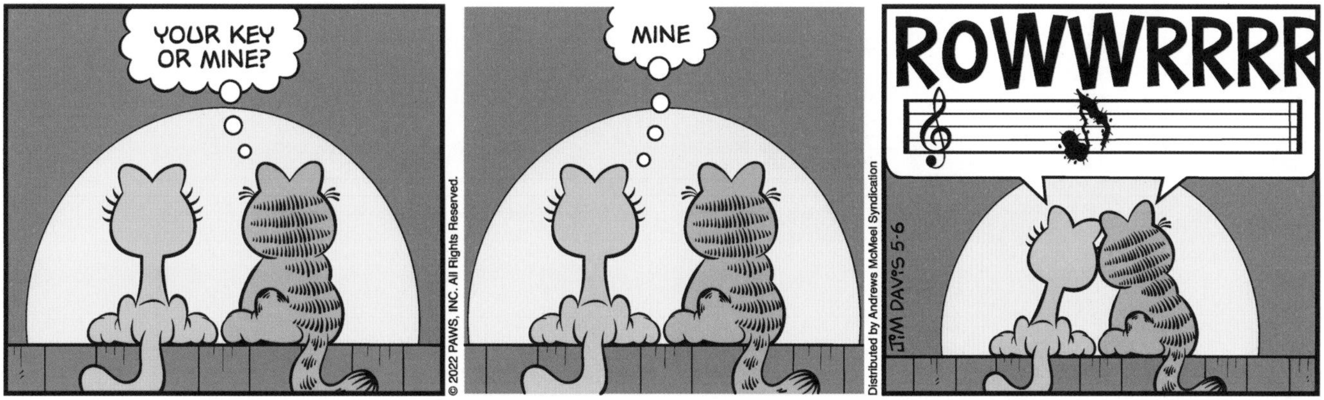
YOUR KEY OR MINE?
© 2022 PAWS, INC. All Rights Reserved.
MINE
Distributed by Andrews McMeel Syndication
JIM DAVIS 5-6
ROWWRRRR

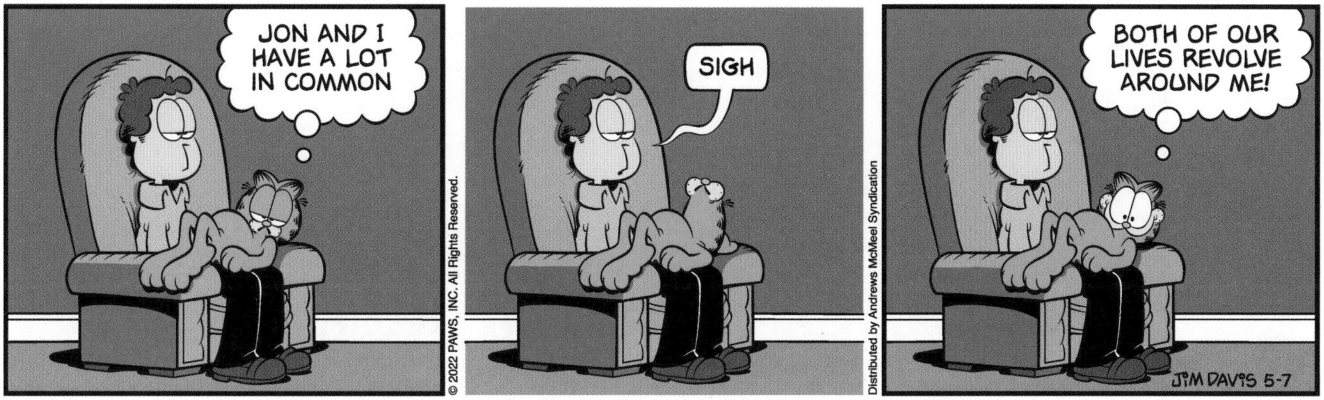
JON AND I HAVE A LOT IN COMMON
© 2022 PAWS, INC. All Rights Reserved.
SIGH
Distributed by Andrews McMeel Syndication
BOTH OF OUR LIVES REVOLVE AROUND ME!
JIM DAVIS 5-7

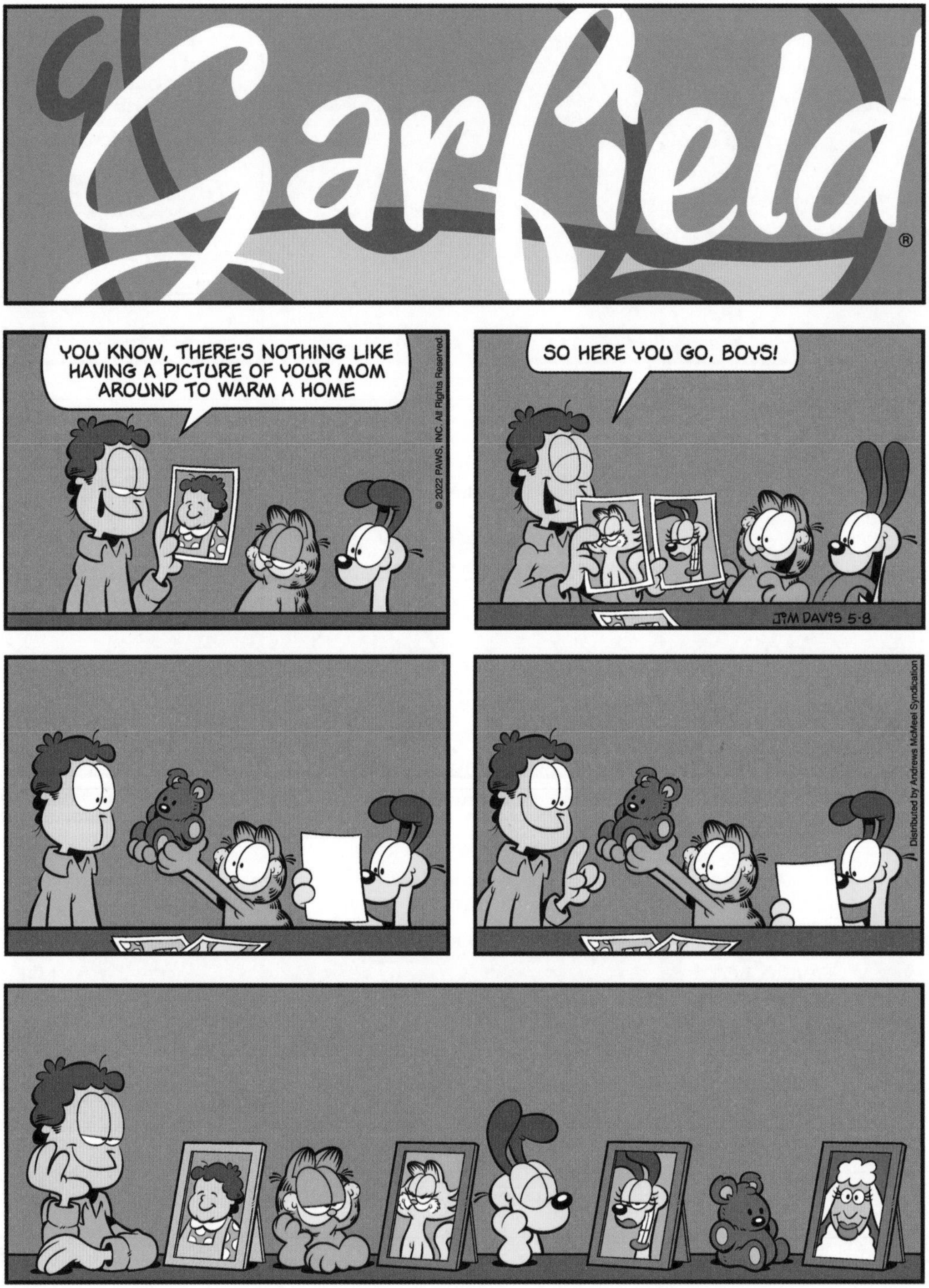
Garfield®
YOU KNOW, THERE'S NOTHING LIKE HAVING A PICTURE OF YOUR MOM AROUND TO WARM A HOME
© 2022 PAWS, INC. All Rights Reserved.
SO HERE YOU GO, BOYS!
JIM DAVIS 5-8
Distributed by Andrews McMeel Syndication

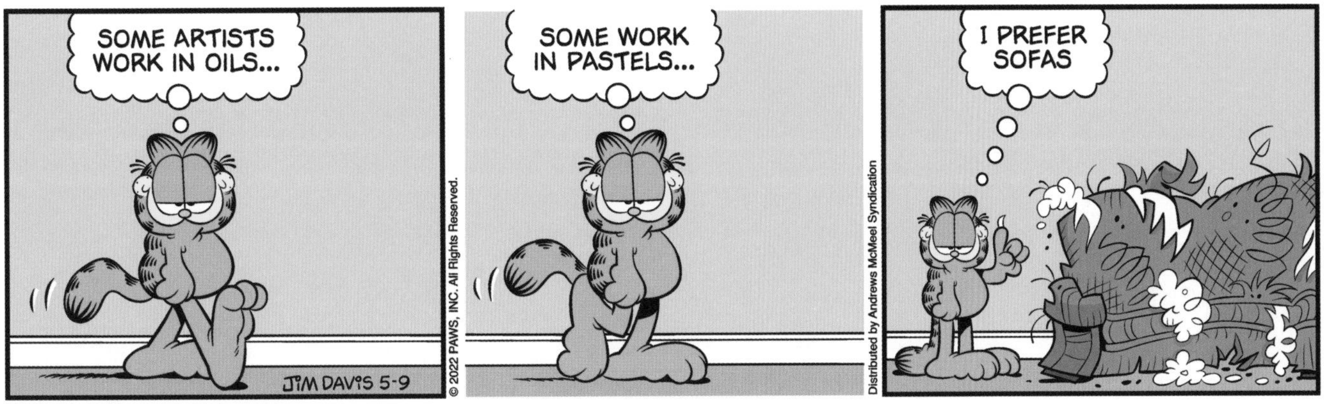
SOME ARTISTS WORK IN OILS...
SOME WORK IN PASTELS...
I PREFER SOFAS
JIM DAVIS 5-9
© 2022 PAWS, INC. All Rights Reserved.
Distributed by Andrews McMeel Syndication

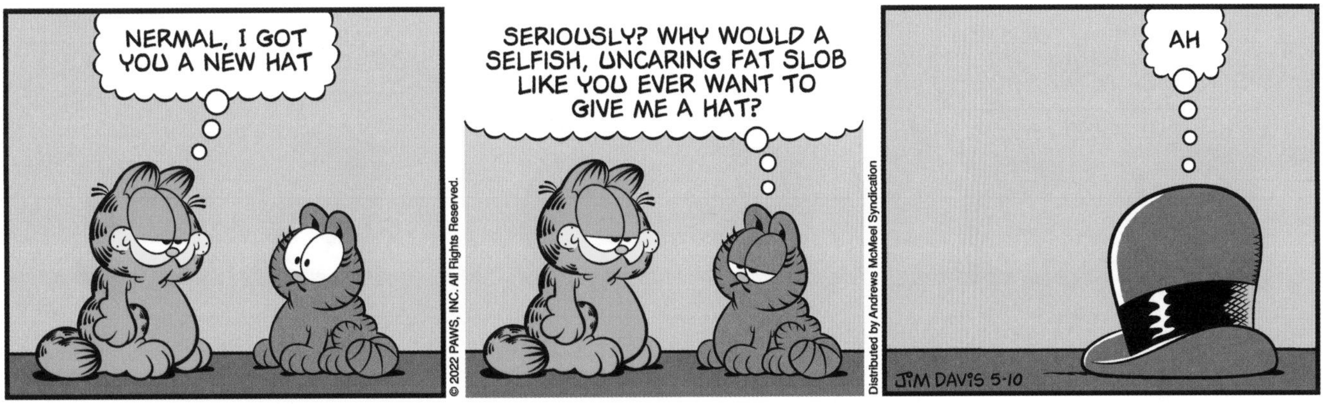
NERMAL, I GOT YOU A NEW HAT
SERIOUSLY? WHY WOULD A SELFISH, UNCARING FAT SLOB LIKE YOU EVER WANT TO GIVE ME A HAT?
AH
JIM DAVIS 5-10
© 2022 PAWS, INC. All Rights Reserved.
Distributed by Andrews McMeel Syndication

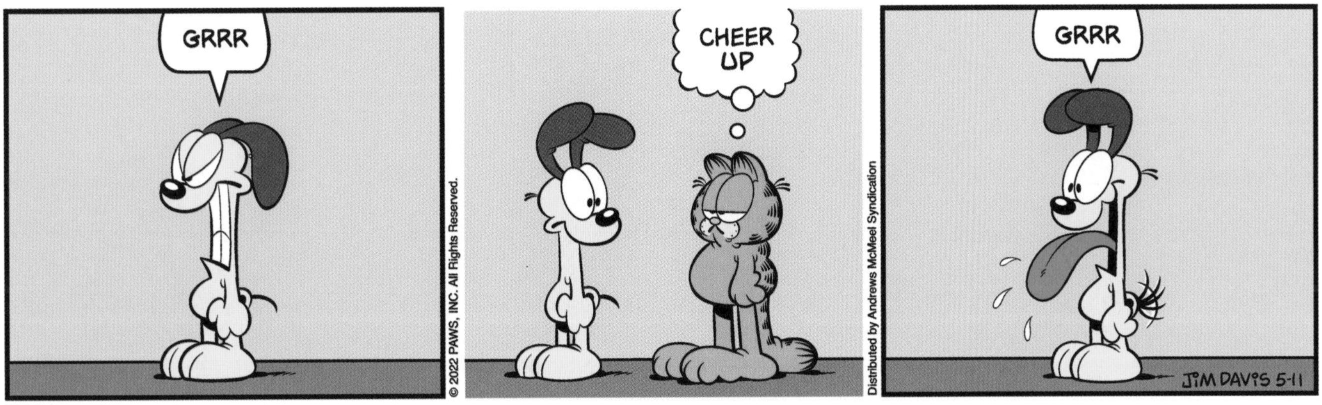
GRRR
CHEER UP
GRRR
JIM DAVIS 5-11
© 2022 PAWS, INC. All Rights Reserved.
Distributed by Andrews McMeel Syndication

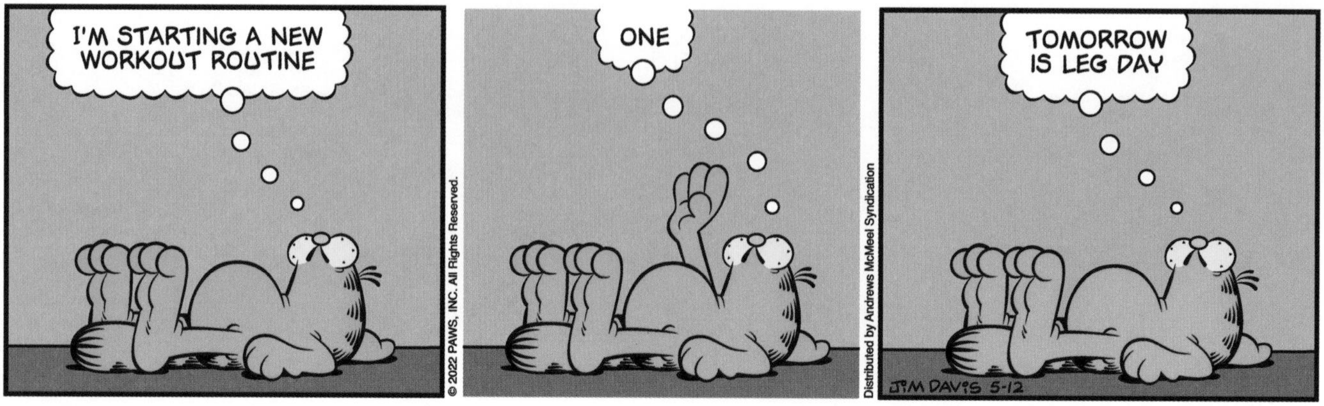
I'M STARTING A NEW WORKOUT ROUTINE
ONE
TOMORROW IS LEG DAY
© 2022 PAWS, INC. All Rights Reserved.
Distributed by Andrews McMeel Syndication
JIM DAVIS 5-12

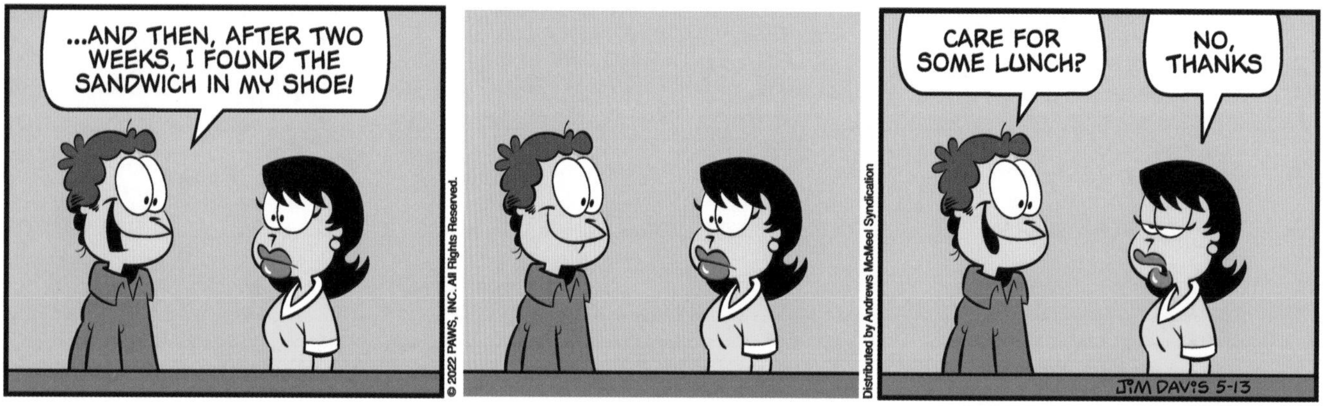
...AND THEN, AFTER TWO WEEKS, I FOUND THE SANDWICH IN MY SHOE!
CARE FOR SOME LUNCH?
NO, THANKS
© 2022 PAWS, INC. All Rights Reserved.
Distributed by Andrews McMeel Syndication
JIM DAVIS 5-13

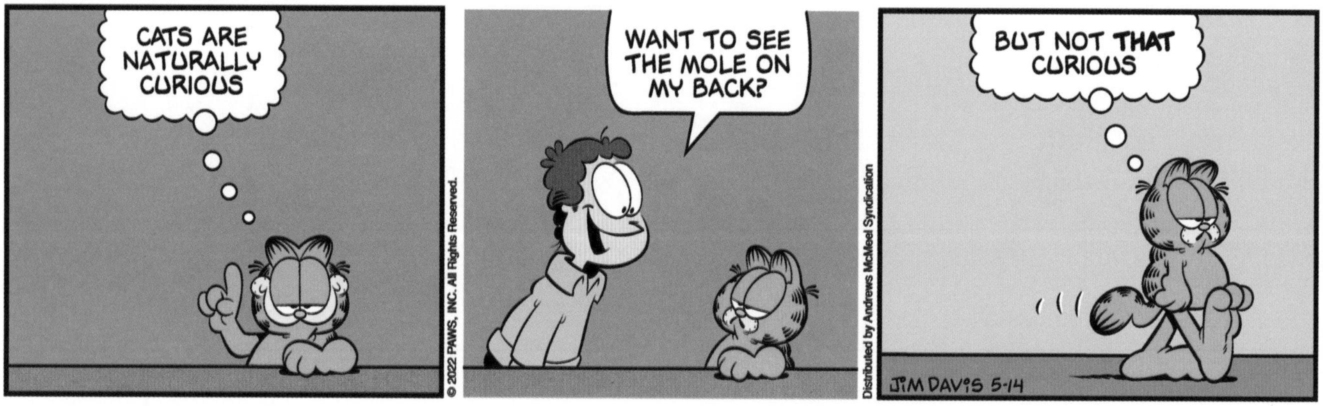
CATS ARE NATURALLY CURIOUS
WANT TO SEE THE MOLE ON MY BACK?
BUT NOT **THAT** CURIOUS
© 2022 PAWS, INC. All Rights Reserved.
Distributed by Andrews McMeel Syndication
JIM DAVIS 5-14

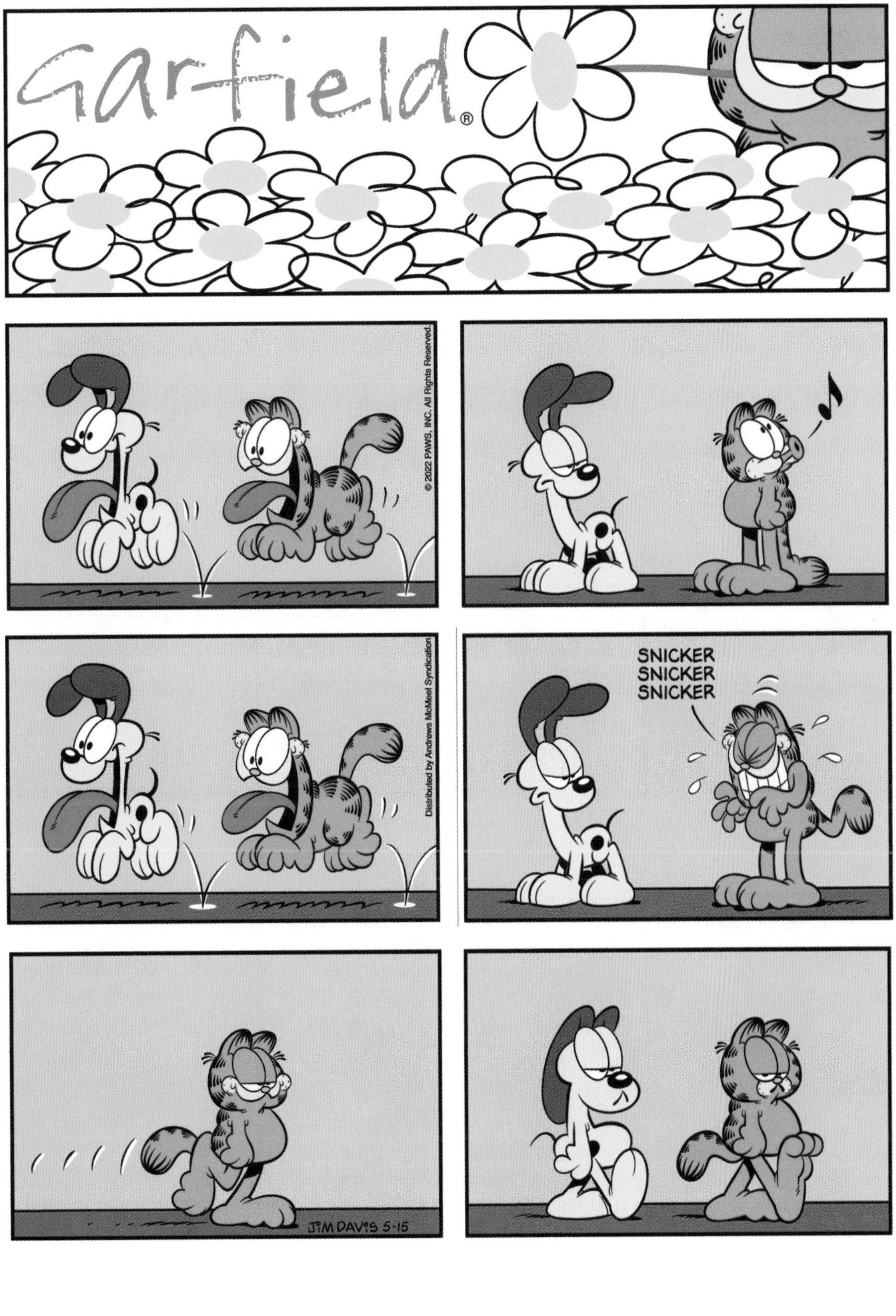
Garfield®
© 2022 PAWS, INC. All Rights Reserved.
Distributed by Andrews McMeel Syndication
SNICKER
SNICKER
SNICKER
JIM DAVIS 5-15

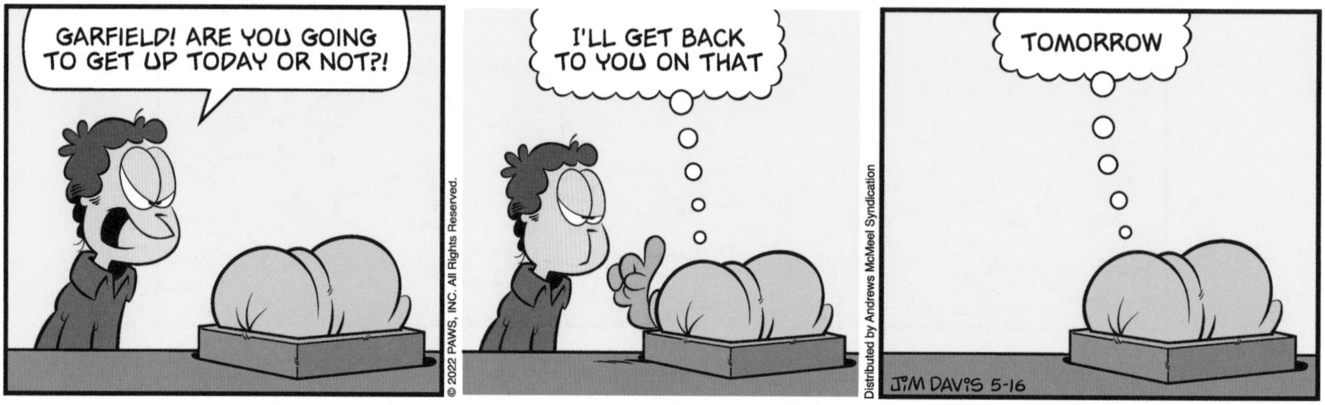
GARFIELD! ARE YOU GOING TO GET UP TODAY OR NOT?!
I'LL GET BACK TO YOU ON THAT
TOMORROW
© 2022 PAWS, INC. All Rights Reserved.
Distributed by Andrews McMeel Syndication
JIM DAVIS 5-16

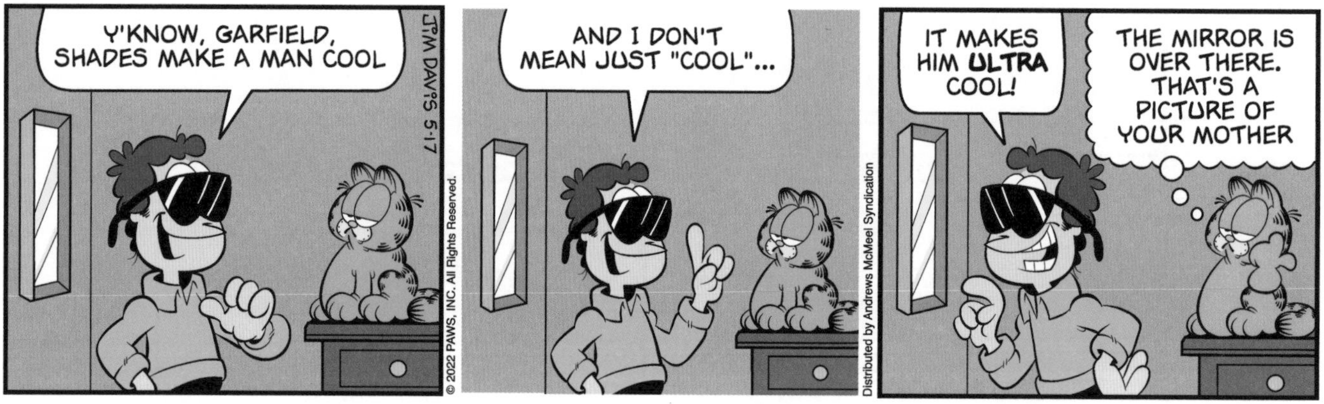
Y'KNOW, GARFIELD, SHADES MAKE A MAN COOL
JIM DAVIS 5-17
AND I DON'T MEAN JUST "COOL"...
IT MAKES HIM **ULTRA** COOL!
THE MIRROR IS OVER THERE. THAT'S A PICTURE OF YOUR MOTHER
© 2022 PAWS, INC. All Rights Reserved.
Distributed by Andrews McMeel Syndication

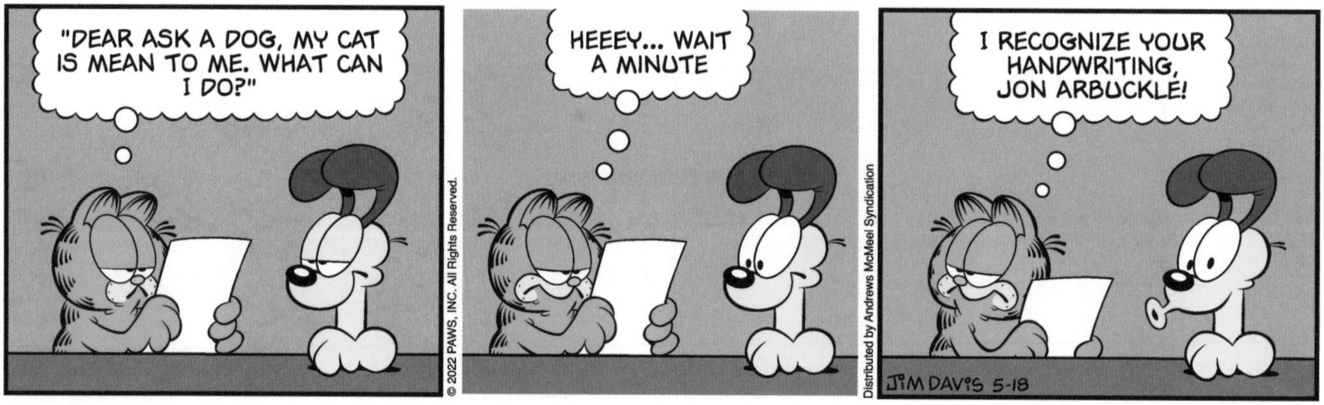
"DEAR ASK A DOG, MY CAT IS MEAN TO ME. WHAT CAN I DO?"
HEEEY... WAIT A MINUTE
I RECOGNIZE YOUR HANDWRITING, JON ARBUCKLE!
© 2022 PAWS, INC. All Rights Reserved.
Distributed by Andrews McMeel Syndication
JIM DAVIS 5-18

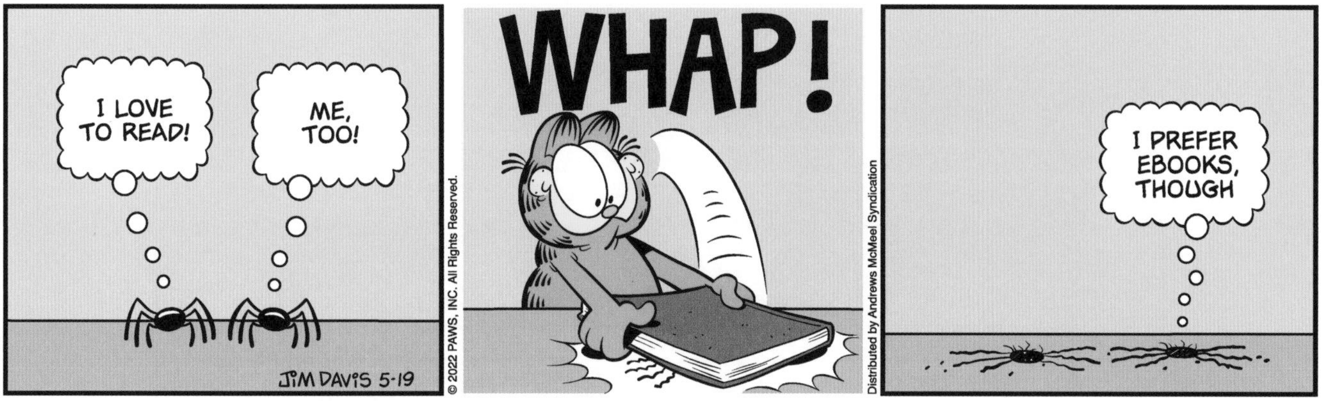
I LOVE TO READ!
ME, TOO!
JIM DAVIS 5-19
© 2022 PAWS, INC. All Rights Reserved.
WHAP!
Distributed by Andrews McMeel Syndication
I PREFER EBOOKS, THOUGH

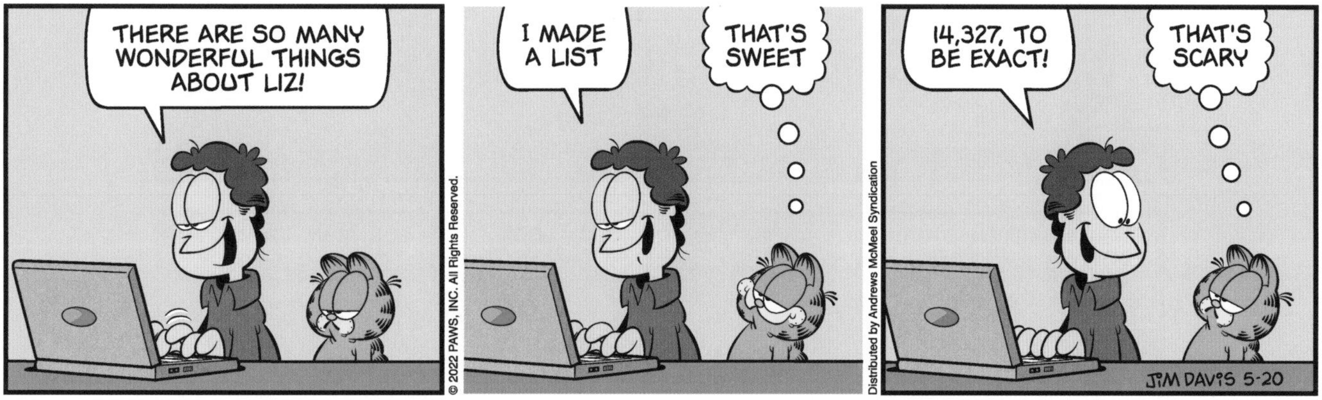
THERE ARE SO MANY WONDERFUL THINGS ABOUT LIZ!
© 2022 PAWS, INC. All Rights Reserved.
I MADE A LIST
THAT'S SWEET
Distributed by Andrews McMeel Syndication
14,327, TO BE EXACT!
THAT'S SCARY
JIM DAVIS 5-20

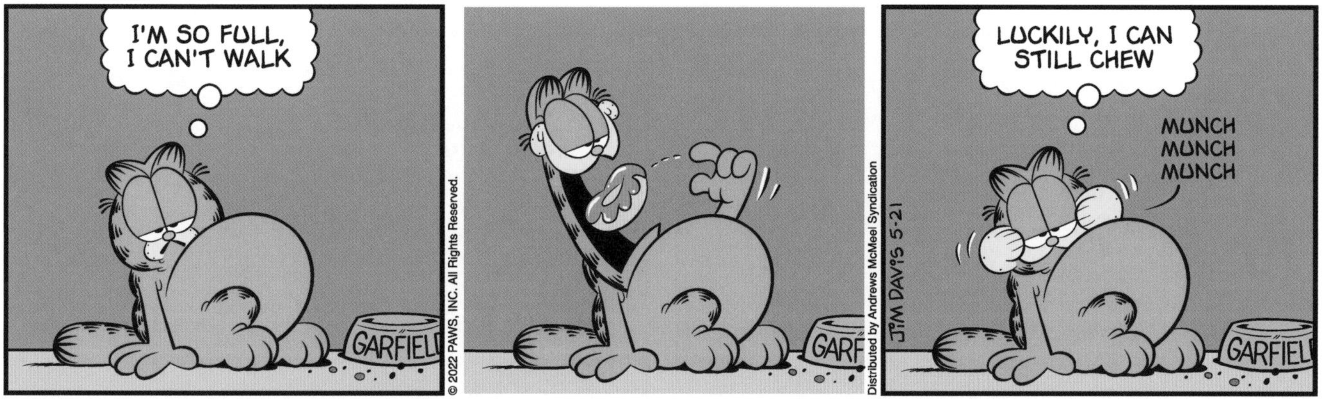
I'M SO FULL, I CAN'T WALK
GARFIELD
© 2022 PAWS, INC. All Rights Reserved.
GARF
Distributed by Andrews McMeel Syndication
JIM DAVIS 5-21
LUCKILY, I CAN STILL CHEW
MUNCH MUNCH MUNCH
GARFIELD

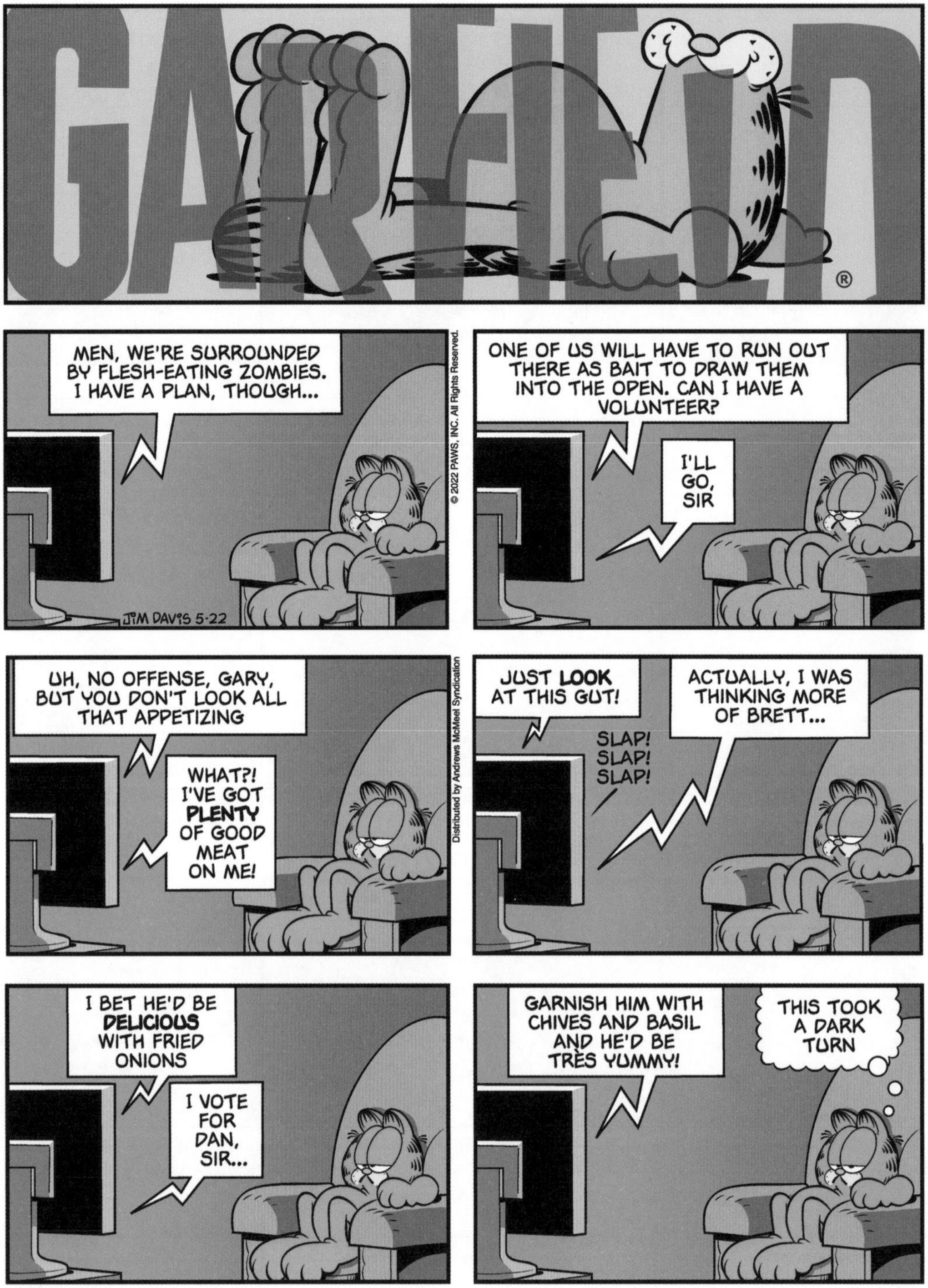
GARFIELD®
MEN, WE'RE SURROUNDED BY FLESH-EATING ZOMBIES. I HAVE A PLAN, THOUGH...
JIM DAVIS 5-22
© 2022 PAWS, INC. All Rights Reserved.
ONE OF US WILL HAVE TO RUN OUT THERE AS BAIT TO DRAW THEM INTO THE OPEN. CAN I HAVE A VOLUNTEER?
I'LL GO, SIR
UH, NO OFFENSE, GARY, BUT YOU DON'T LOOK ALL THAT APPETIZING
WHAT?! I'VE GOT PLENTY OF GOOD MEAT ON ME!
Distributed by Andrews McMeel Syndication
JUST LOOK AT THIS GUT!
SLAP! SLAP! SLAP!
ACTUALLY, I WAS THINKING MORE OF BRETT...
I BET HE'D BE DELICIOUS WITH FRIED ONIONS
I VOTE FOR DAN, SIR...
GARNISH HIM WITH CHIVES AND BASIL AND HE'D BE TRÈS YUMMY!
THIS TOOK A DARK TURN

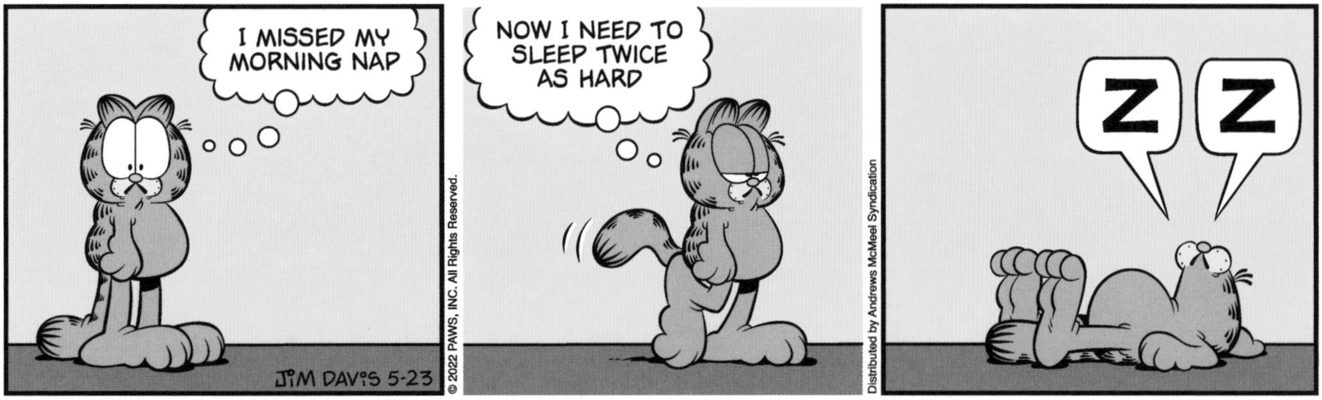
I MISSED MY MORNING NAP
JIM DAVIS 5-23
© 2022 PAWS, INC. All Rights Reserved.
NOW I NEED TO SLEEP TWICE AS HARD
Distributed by Andrews McMeel Syndication
Z Z

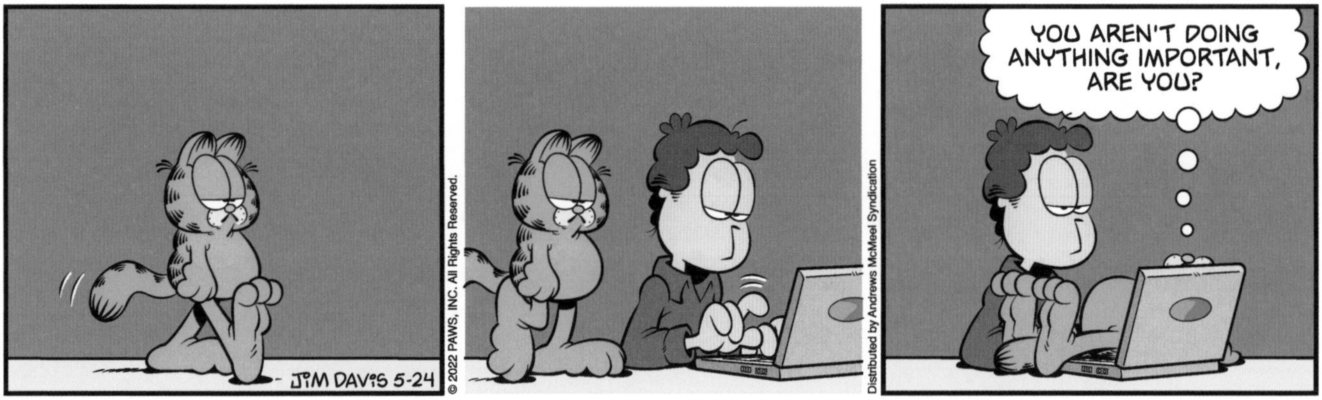
JIM DAVIS 5-24
© 2022 PAWS, INC. All Rights Reserved.
Distributed by Andrews McMeel Syndication
YOU AREN'T DOING ANYTHING IMPORTANT, ARE YOU?

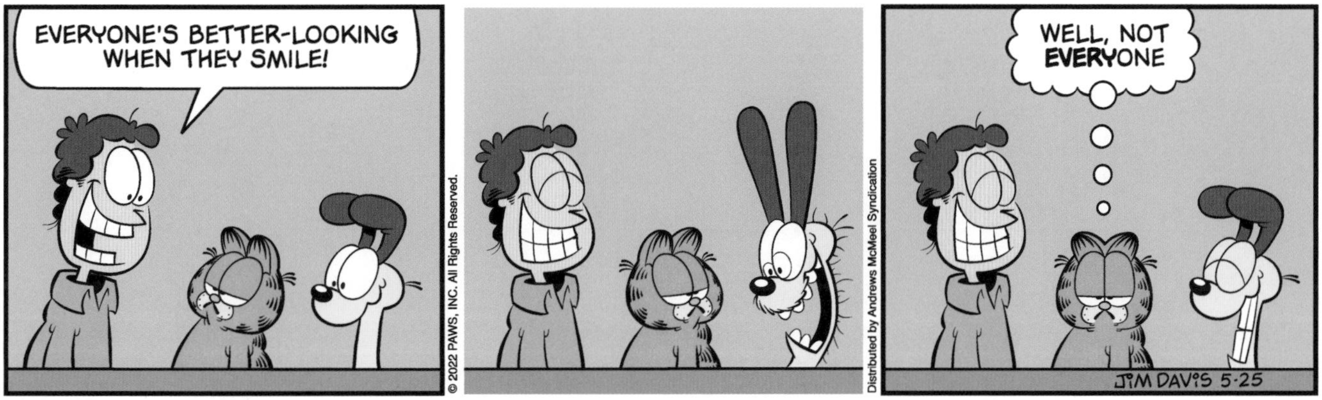
EVERYONE'S BETTER-LOOKING WHEN THEY SMILE!
© 2022 PAWS, INC. All Rights Reserved.
Distributed by Andrews McMeel Syndication
WELL, NOT **EVERY**ONE
JIM DAVIS 5-25

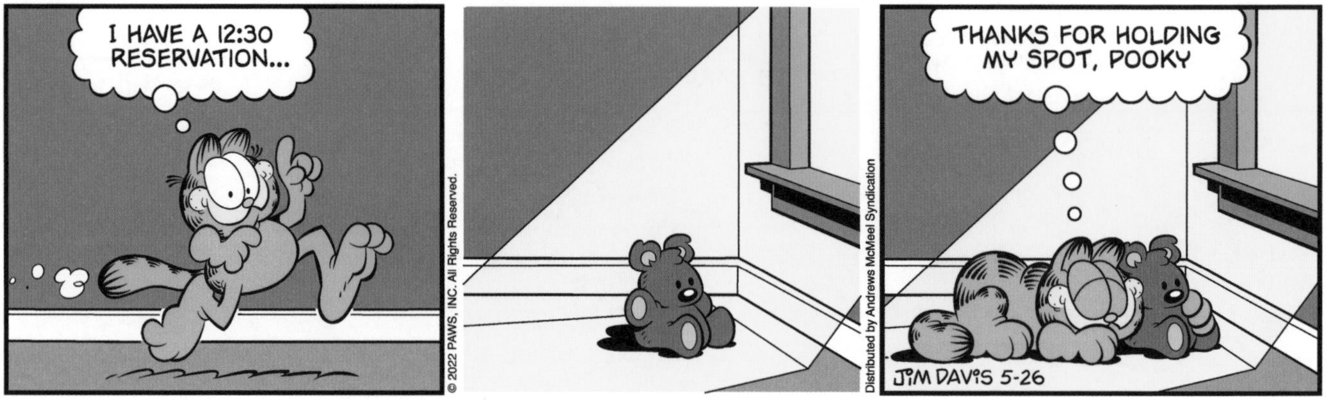
I HAVE A 12:30 RESERVATION...
© 2022 PAWS, INC. All Rights Reserved.
Distributed by Andrews McMeel Syndication
THANKS FOR HOLDING MY SPOT, POOKY
JIM DAVIS 5-26

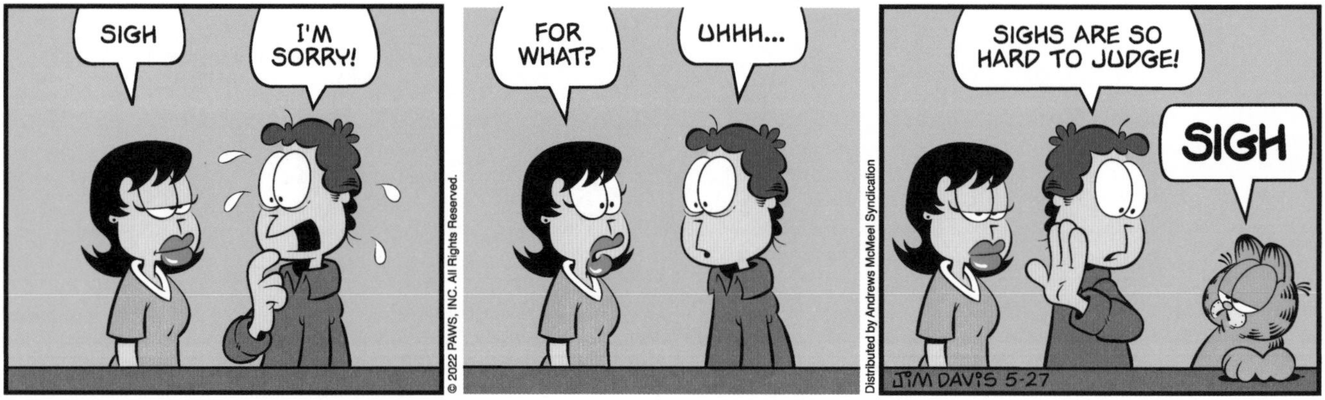
SIGH
I'M SORRY!
© 2022 PAWS, INC. All Rights Reserved.
FOR WHAT?
UHHH...
Distributed by Andrews McMeel Syndication
SIGHS ARE SO HARD TO JUDGE!
SIGH
JIM DAVIS 5-27

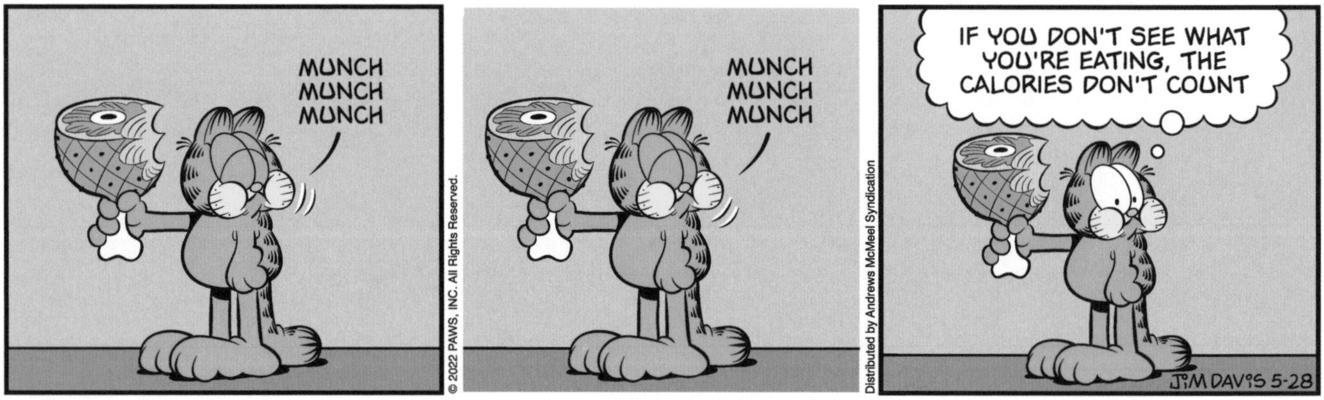
MUNCH MUNCH MUNCH
© 2022 PAWS, INC. All Rights Reserved.
MUNCH MUNCH MUNCH
Distributed by Andrews McMeel Syndication
IF YOU DON'T SEE WHAT YOU'RE EATING, THE CALORIES DON'T COUNT
JIM DAVIS 5-28

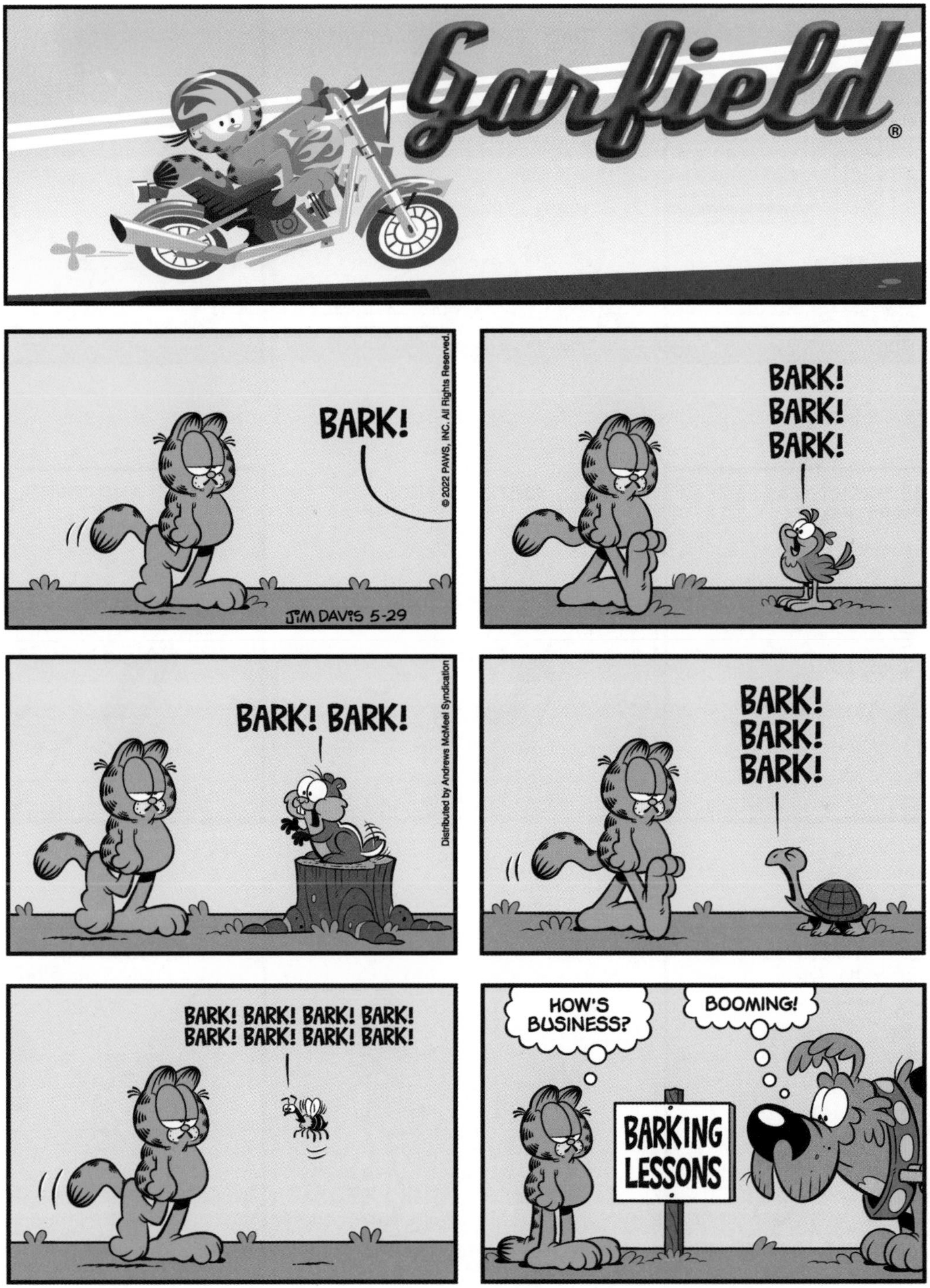
Garfield®
BARK!
© 2022 PAWS, INC. All Rights Reserved.
JIM DAVIS 5-29
BARK! BARK! BARK!
BARK! BARK!
Distributed by Andrews McMeel Syndication
BARK! BARK! BARK!
BARK! BARK! BARK! BARK! BARK! BARK! BARK! BARK!
HOW'S BUSINESS?
BOOMING!
BARKING LESSONS

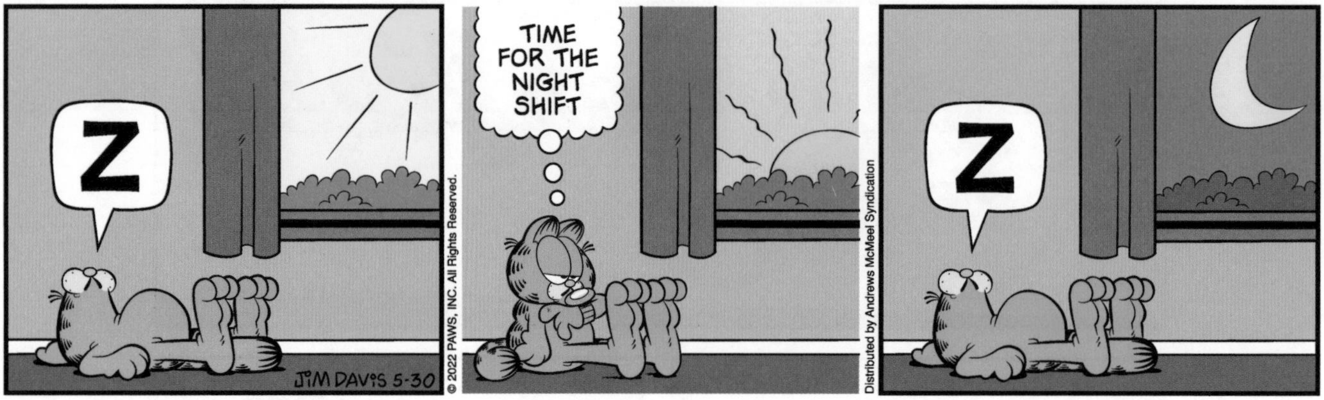
Z
JIM DAVIS 5-30
© 2022 PAWS, INC. All Rights Reserved.
TIME FOR THE NIGHT SHIFT
Distributed by Andrews McMeel Syndication
Z

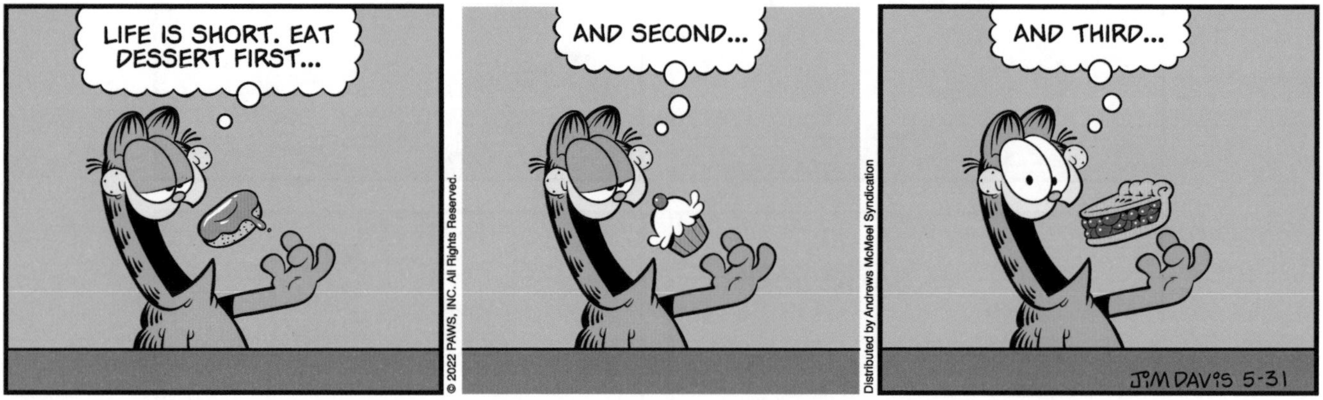
LIFE IS SHORT. EAT DESSERT FIRST...
© 2022 PAWS, INC. All Rights Reserved.
AND SECOND...
Distributed by Andrews McMeel Syndication
AND THIRD...
JIM DAVIS 5-31

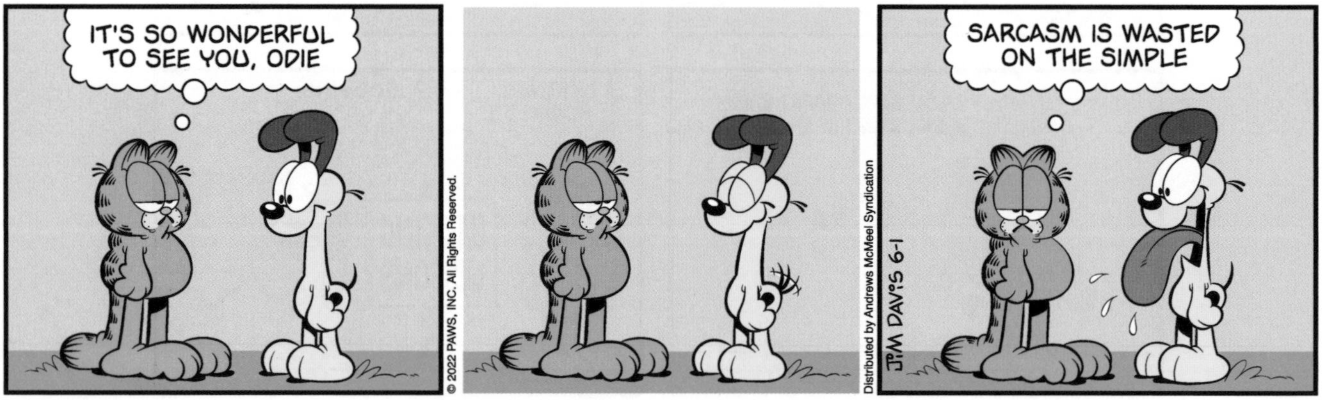
IT'S SO WONDERFUL TO SEE YOU, ODIE
© 2022 PAWS, INC. All Rights Reserved.
Distributed by Andrews McMeel Syndication
JIM DAVIS 6-1
SARCASM IS WASTED ON THE SIMPLE

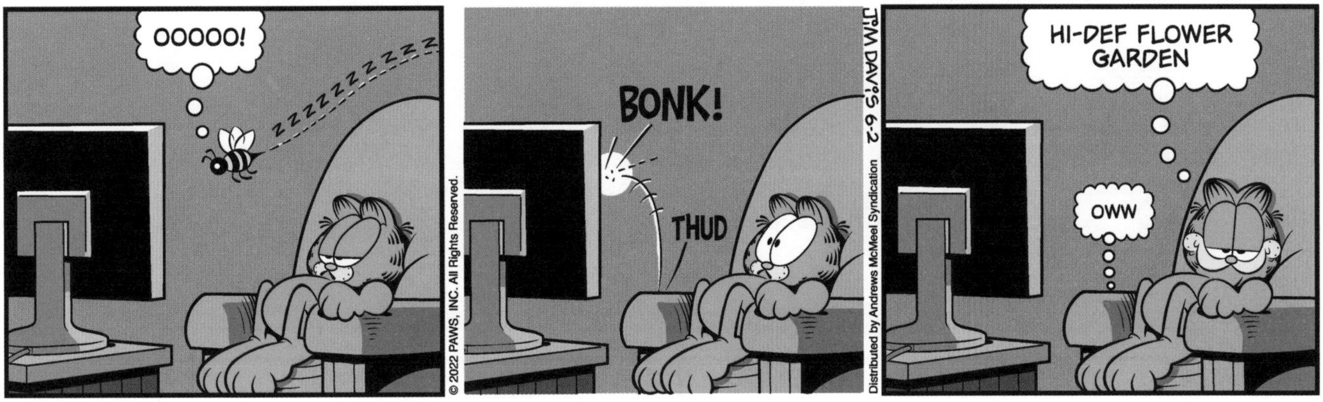
OOOOO!
BONK!
THUD
© 2022 PAWS, INC. All Rights Reserved.
JIM DAVIS 6-2
Distributed by Andrews McMeel Syndication
HI-DEF FLOWER GARDEN
OWW

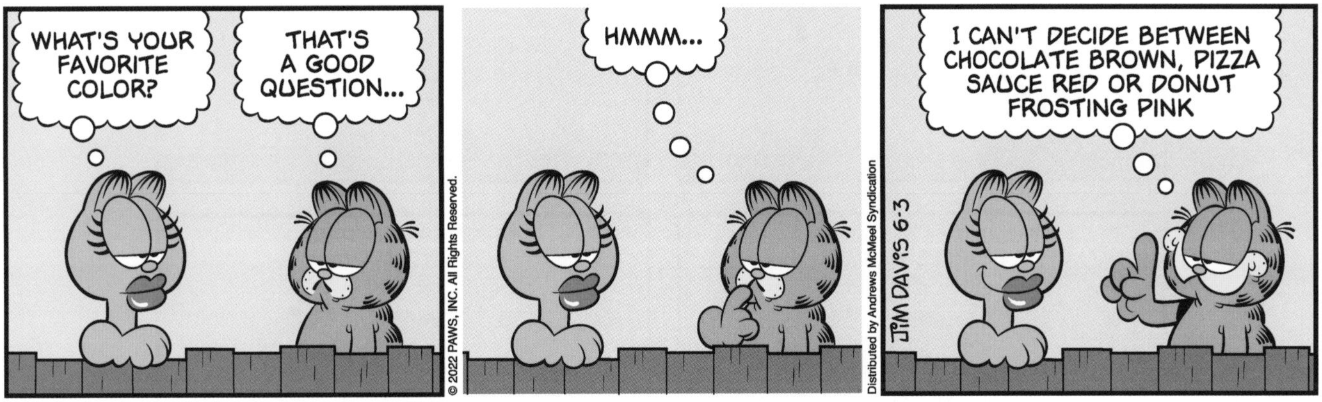
WHAT'S YOUR FAVORITE COLOR?
THAT'S A GOOD QUESTION...
© 2022 PAWS, INC. All Rights Reserved.
HMMM...
Distributed by Andrews McMeel Syndication
JIM DAVIS 6-3
I CAN'T DECIDE BETWEEN CHOCOLATE BROWN, PIZZA SAUCE RED OR DONUT FROSTING PINK

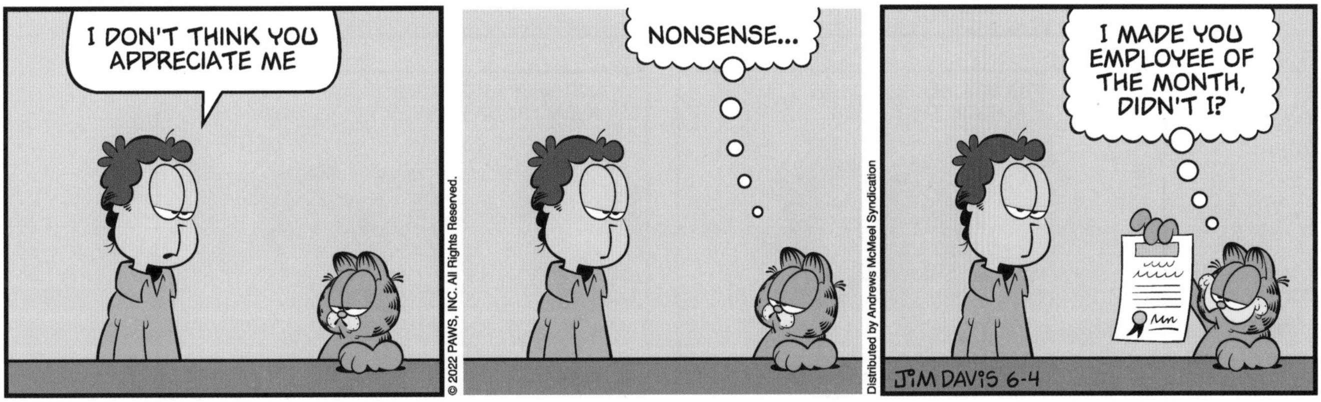
I DON'T THINK YOU APPRECIATE ME
© 2022 PAWS, INC. All Rights Reserved.
NONSENSE...
Distributed by Andrews McMeel Syndication
I MADE YOU EMPLOYEE OF THE MONTH, DIDN'T I?
JIM DAVIS 6-4

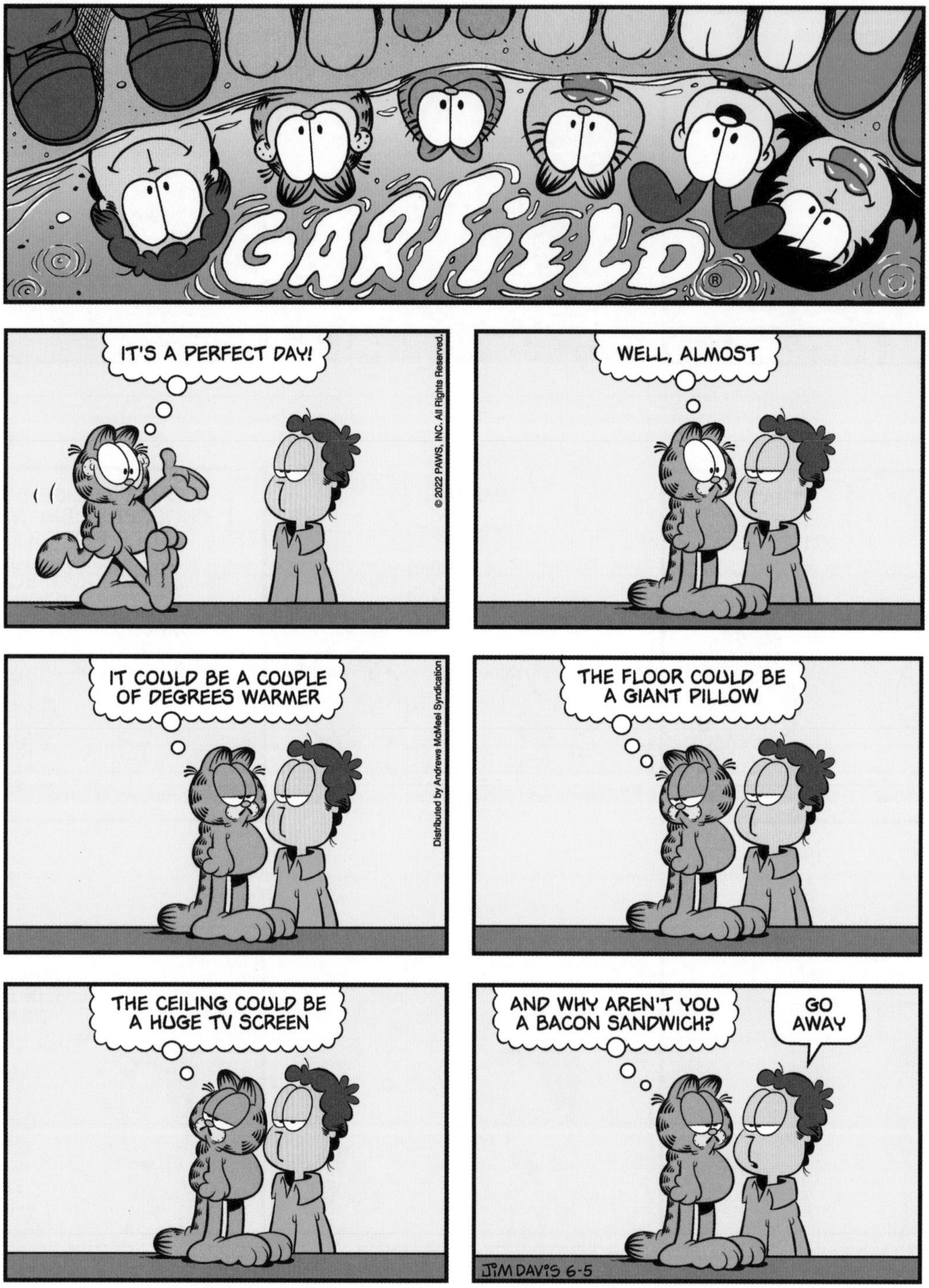
GARFIELD®
IT'S A PERFECT DAY!
© 2022 PAWS, INC. All Rights Reserved.
WELL, ALMOST
IT COULD BE A COUPLE OF DEGREES WARMER
Distributed by Andrews McMeel Syndication
THE FLOOR COULD BE A GIANT PILLOW
THE CEILING COULD BE A HUGE TV SCREEN
AND WHY AREN'T YOU A BACON SANDWICH?
GO AWAY
JIM DAVIS 6-5

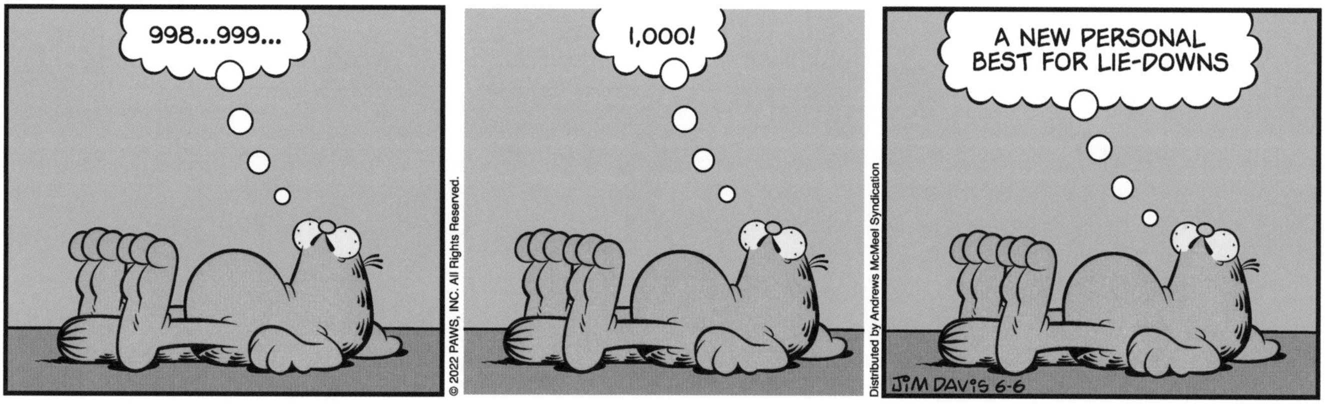
998...999...
1,000!
A NEW PERSONAL BEST FOR LIE-DOWNS
© 2022 PAWS, INC. All Rights Reserved.
Distributed by Andrews McMeel Syndication
JIM DAVIS 6-6

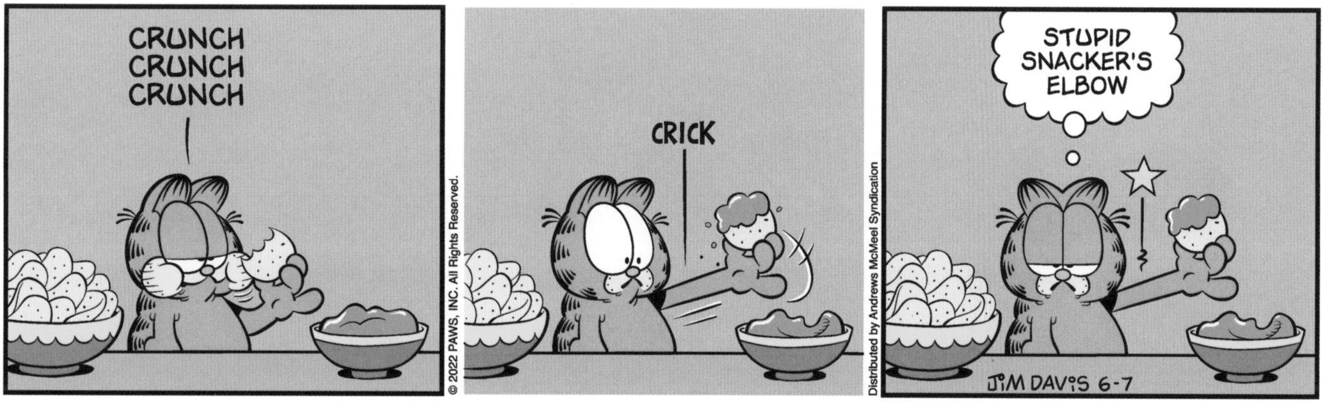
CRUNCH CRUNCH CRUNCH
CRICK
STUPID SNACKER'S ELBOW
© 2022 PAWS, INC. All Rights Reserved.
Distributed by Andrews McMeel Syndication
JIM DAVIS 6-7

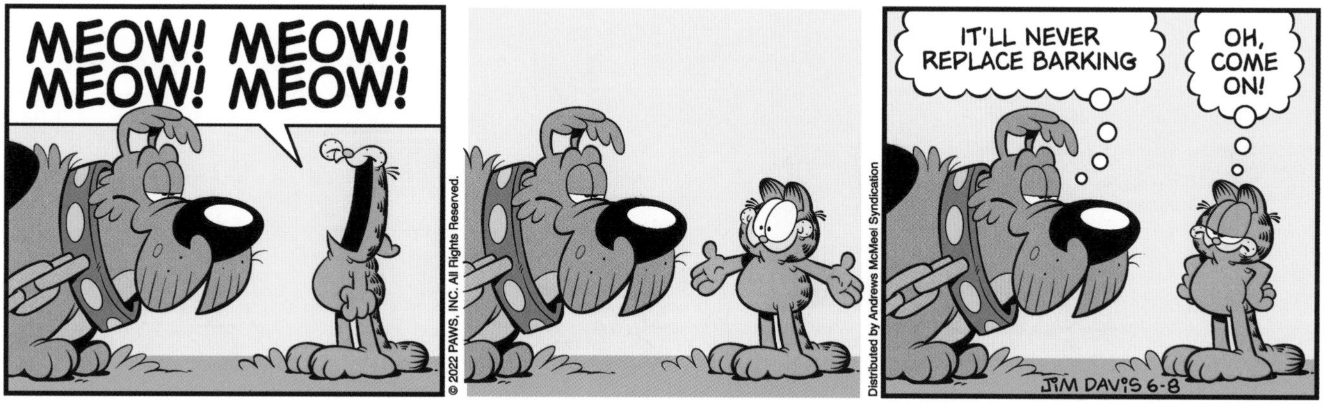
MEOW! MEOW! MEOW! MEOW!
IT'LL NEVER REPLACE BARKING
OH, COME ON!
© 2022 PAWS, INC. All Rights Reserved.
Distributed by Andrews McMeel Syndication
JIM DAVIS 6-8

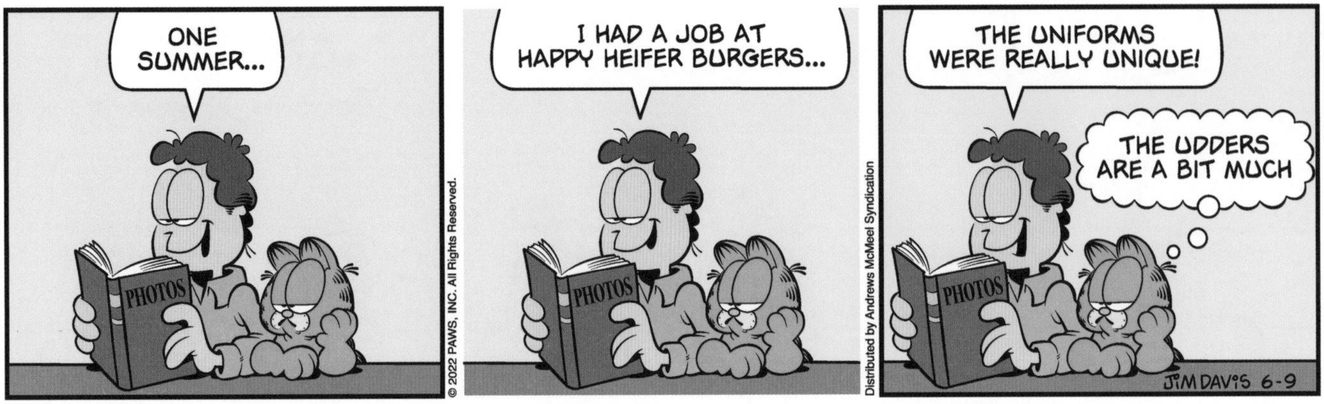
ONE SUMMER...
I HAD A JOB AT HAPPY HEIFER BURGERS...
THE UNIFORMS WERE REALLY UNIQUE!
THE UDDERS ARE A BIT MUCH
PHOTOS
JIM DAVIS 6-9
© 2022 PAWS, INC. All Rights Reserved.
Distributed by Andrews McMeel Syndication

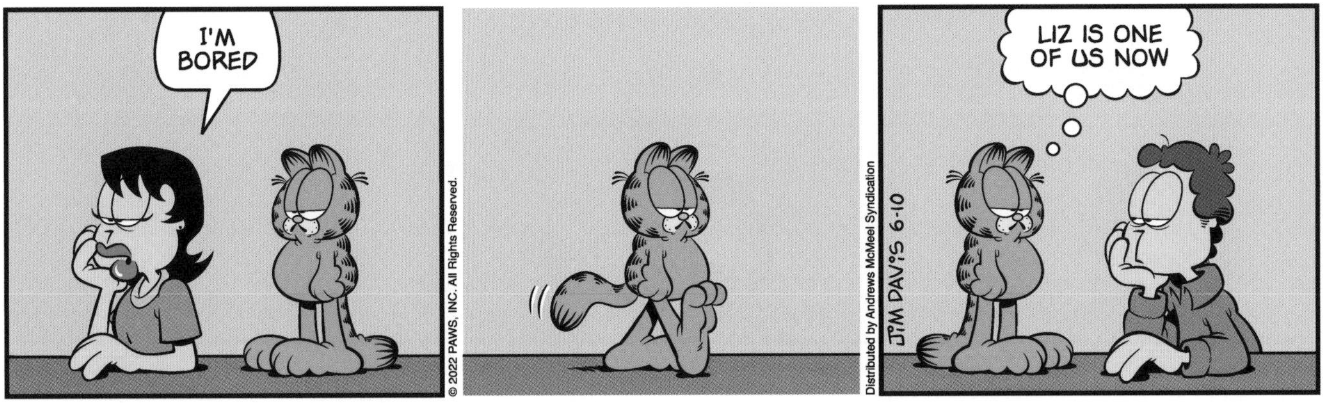
I'M BORED
LIZ IS ONE OF US NOW
JIM DAVIS 6-10
© 2022 PAWS, INC. All Rights Reserved.
Distributed by Andrews McMeel Syndication

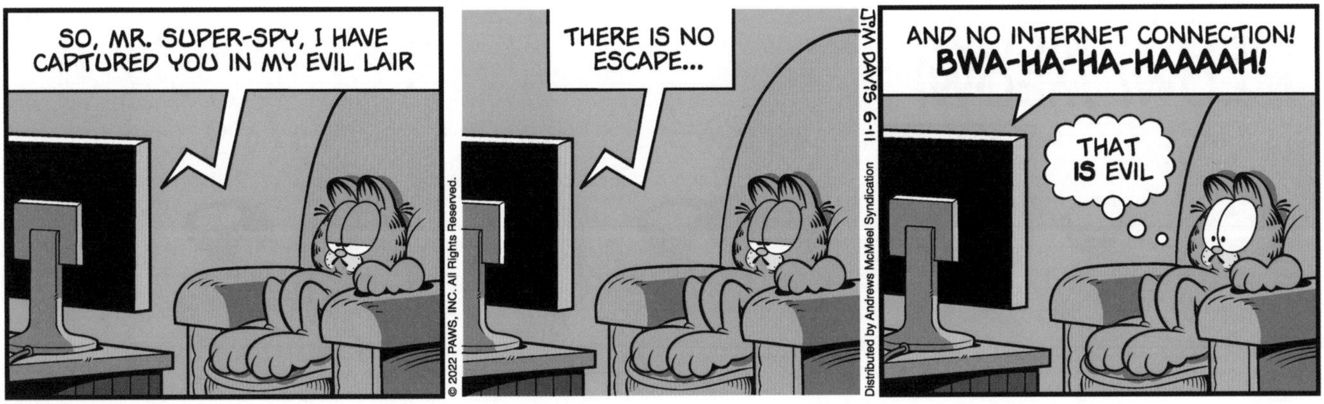
SO, MR. SUPER-SPY, I HAVE CAPTURED YOU IN MY EVIL LAIR
THERE IS NO ESCAPE...
AND NO INTERNET CONNECTION! **BWA-HA-HA-HAAAAH!**
THAT **IS** EVIL
JIM DAVIS 6-11
© 2022 PAWS, INC. All Rights Reserved.
Distributed by Andrews McMeel Syndication

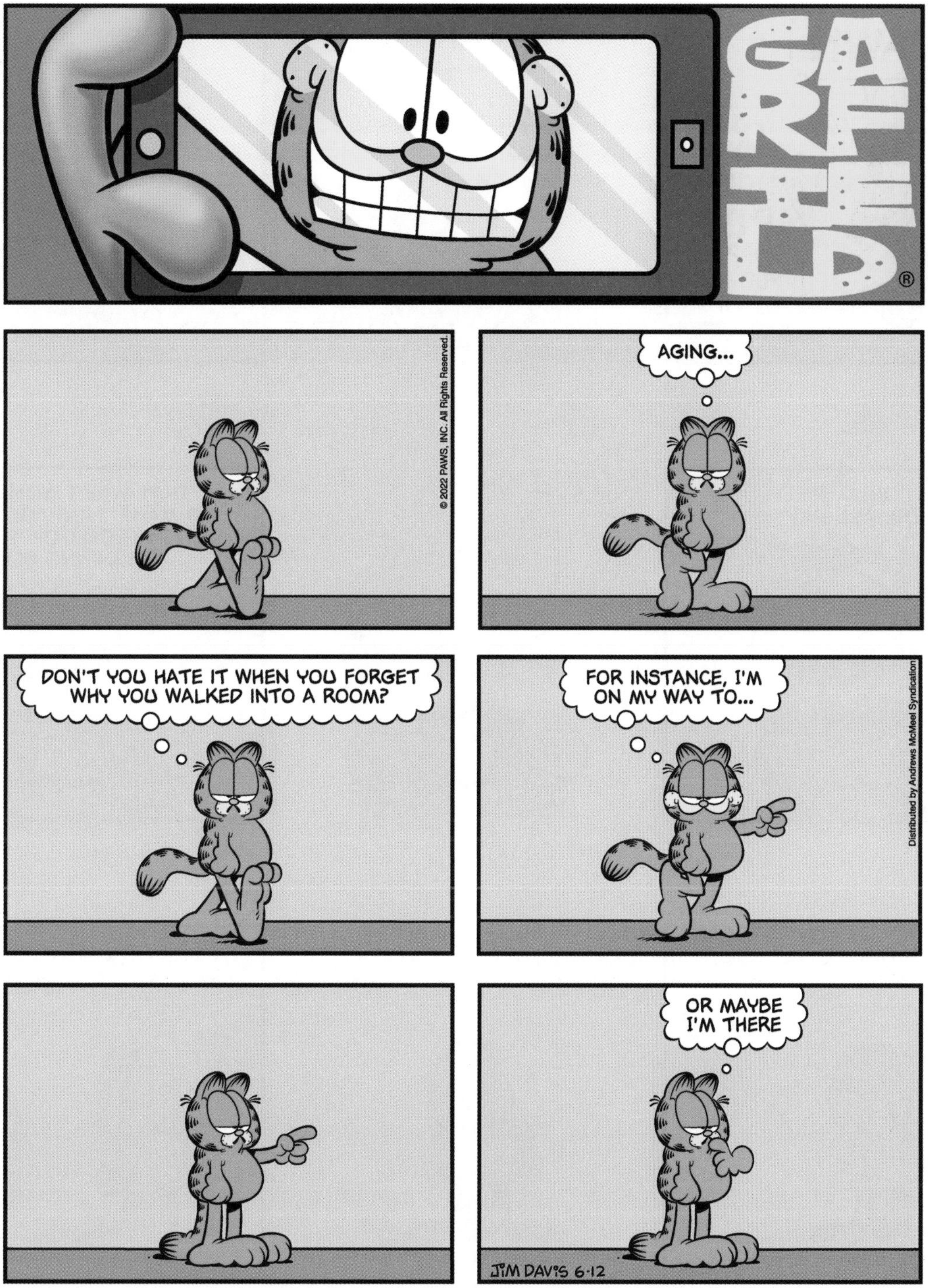
GARFIELD®
© 2022 PAWS, INC. All Rights Reserved.
AGING...
DON'T YOU HATE IT WHEN YOU FORGET WHY YOU WALKED INTO A ROOM?
FOR INSTANCE, I'M ON MY WAY TO...
Distributed by Andrews McMeel Syndication
OR MAYBE I'M THERE
JIM DAVIS 6-12

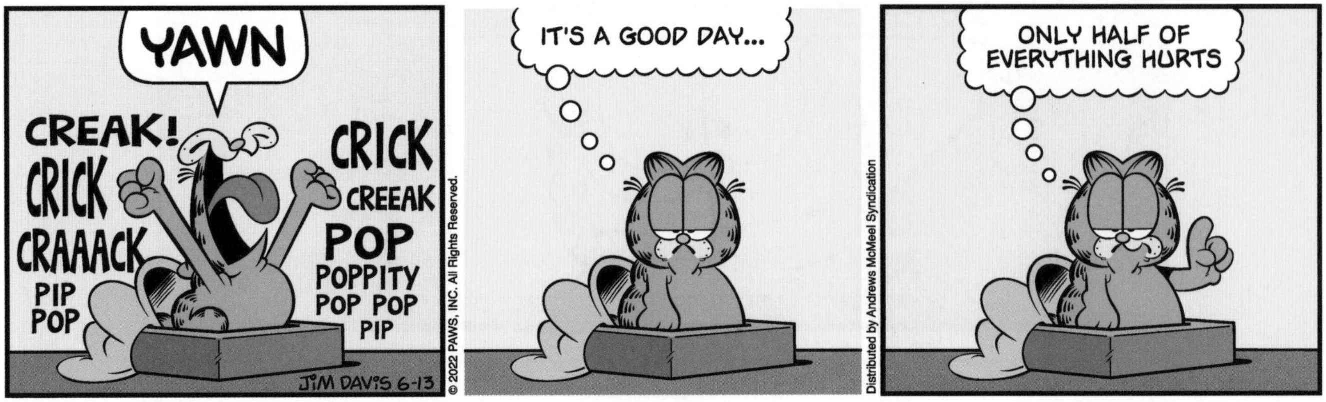
YAWN
CREAK!
CRICK
CRAAACK
PIP
POP
CRICK
CREEAK
POP
POPPITY
POP POP
PIP
JIM DAVIS 6-13
IT'S A GOOD DAY...
ONLY HALF OF EVERYTHING HURTS

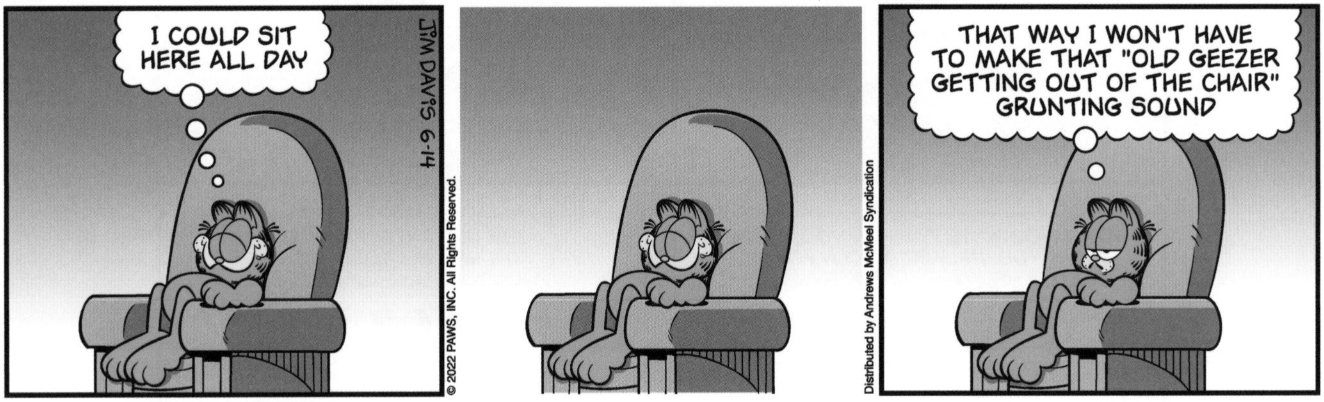
I COULD SIT HERE ALL DAY
JIM DAVIS 6-14
THAT WAY I WON'T HAVE TO MAKE THAT "OLD GEEZER GETTING OUT OF THE CHAIR" GRUNTING SOUND

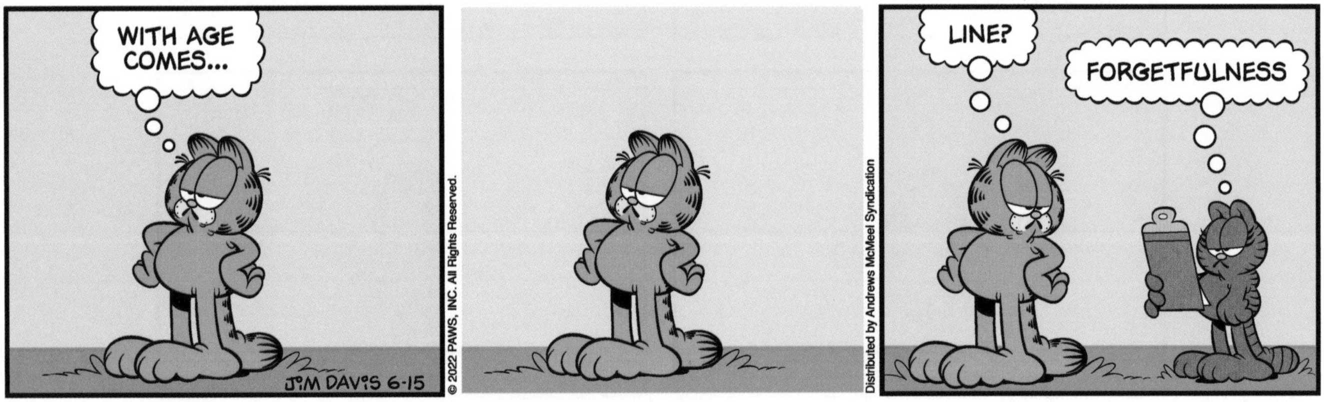
WITH AGE COMES...
JIM DAVIS 6-15
LINE?
FORGETFULNESS

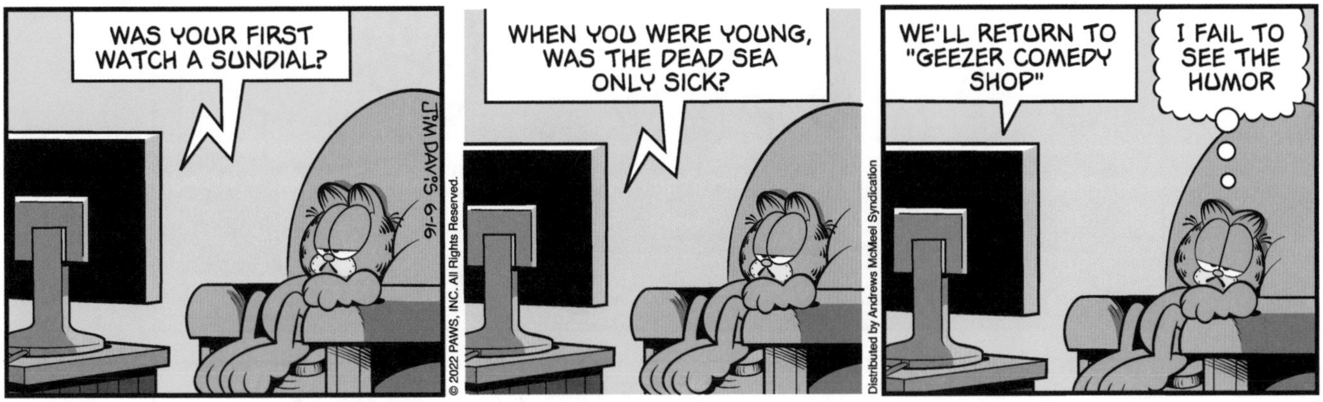
WAS YOUR FIRST WATCH A SUNDIAL?
JIM DAVIS 6-16
WHEN YOU WERE YOUNG, WAS THE DEAD SEA ONLY SICK?
© 2022 PAWS, INC. All Rights Reserved.
WE'LL RETURN TO "GEEZER COMEDY SHOP"
I FAIL TO SEE THE HUMOR
Distributed by Andrews McMeel Syndication

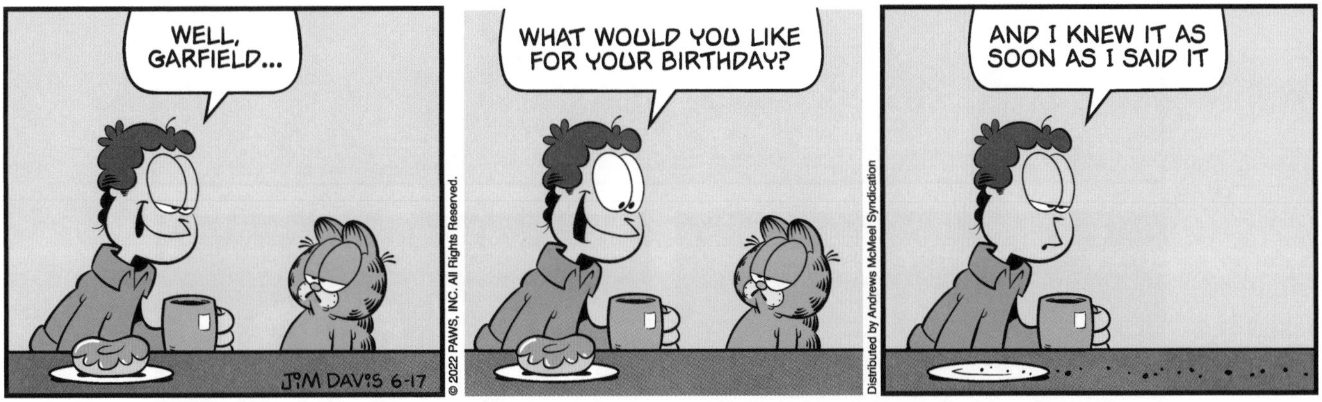
WELL, GARFIELD...
JIM DAVIS 6-17
WHAT WOULD YOU LIKE FOR YOUR BIRTHDAY?
© 2022 PAWS, INC. All Rights Reserved.
AND I KNEW IT AS SOON AS I SAID IT
Distributed by Andrews McMeel Syndication

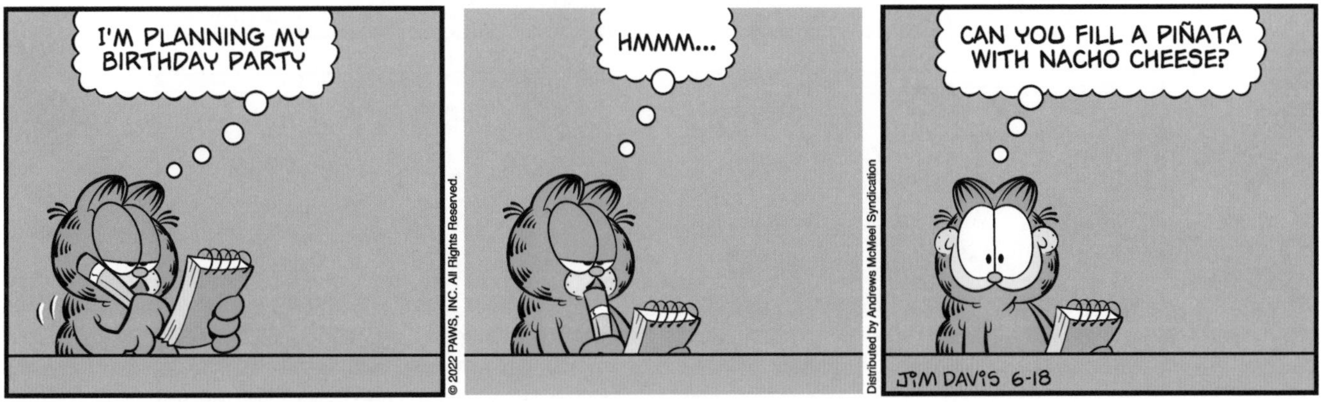
I'M PLANNING MY BIRTHDAY PARTY
HMMM...
© 2022 PAWS, INC. All Rights Reserved.
CAN YOU FILL A PIÑATA WITH NACHO CHEESE?
JIM DAVIS 6-18
Distributed by Andrews McMeel Syndication

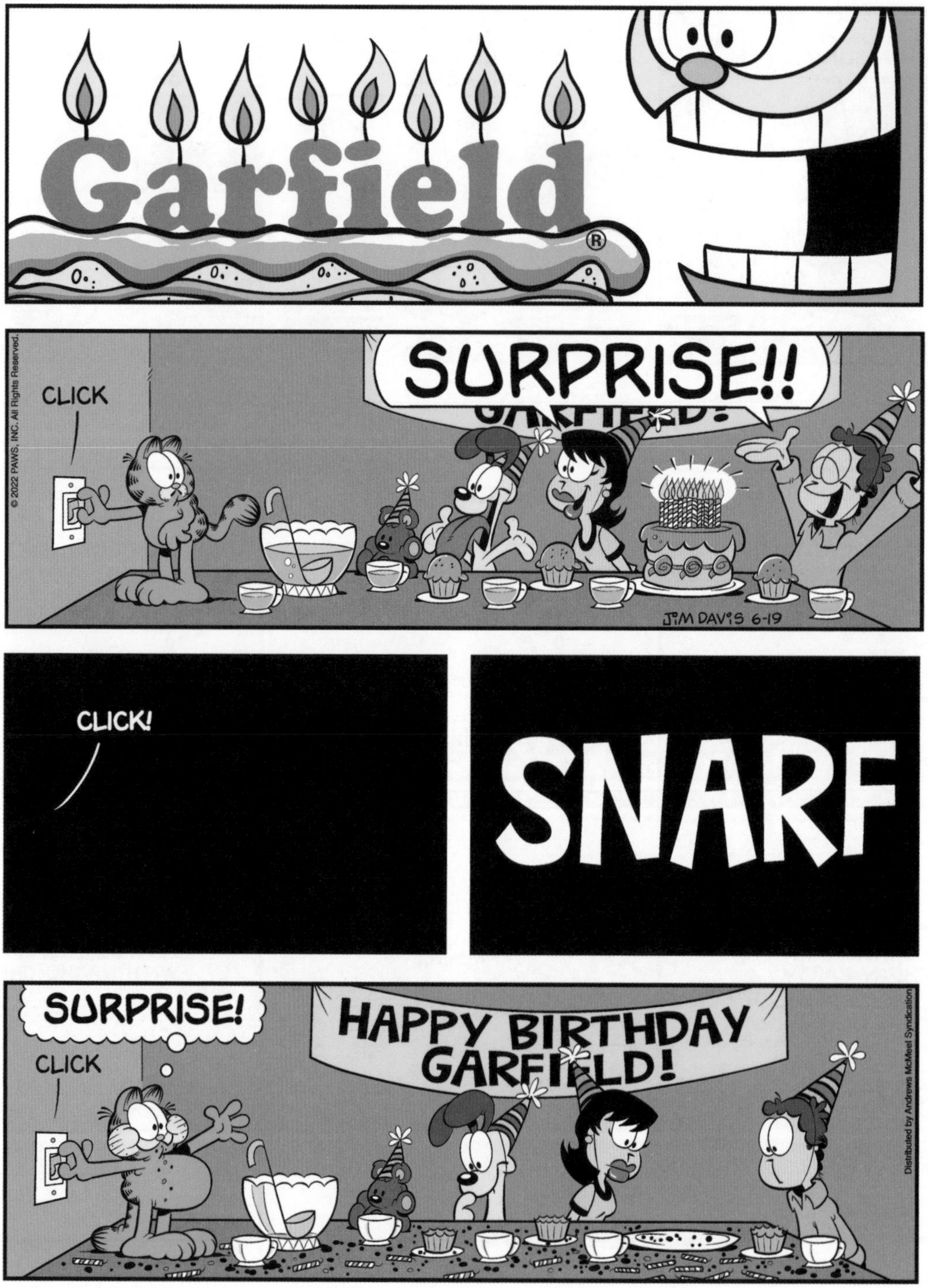
Garfield
© 2022 PAWS, INC. All Rights Reserved.
CLICK
SURPRISE!!
JIM DAVIS 6-19
CLICK!
SNARF
SURPRISE!
CLICK
HAPPY BIRTHDAY GARFIELD!
Distributed by Andrews McMeel Syndication

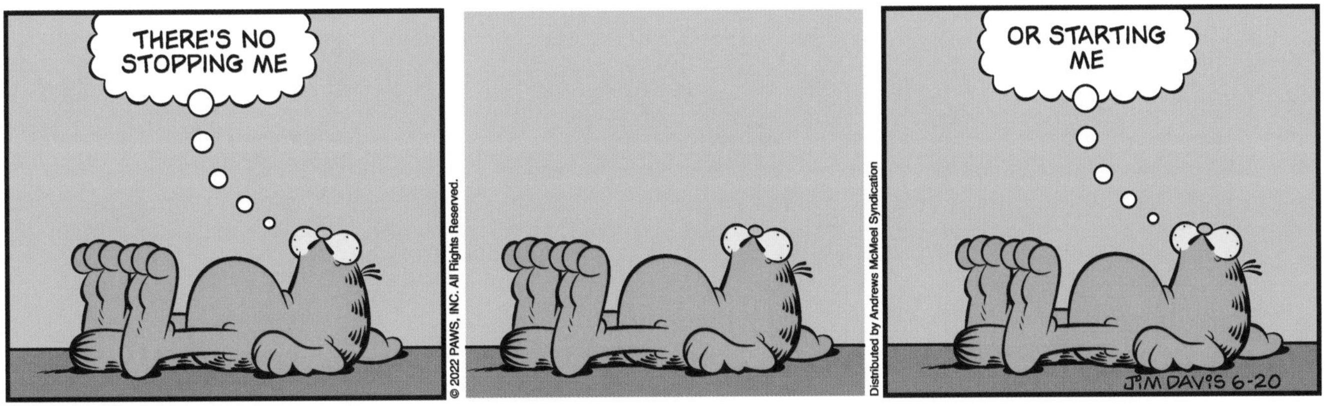
THERE'S NO STOPPING ME
© 2022 PAWS, INC. All Rights Reserved.
Distributed by Andrews McMeel Syndication
OR STARTING ME
JIM DAVIS 6-20

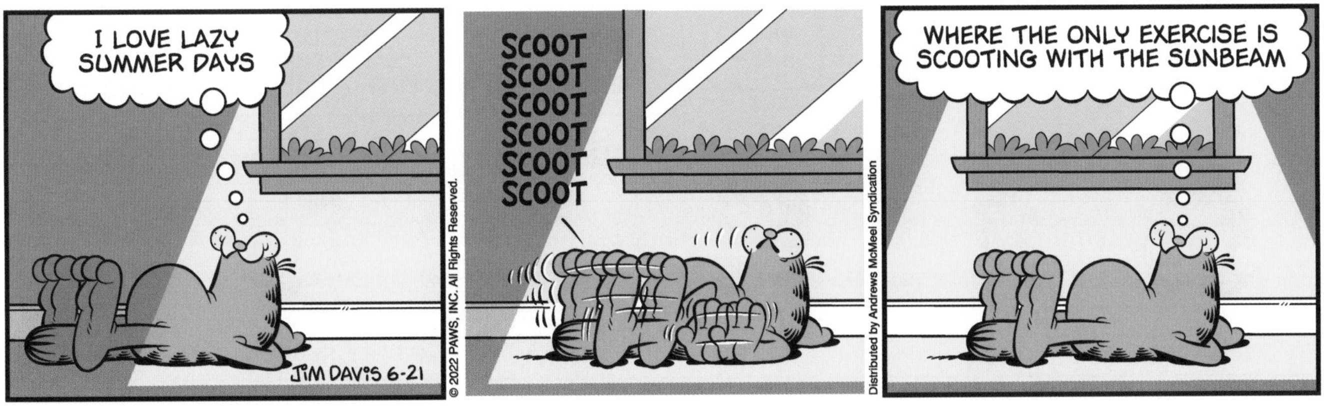
I LOVE LAZY SUMMER DAYS
JIM DAVIS 6-21
© 2022 PAWS, INC. All Rights Reserved.
SCOOT SCOOT SCOOT SCOOT SCOOT SCOOT SCOOT
Distributed by Andrews McMeel Syndication
WHERE THE ONLY EXERCISE IS SCOOTING WITH THE SUNBEAM

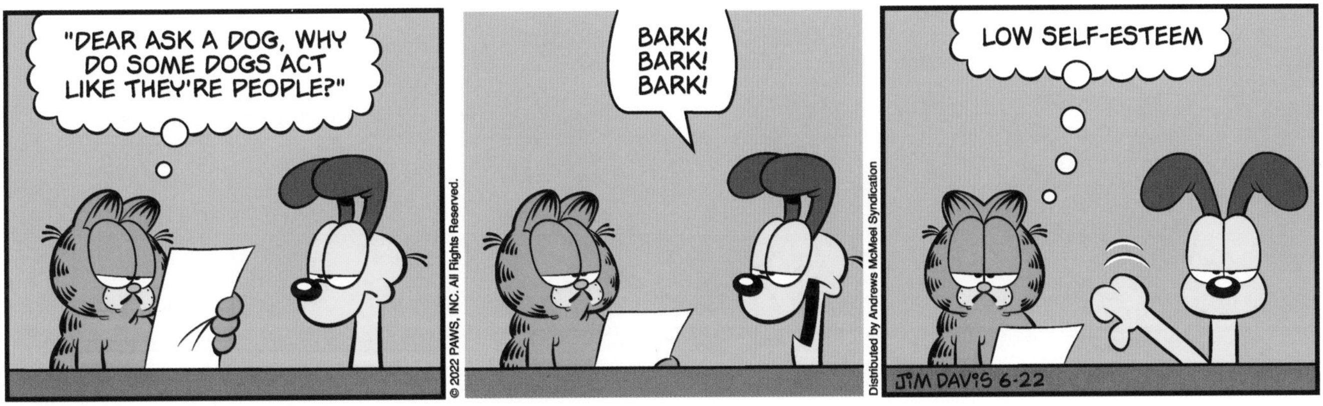
"DEAR ASK A DOG, WHY DO SOME DOGS ACT LIKE THEY'RE PEOPLE?"
© 2022 PAWS, INC. All Rights Reserved.
BARK! BARK! BARK!
Distributed by Andrews McMeel Syndication
LOW SELF-ESTEEM
JIM DAVIS 6-22

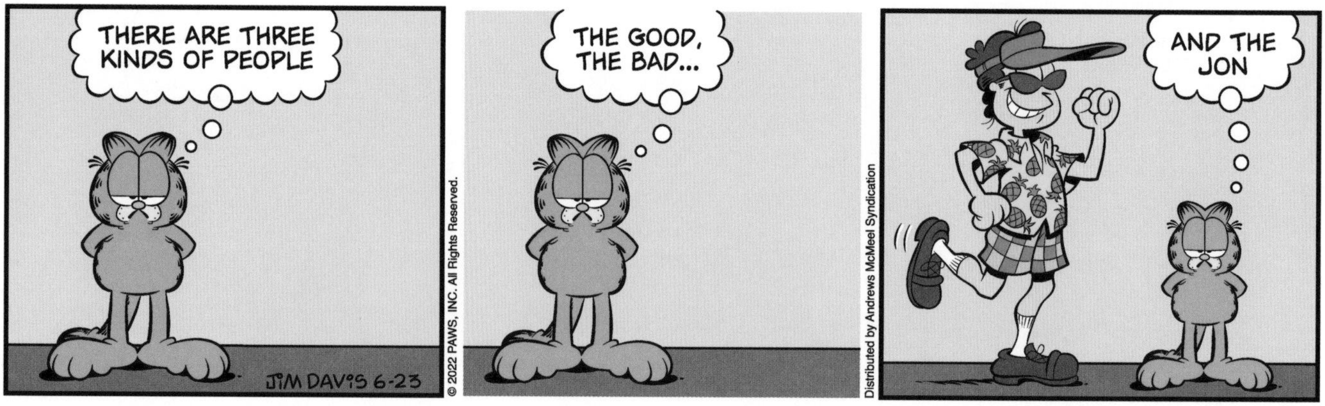
THERE ARE THREE KINDS OF PEOPLE
JIM DAVIS 6-23
© 2022 PAWS, INC. All Rights Reserved.
THE GOOD, THE BAD...
Distributed by Andrews McMeel Syndication
AND THE JON

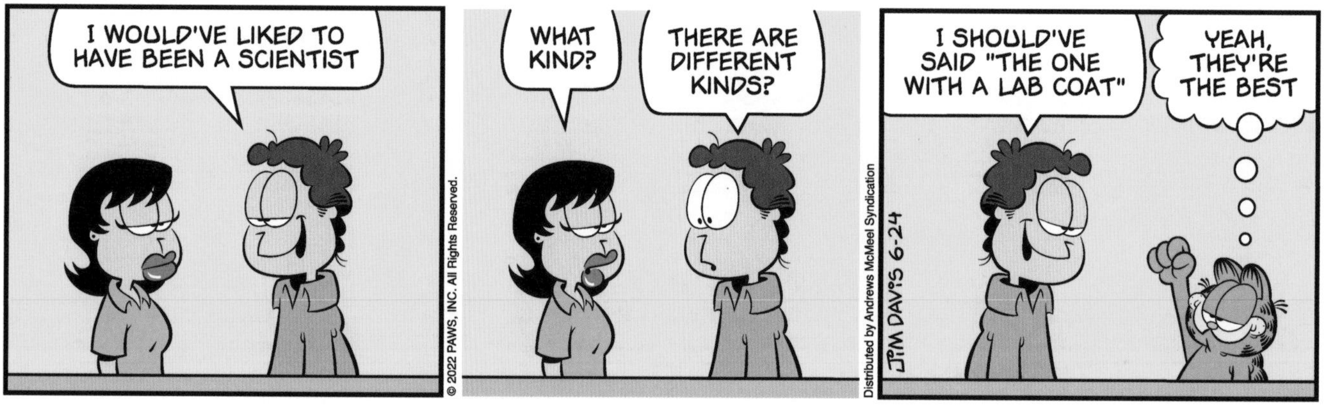
I WOULD'VE LIKED TO HAVE BEEN A SCIENTIST
© 2022 PAWS, INC. All Rights Reserved.
WHAT KIND?
THERE ARE DIFFERENT KINDS?
Distributed by Andrews McMeel Syndication
JIM DAVIS 6-24
I SHOULD'VE SAID "THE ONE WITH A LAB COAT"
YEAH, THEY'RE THE BEST

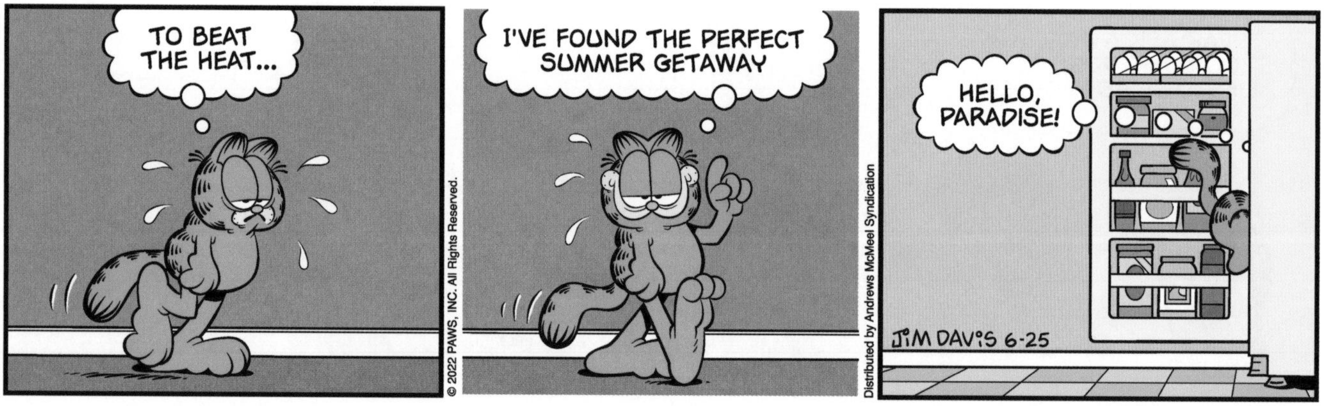
TO BEAT THE HEAT...
© 2022 PAWS, INC. All Rights Reserved.
I'VE FOUND THE PERFECT SUMMER GETAWAY
Distributed by Andrews McMeel Syndication
HELLO, PARADISE!
JIM DAVIS 6-25

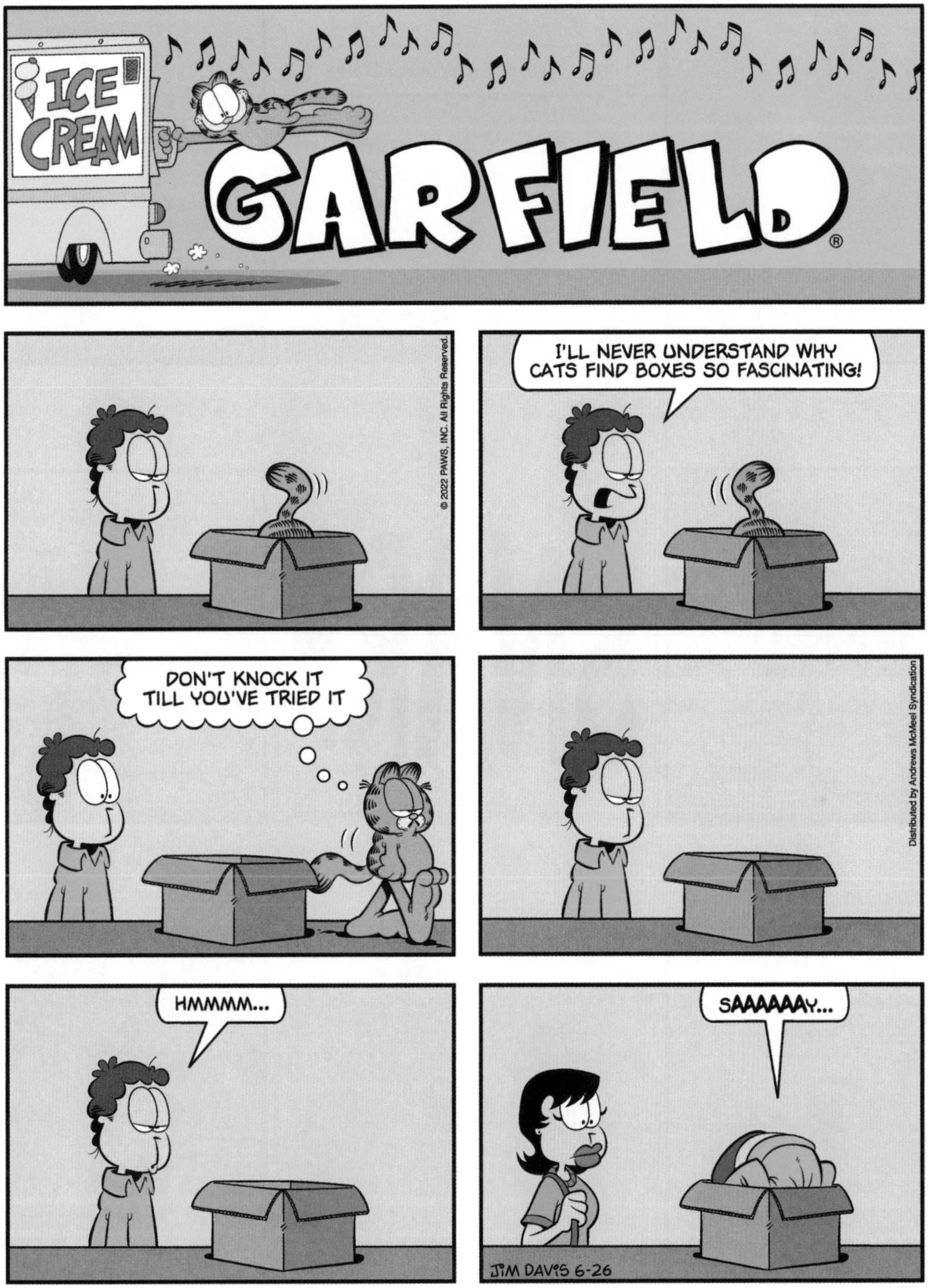
ICE CREAM
GARFIELD®
© 2022 PAWS, INC. All Rights Reserved.
I'LL NEVER UNDERSTAND WHY CATS FIND BOXES SO FASCINATING!
DON'T KNOCK IT TILL YOU'VE TRIED IT
Distributed by Andrews McMeel Syndication
HMMMM...
SAAAAAAY...
JIM DAVIS 6-26

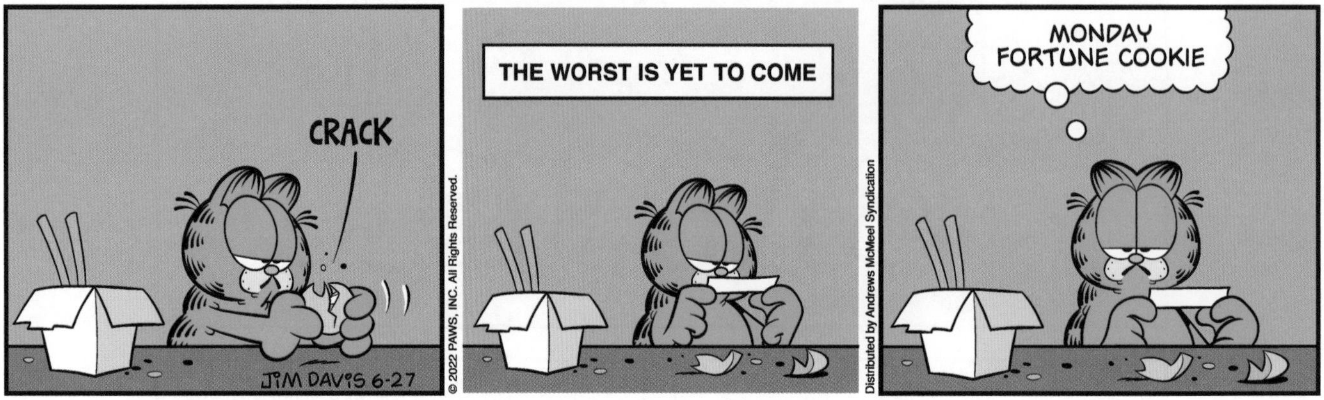
CRACK
JIM DAVIS 6-27
© 2022 PAWS, INC. All Rights Reserved.
THE WORST IS YET TO COME
Distributed by Andrews McMeel Syndication
MONDAY FORTUNE COOKIE

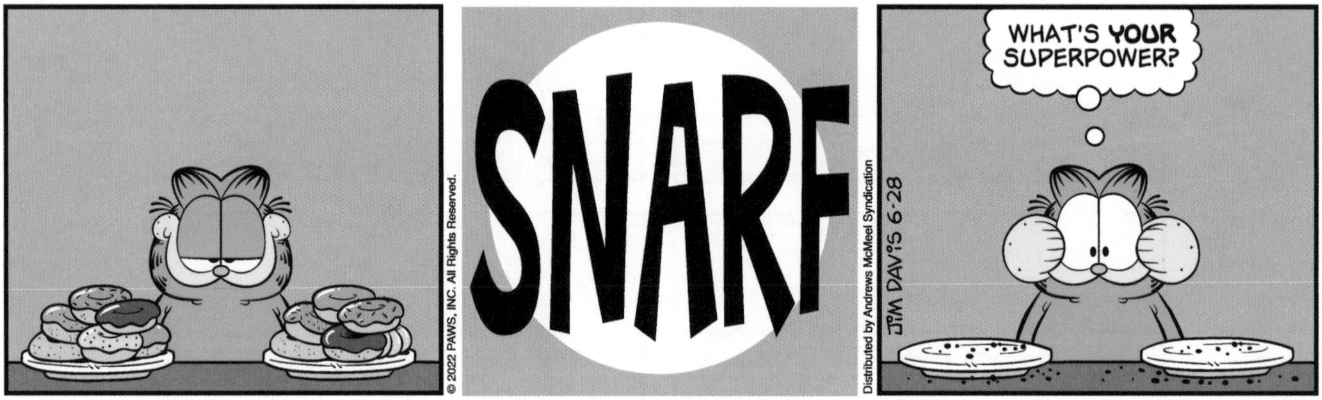
© 2022 PAWS, INC. All Rights Reserved.
SNARF
Distributed by Andrews McMeel Syndication
JIM DAVIS 6-28
WHAT'S **YOUR** SUPERPOWER?

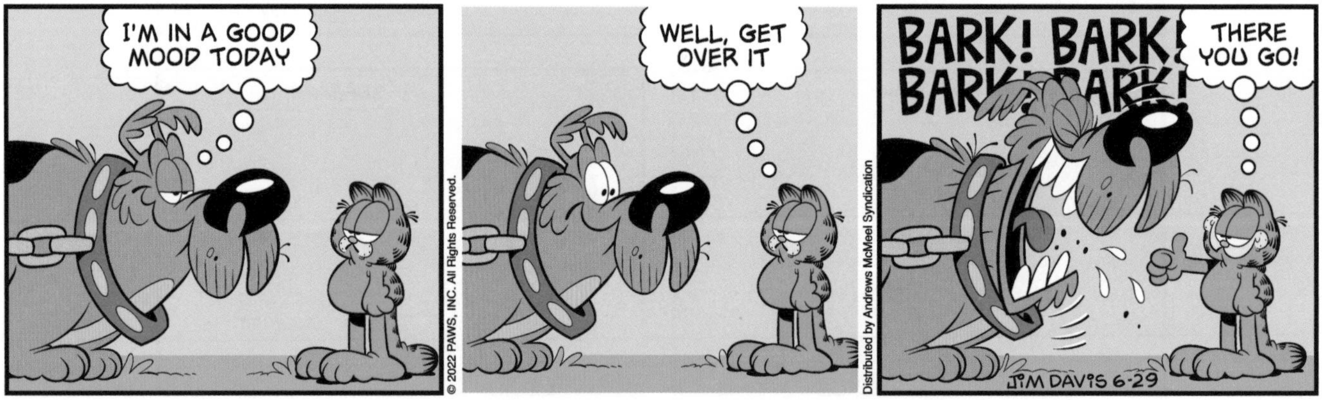
I'M IN A GOOD MOOD TODAY
© 2022 PAWS, INC. All Rights Reserved.
WELL, GET OVER IT
Distributed by Andrews McMeel Syndication
BARK! BARK! BARK! BARK!
THERE YOU GO!
JIM DAVIS 6-29

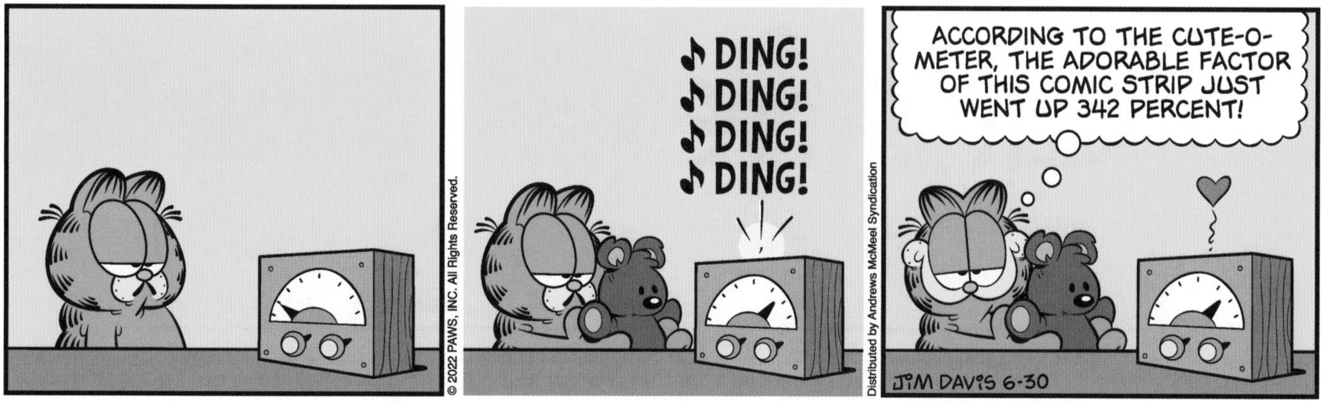
♪ DING! ♪ DING! ♪ DING! ♪ DING!
ACCORDING TO THE CUTE-O-METER, THE ADORABLE FACTOR OF THIS COMIC STRIP JUST WENT UP 342 PERCENT!
JIM DAVIS 6-30

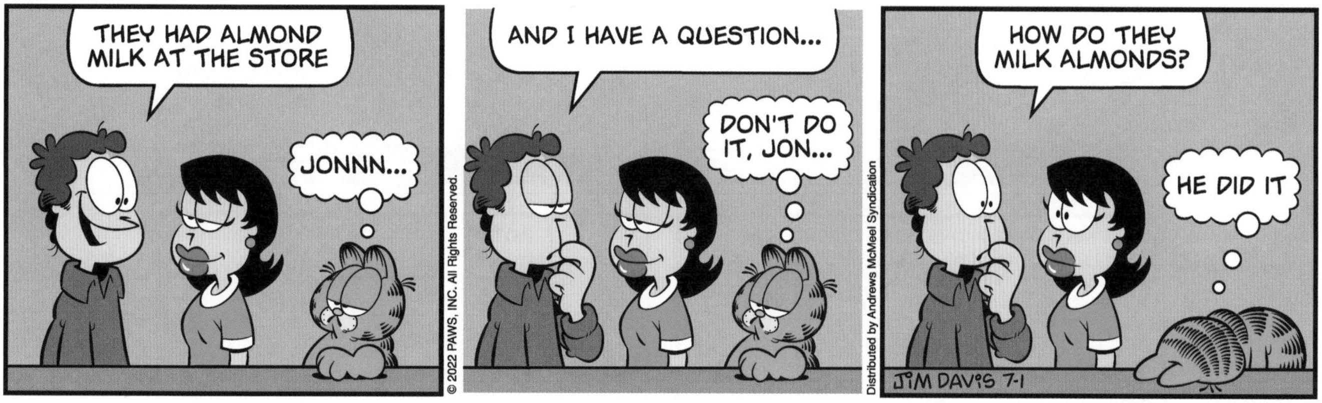
THEY HAD ALMOND MILK AT THE STORE
JONNN...
AND I HAVE A QUESTION...
DON'T DO IT, JON...
HOW DO THEY MILK ALMONDS?
HE DID IT
JIM DAVIS 7-1

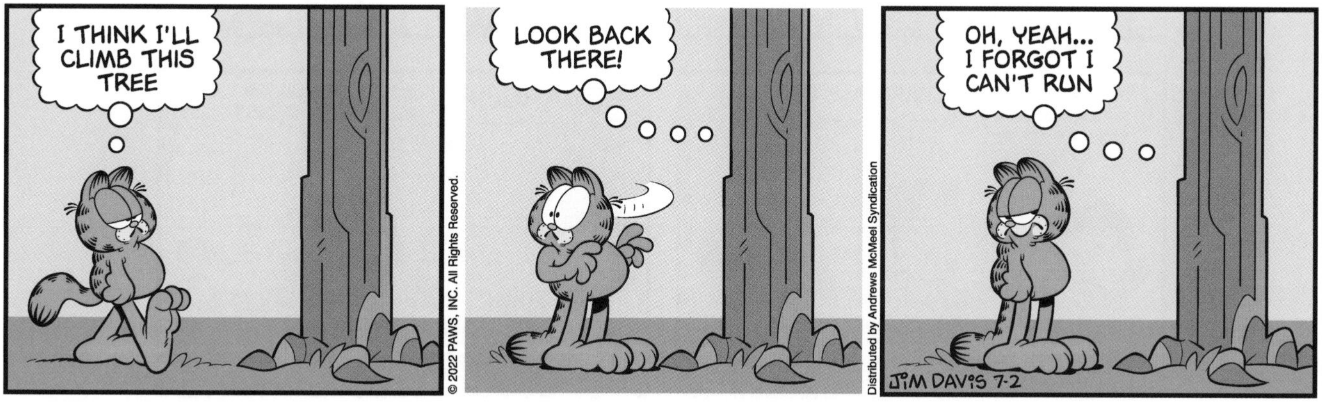
I THINK I'LL CLIMB THIS TREE
LOOK BACK THERE!
OH, YEAH... I FORGOT I CAN'T RUN
JIM DAVIS 7-2

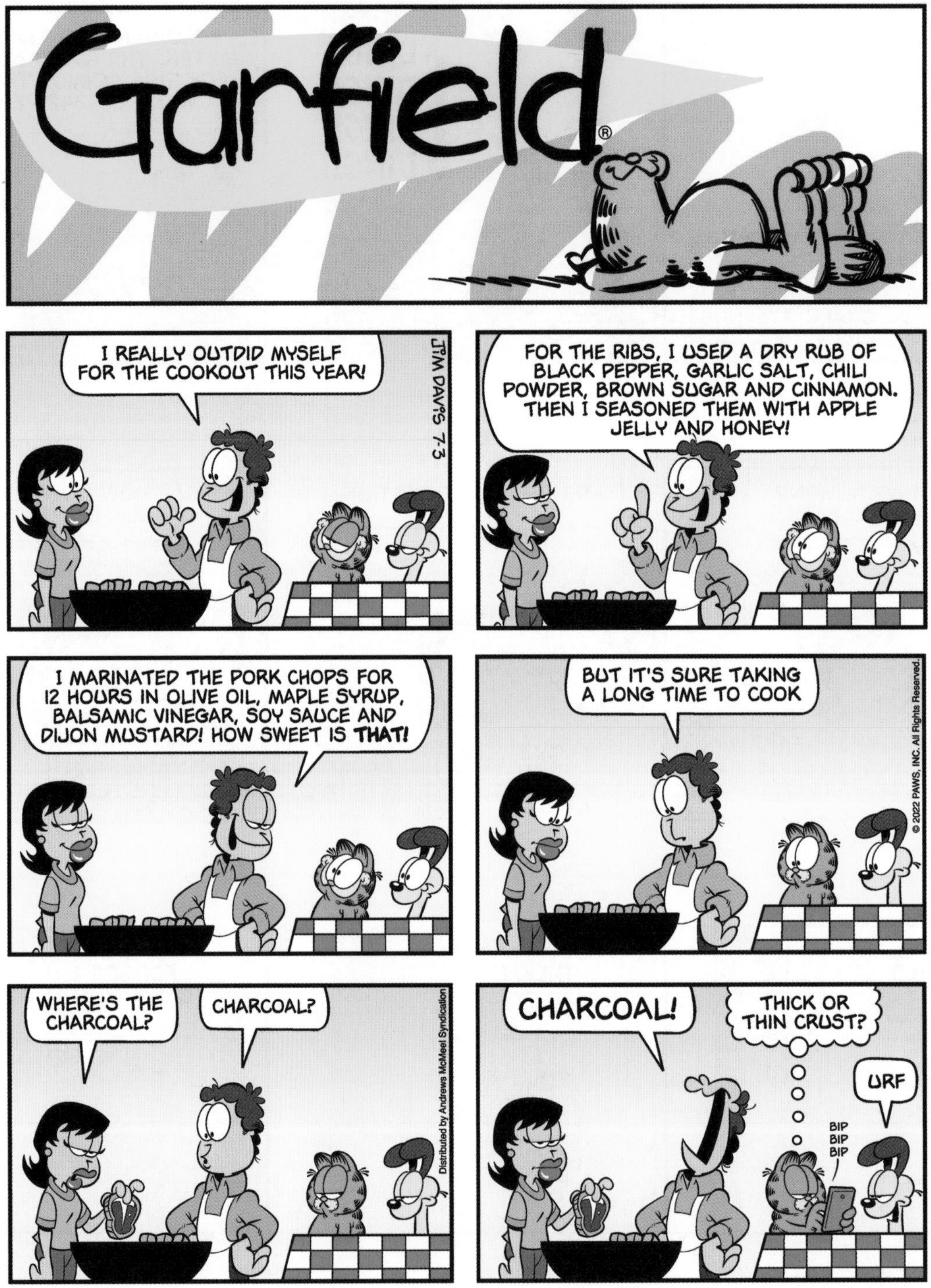
Garfield®
JIM DAVIS 7-3
I REALLY OUTDID MYSELF FOR THE COOKOUT THIS YEAR!
FOR THE RIBS, I USED A DRY RUB OF BLACK PEPPER, GARLIC SALT, CHILI POWDER, BROWN SUGAR AND CINNAMON. THEN I SEASONED THEM WITH APPLE JELLY AND HONEY!
I MARINATED THE PORK CHOPS FOR 12 HOURS IN OLIVE OIL, MAPLE SYRUP, BALSAMIC VINEGAR, SOY SAUCE AND DIJON MUSTARD! HOW SWEET IS THAT!
BUT IT'S SURE TAKING A LONG TIME TO COOK
© 2022 PAWS, INC. All Rights Reserved.
WHERE'S THE CHARCOAL?
CHARCOAL?
Distributed by Andrews McMeel Syndication
CHARCOAL!
THICK OR THIN CRUST?
BIP BIP BIP
URF

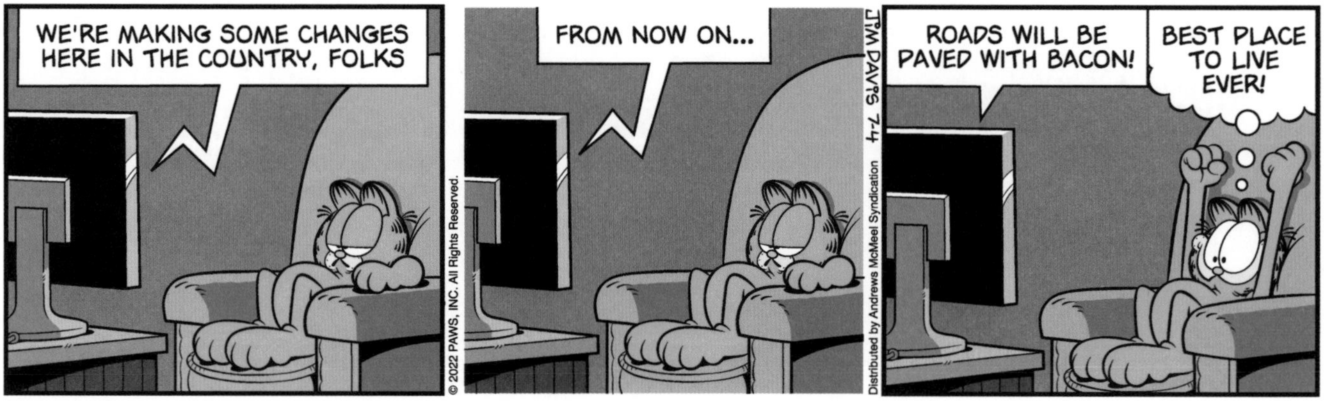
WE'RE MAKING SOME CHANGES HERE IN THE COUNTRY, FOLKS
FROM NOW ON...
JIM DAVIS 7-4
ROADS WILL BE PAVED WITH BACON!
BEST PLACE TO LIVE EVER!
© 2022 PAWS, INC. All Rights Reserved.
Distributed by Andrews McMeel Syndication

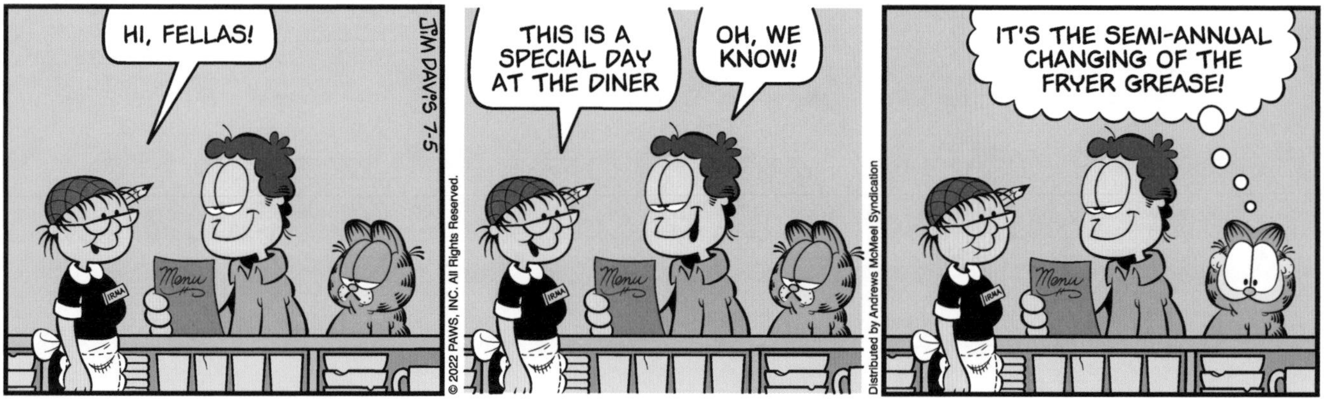
HI, FELLAS!
JIM DAVIS 7-5
IRMA
Menu
THIS IS A SPECIAL DAY AT THE DINER
OH, WE KNOW!
IT'S THE SEMI-ANNUAL CHANGING OF THE FRYER GREASE!
© 2022 PAWS, INC. All Rights Reserved.
Distributed by Andrews McMeel Syndication

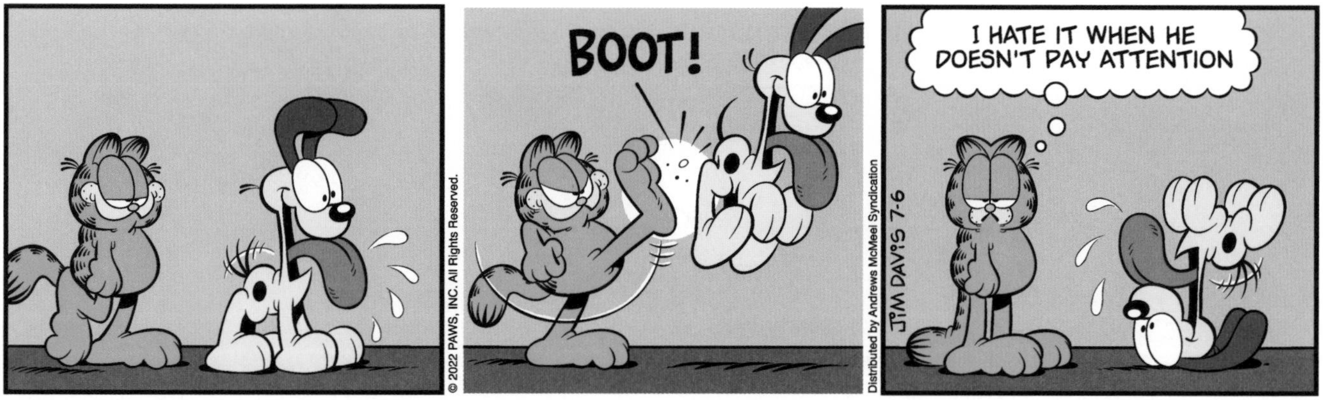
BOOT!
JIM DAVIS 7-6
I HATE IT WHEN HE DOESN'T PAY ATTENTION
© 2022 PAWS, INC. All Rights Reserved.
Distributed by Andrews McMeel Syndication

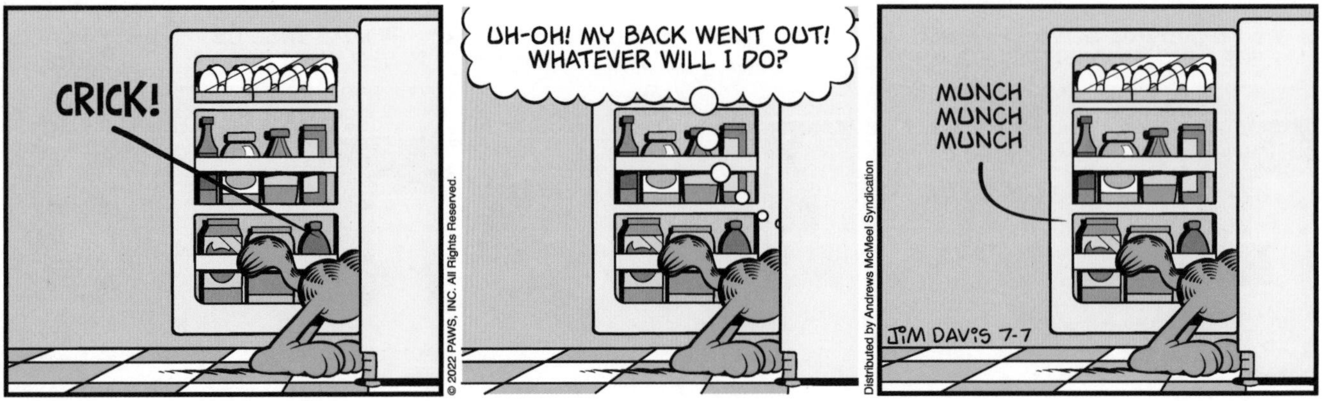
CRICK!
UH-OH! MY BACK WENT OUT! WHATEVER WILL I DO?
MUNCH MUNCH MUNCH
JIM DAVIS 7-7
© 2022 PAWS, INC. All Rights Reserved.
Distributed by Andrews McMeel Syndication

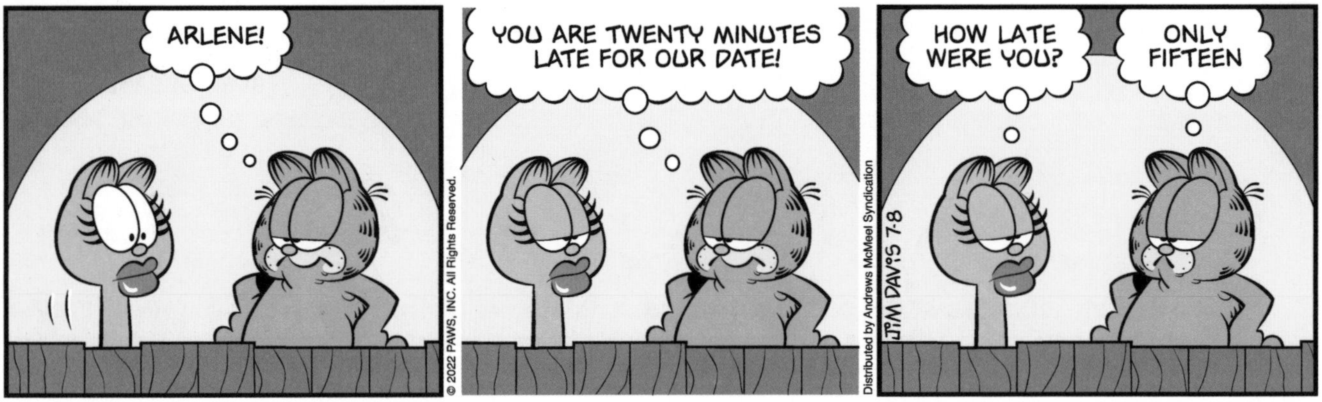
ARLENE!
YOU ARE TWENTY MINUTES LATE FOR OUR DATE!
HOW LATE WERE YOU?
ONLY FIFTEEN
JIM DAVIS 7-8
© 2022 PAWS, INC. All Rights Reserved.
Distributed by Andrews McMeel Syndication

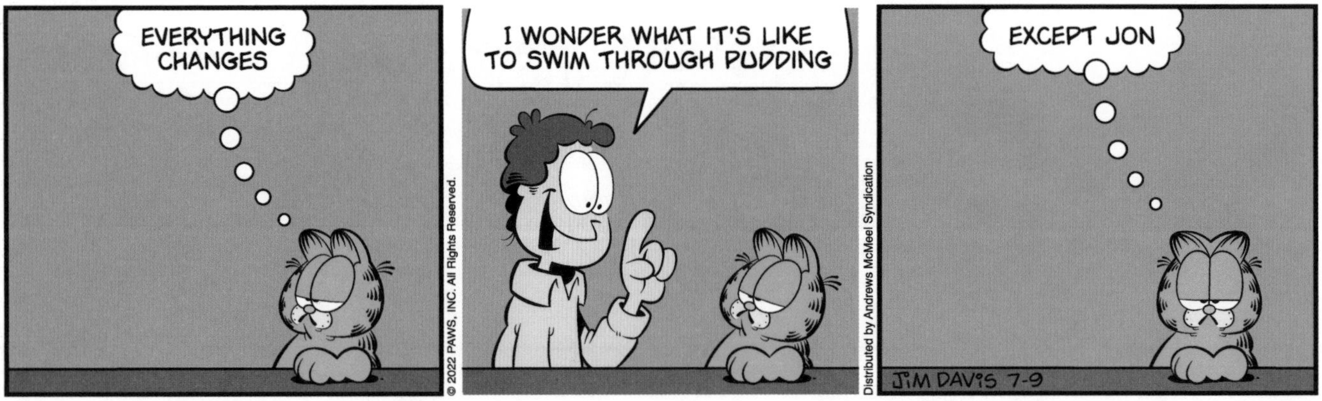
EVERYTHING CHANGES
I WONDER WHAT IT'S LIKE TO SWIM THROUGH PUDDING
EXCEPT JON
JIM DAVIS 7-9
© 2022 PAWS, INC. All Rights Reserved.
Distributed by Andrews McMeel Syndication

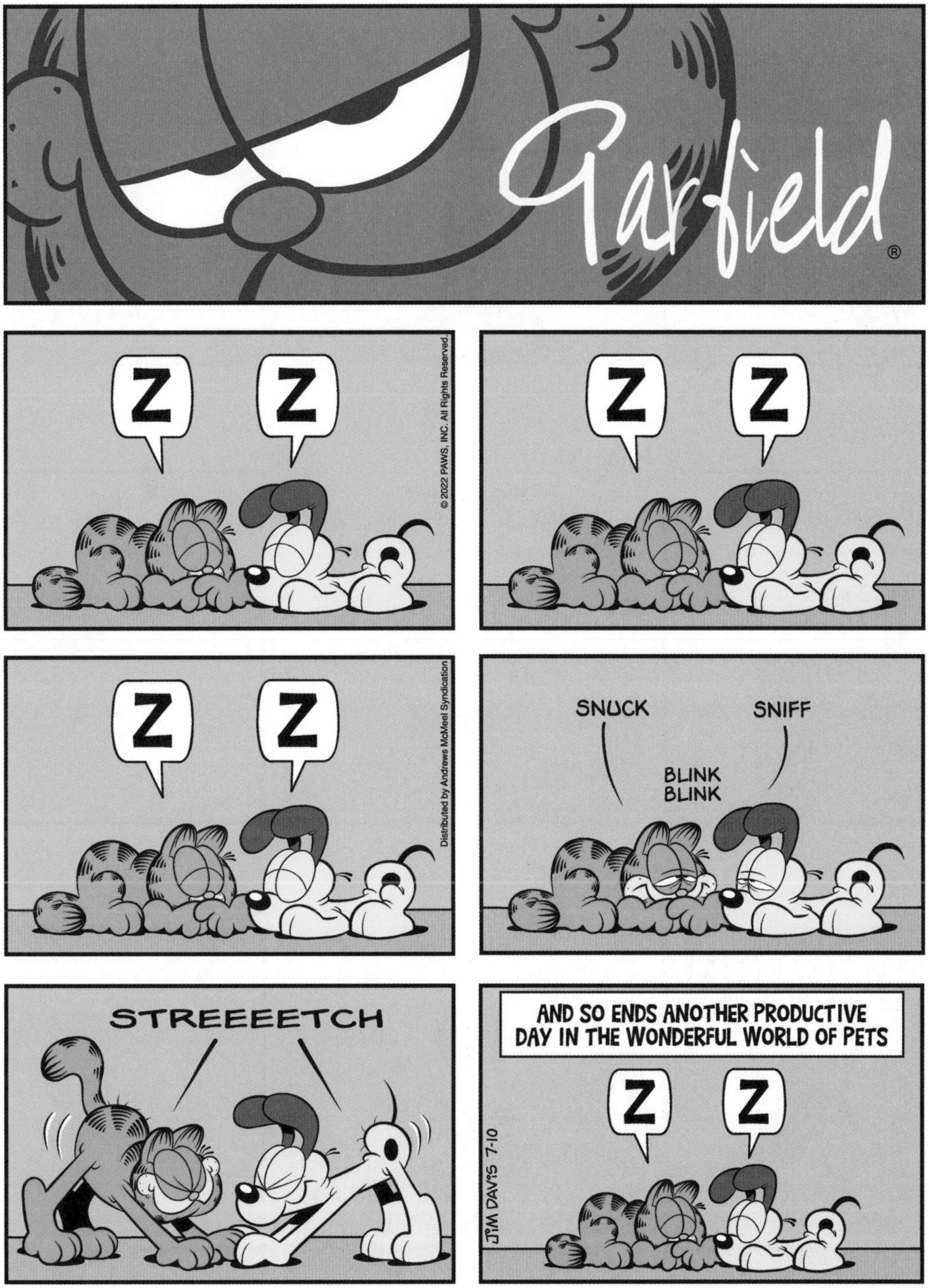
Garfield®
Z
Z
© 2022 PAWS, INC. All Rights Reserved.
Z
Z
Z
Z
Distributed by Andrews McMeel Syndication
SNUCK
SNIFF
BLINK
BLINK
STREEEEETCH
JIM DAVIS 7-10
AND SO ENDS ANOTHER PRODUCTIVE
DAY IN THE WONDERFUL WORLD OF PETS
Z
Z

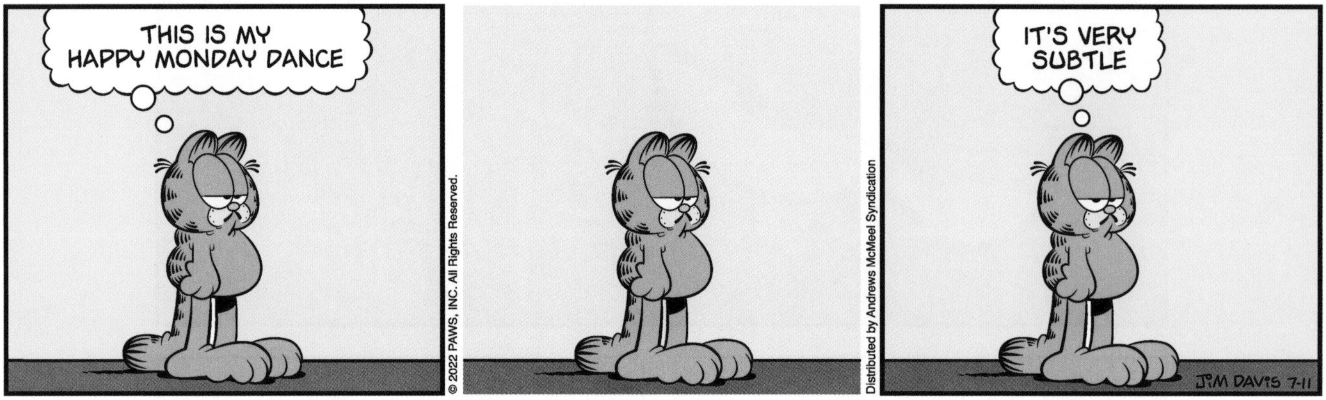
THIS IS MY HAPPY MONDAY DANCE
IT'S VERY SUBTLE
© 2022 PAWS, INC. All Rights Reserved.
Distributed by Andrews McMeel Syndication
JIM DAVIS 7-11

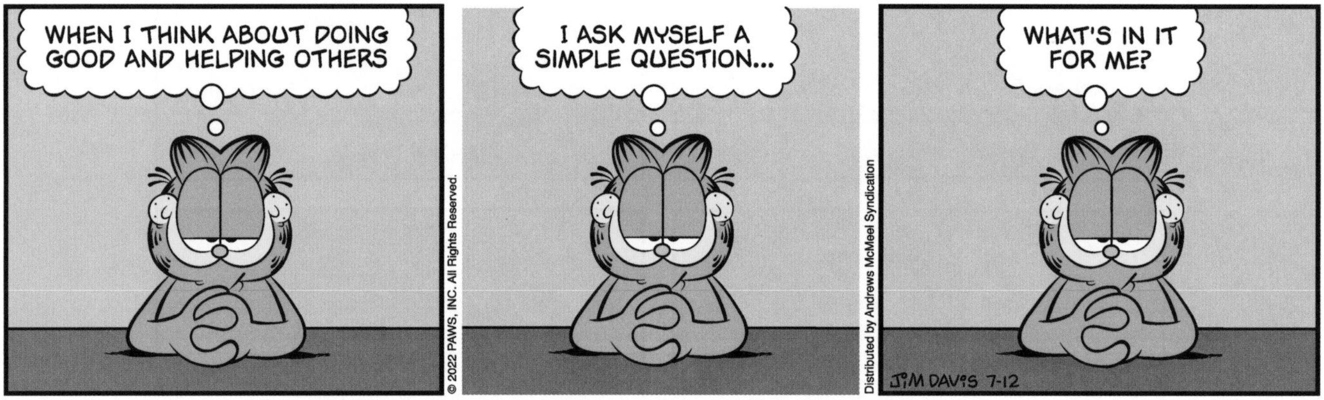
WHEN I THINK ABOUT DOING GOOD AND HELPING OTHERS
I ASK MYSELF A SIMPLE QUESTION...
WHAT'S IN IT FOR ME?
© 2022 PAWS, INC. All Rights Reserved.
Distributed by Andrews McMeel Syndication
JIM DAVIS 7-12

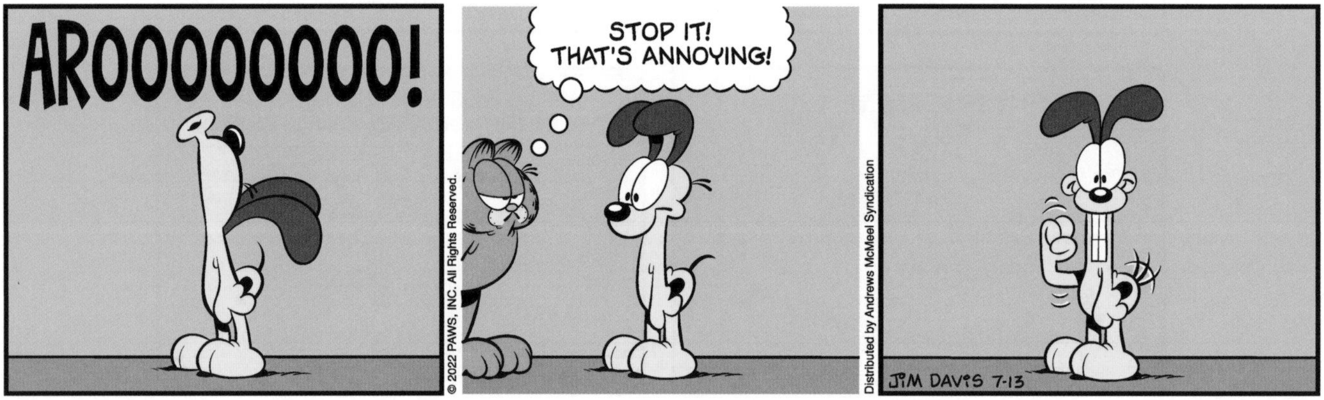
AROOOOOOOO!
STOP IT! THAT'S ANNOYING!
© 2022 PAWS, INC. All Rights Reserved.
Distributed by Andrews McMeel Syndication
JIM DAVIS 7-13

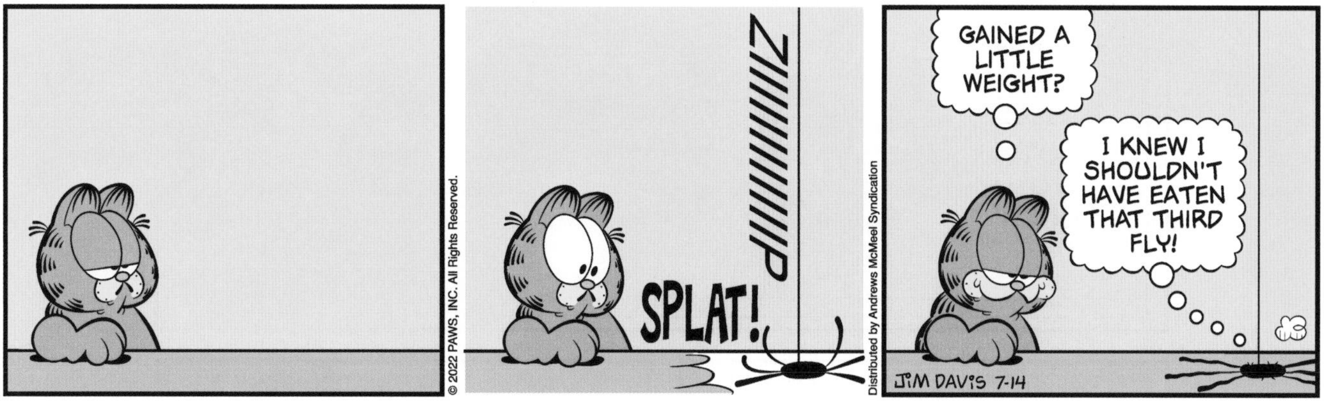

© 2022 PAWS, INC. All Rights Reserved.
ZIIIIIIIIIIIIP
SPLAT!
Distributed by Andrews McMeel Syndication
GAINED A LITTLE WEIGHT?
I KNEW I SHOULDN'T HAVE EATEN THAT THIRD FLY!
JIM DAVIS 7-14

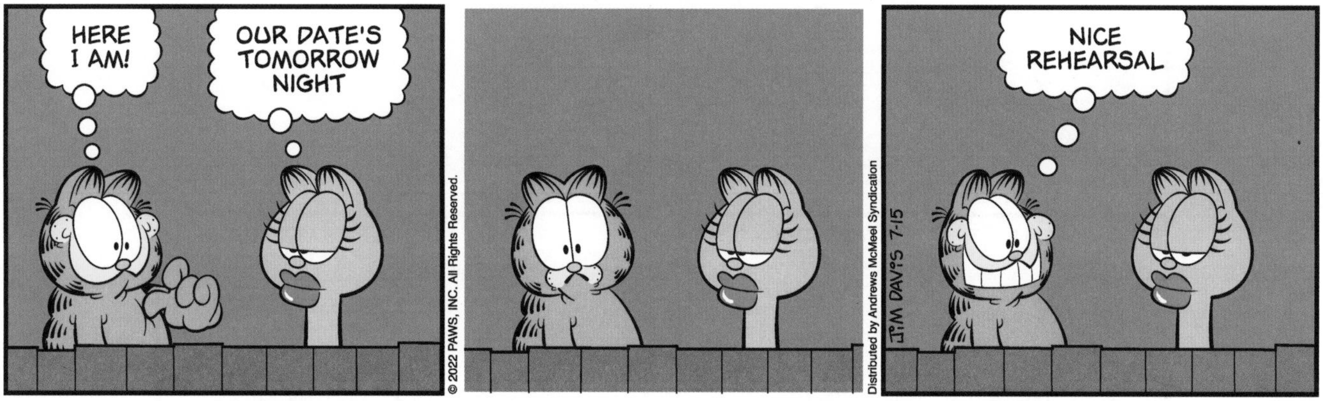

HERE I AM!
OUR DATE'S TOMORROW NIGHT
© 2022 PAWS, INC. All Rights Reserved.
Distributed by Andrews McMeel Syndication
JIM DAVIS 7-15
NICE REHEARSAL

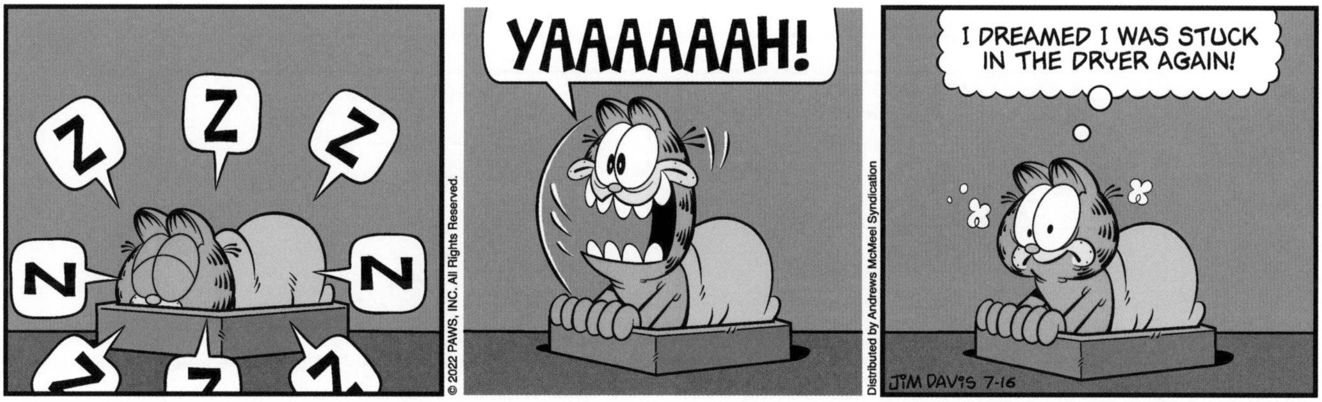

Z
Z
Z
N
N
© 2022 PAWS, INC. All Rights Reserved.
YAAAAAAH!
Distributed by Andrews McMeel Syndication
I DREAMED I WAS STUCK IN THE DRYER AGAIN!
JIM DAVIS 7-16

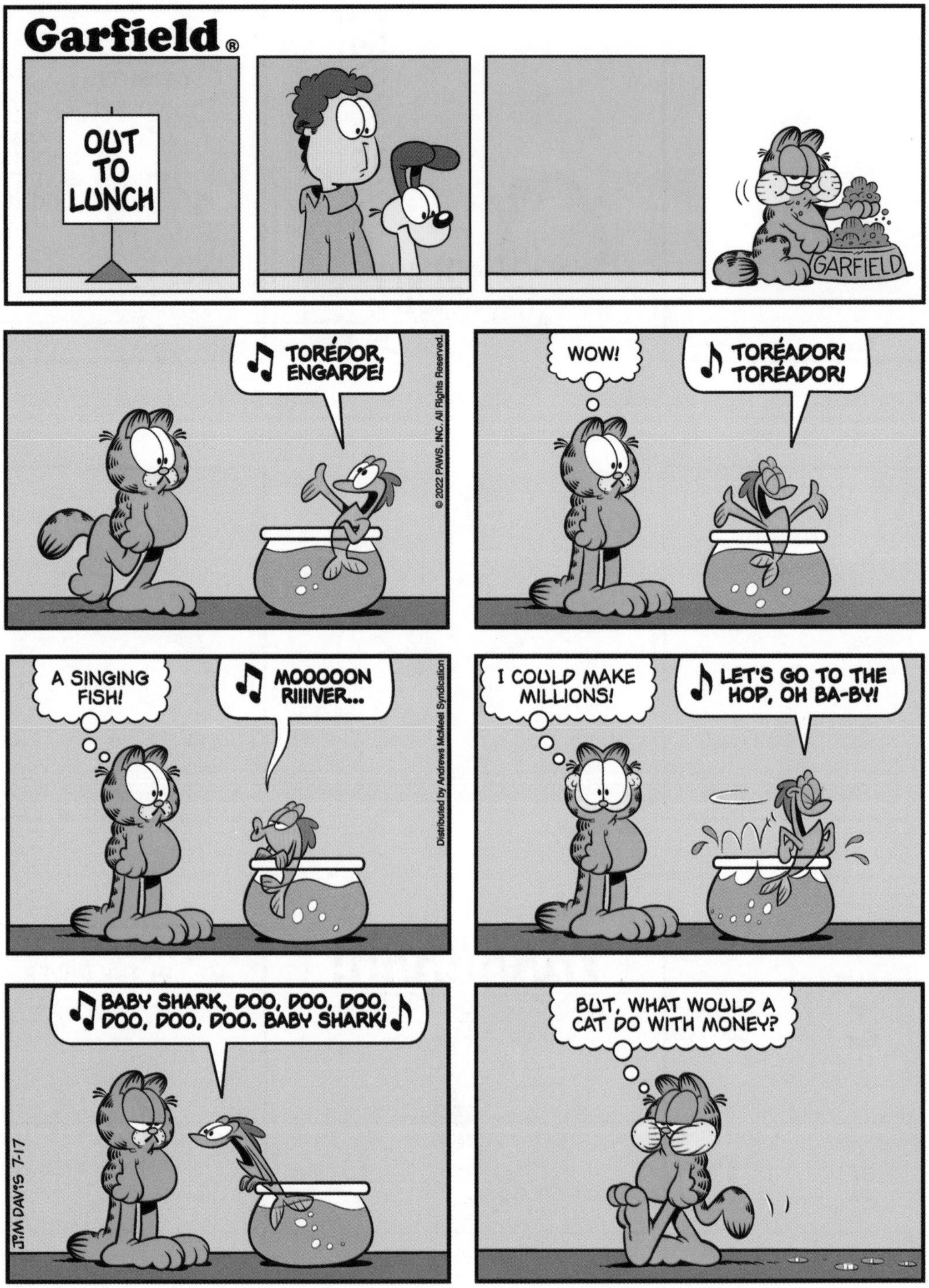
Garfield®
OUT TO LUNCH
GARFIELD
© 2022 PAWS, INC. All Rights Reserved.
TORÉDOR, ENGARDE!
WOW!
TORÉADOR! TORÉADOR!
Distributed by Andrews McMeel Syndication
A SINGING FISH!
MOOOOON RIIIIVER...
I COULD MAKE MILLIONS!
LET'S GO TO THE HOP, OH BA-BY!
BABY SHARK, DOO, DOO, DOO, DOO, DOO, DOO. BABY SHARK!
JIM DAVIS 7-17
BUT, WHAT WOULD A CAT DO WITH MONEY?

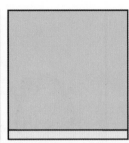

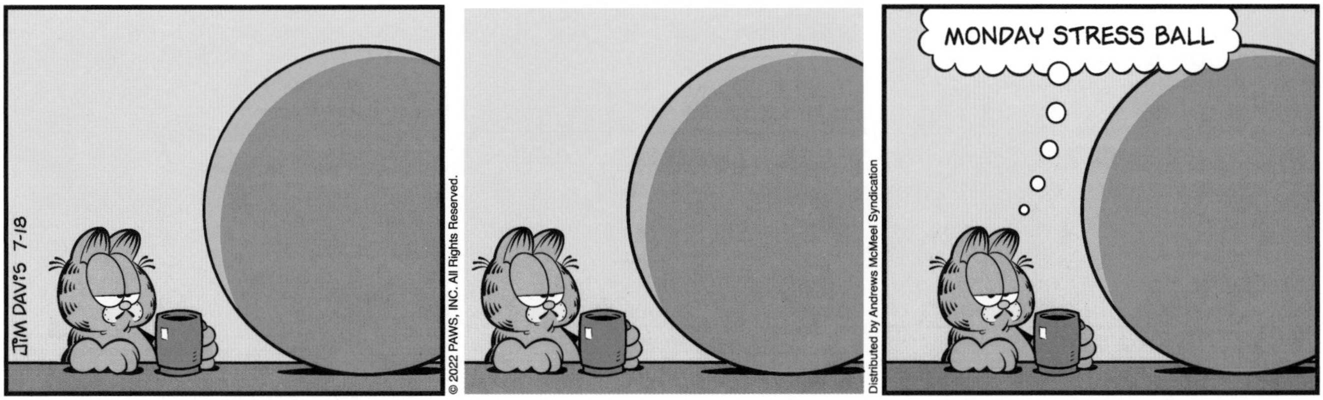
JIM DAVIS 7-18
© 2022 PAWS, INC. All Rights Reserved.
Distributed by Andrews McMeel Syndication
MONDAY STRESS BALL

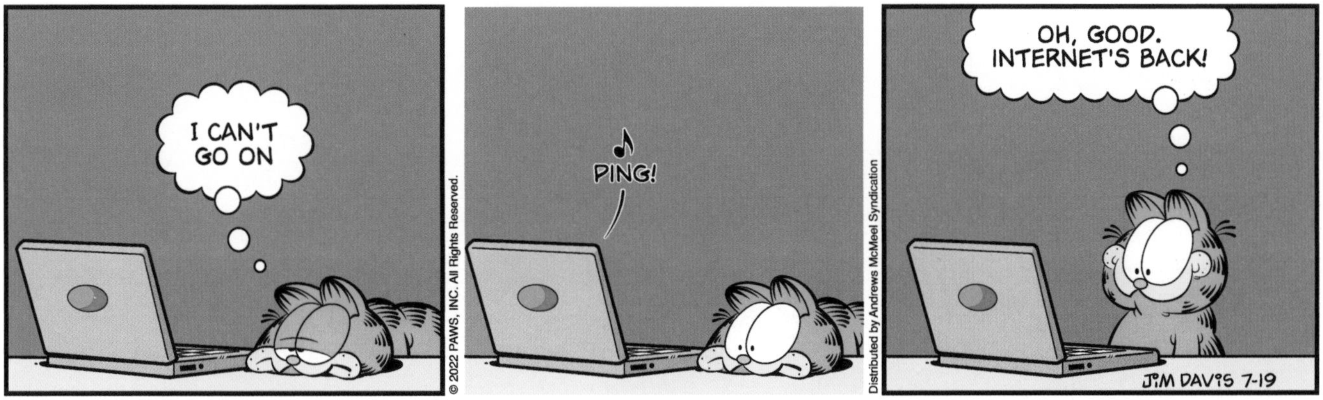
I CAN'T GO ON
© 2022 PAWS, INC. All Rights Reserved.
PING!
Distributed by Andrews McMeel Syndication
OH, GOOD. INTERNET'S BACK!
JIM DAVIS 7-19

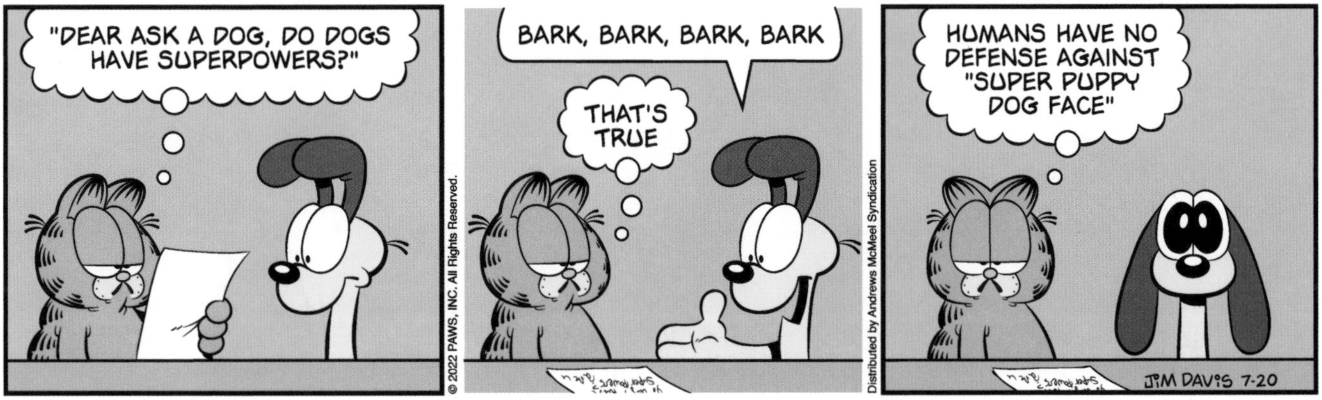
"DEAR ASK A DOG, DO DOGS HAVE SUPERPOWERS?"
© 2022 PAWS, INC. All Rights Reserved.
BARK, BARK, BARK, BARK
THAT'S TRUE
Distributed by Andrews McMeel Syndication
HUMANS HAVE NO DEFENSE AGAINST "SUPER PUPPY DOG FACE"
JIM DAVIS 7-20

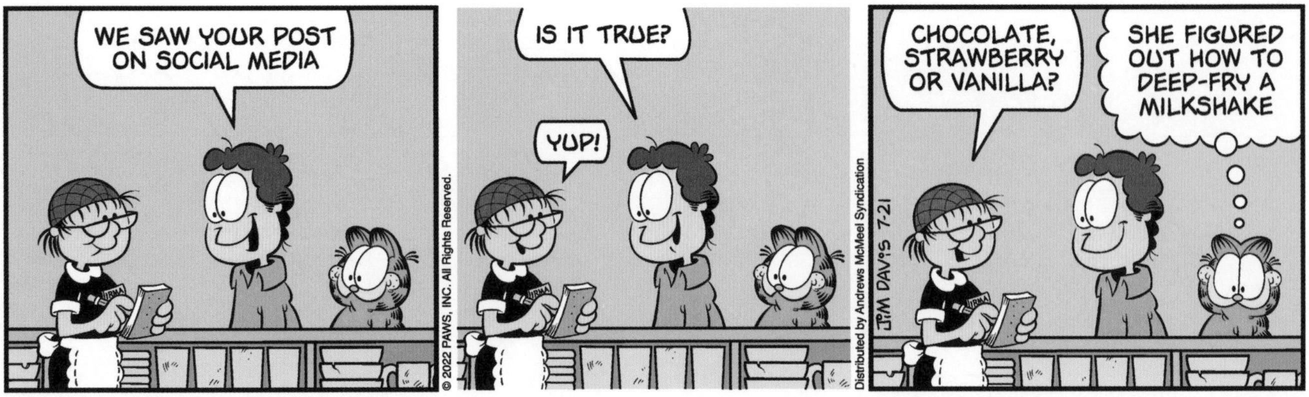
WE SAW YOUR POST ON SOCIAL MEDIA
IS IT TRUE?
YUP!
CHOCOLATE, STRAWBERRY OR VANILLA?
SHE FIGURED OUT HOW TO DEEP-FRY A MILKSHAKE
© 2022 PAWS, INC. All Rights Reserved.
Distributed by Andrews McMeel Syndication
JIM DAVIS 7-21

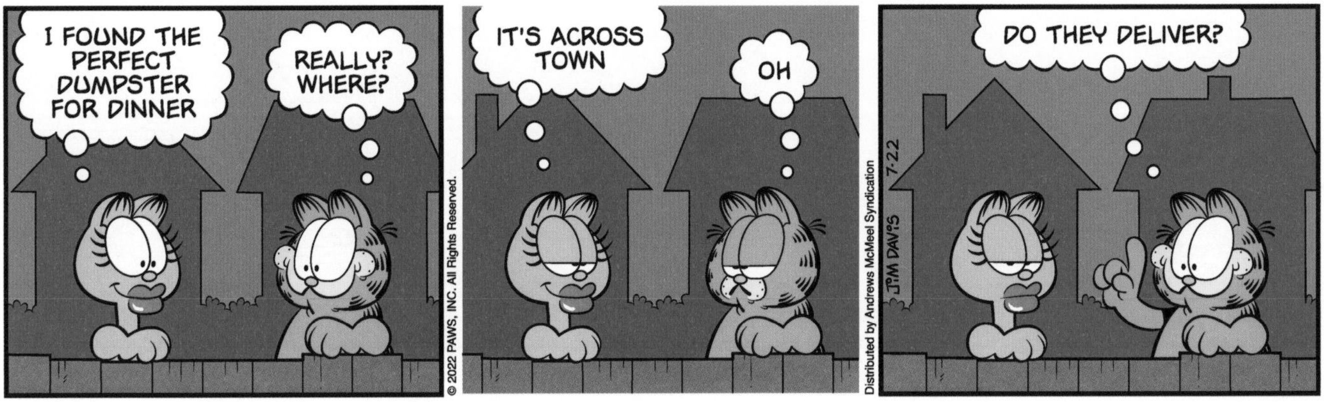
I FOUND THE PERFECT DUMPSTER FOR DINNER
REALLY? WHERE?
IT'S ACROSS TOWN
OH
DO THEY DELIVER?
© 2022 PAWS, INC. All Rights Reserved.
Distributed by Andrews McMeel Syndication
JIM DAVIS 7-22

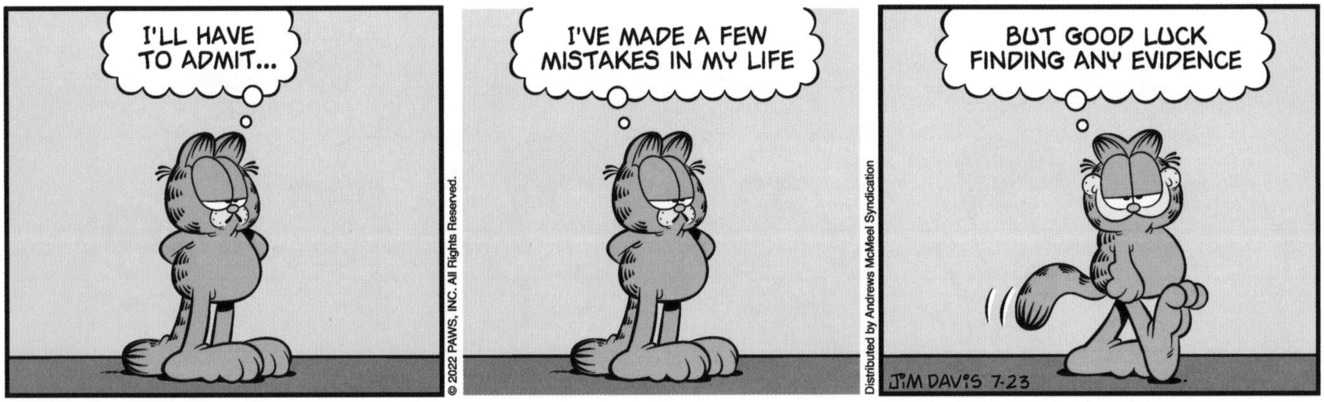
I'LL HAVE TO ADMIT...
I'VE MADE A FEW MISTAKES IN MY LIFE
BUT GOOD LUCK FINDING ANY EVIDENCE
© 2022 PAWS, INC. All Rights Reserved.
Distributed by Andrews McMeel Syndication
JIM DAVIS 7-23

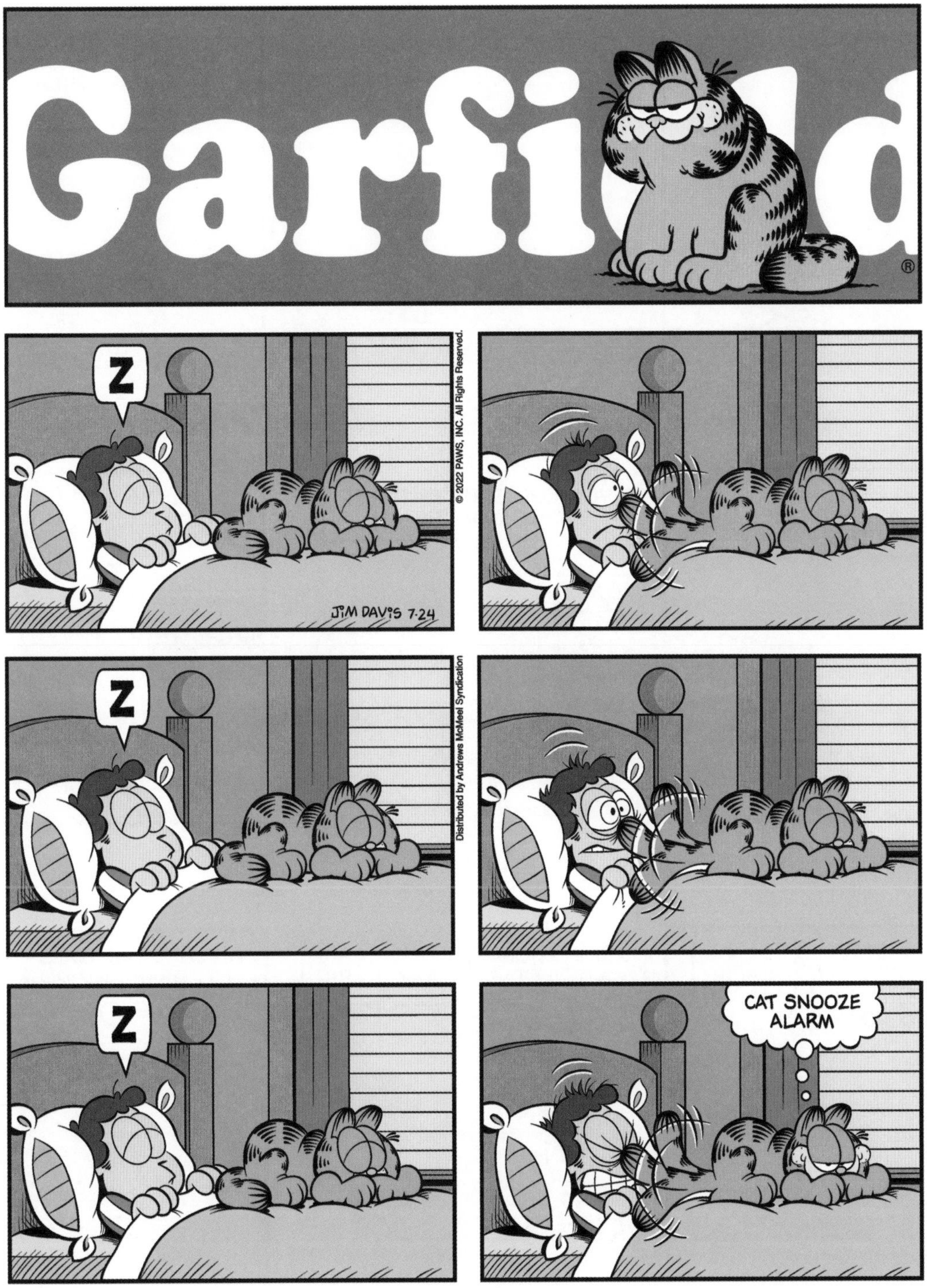
Garfield®
Z
JIM DAVIS 7-24
© 2022 PAWS, INC. All Rights Reserved.
Distributed by Andrews McMeel Syndication
Z
Z
CAT SNOOZE ALARM

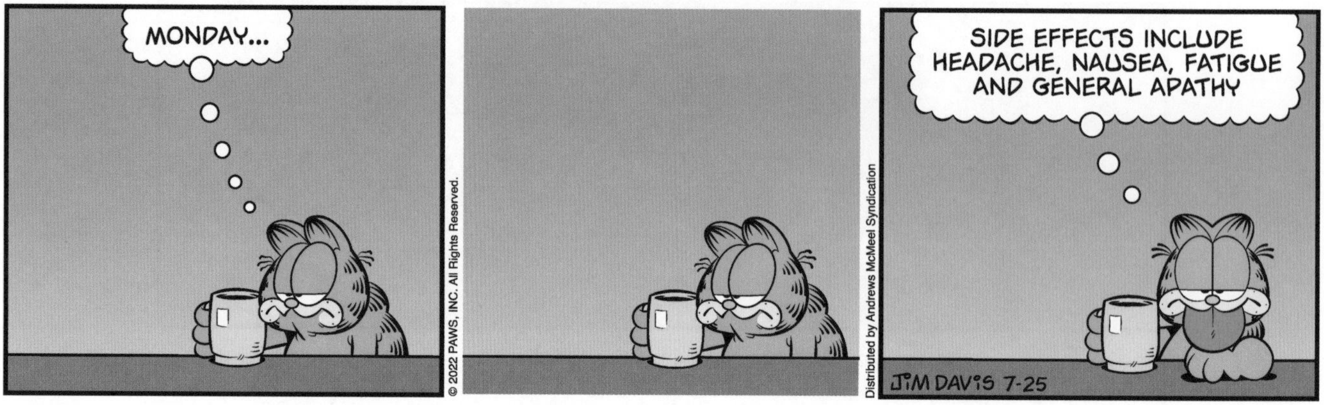
MONDAY...
SIDE EFFECTS INCLUDE HEADACHE, NAUSEA, FATIGUE AND GENERAL APATHY
JIM DAVIS 7-25
© 2022 PAWS, INC. All Rights Reserved.
Distributed by Andrews McMeel Syndication

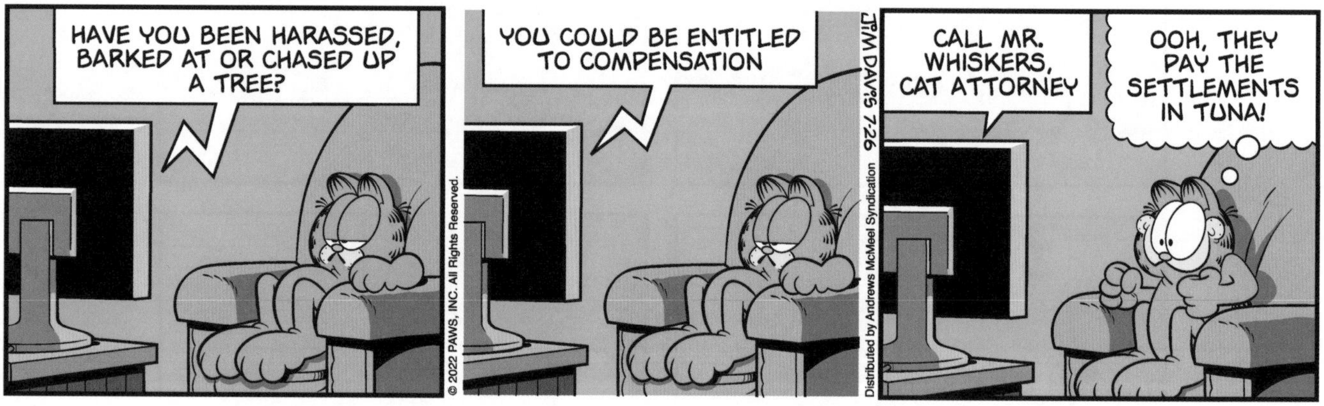
HAVE YOU BEEN HARASSED, BARKED AT OR CHASED UP A TREE?
YOU COULD BE ENTITLED TO COMPENSATION
CALL MR. WHISKERS, CAT ATTORNEY
OOH, THEY PAY THE SETTLEMENTS IN TUNA!
JIM DAVIS 7-26
© 2022 PAWS, INC. All Rights Reserved.
Distributed by Andrews McMeel Syndication

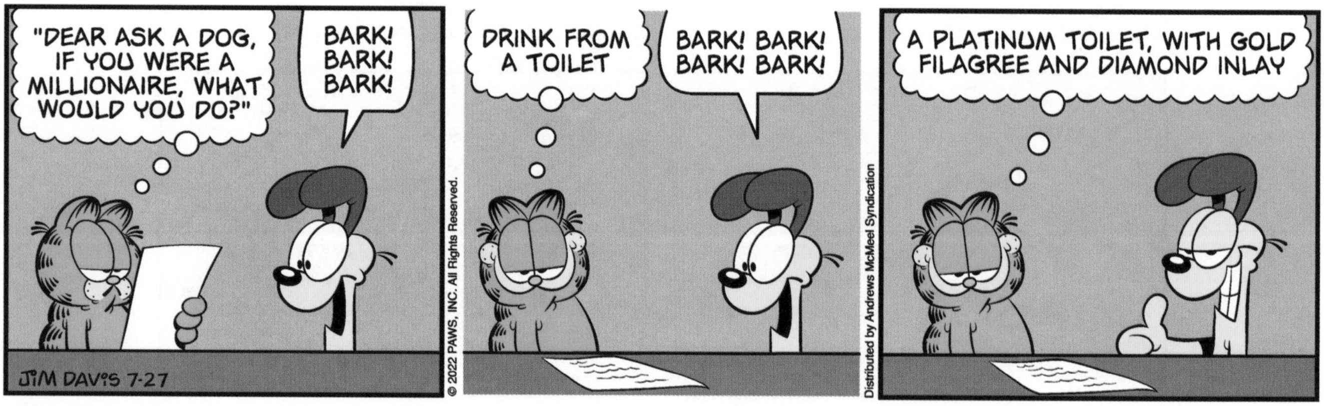
"DEAR ASK A DOG, IF YOU WERE A MILLIONAIRE, WHAT WOULD YOU DO?"
BARK! BARK! BARK!
DRINK FROM A TOILET
BARK! BARK! BARK! BARK!
A PLATINUM TOILET, WITH GOLD FILAGREE AND DIAMOND INLAY
JIM DAVIS 7-27
© 2022 PAWS, INC. All Rights Reserved.
Distributed by Andrews McMeel Syndication

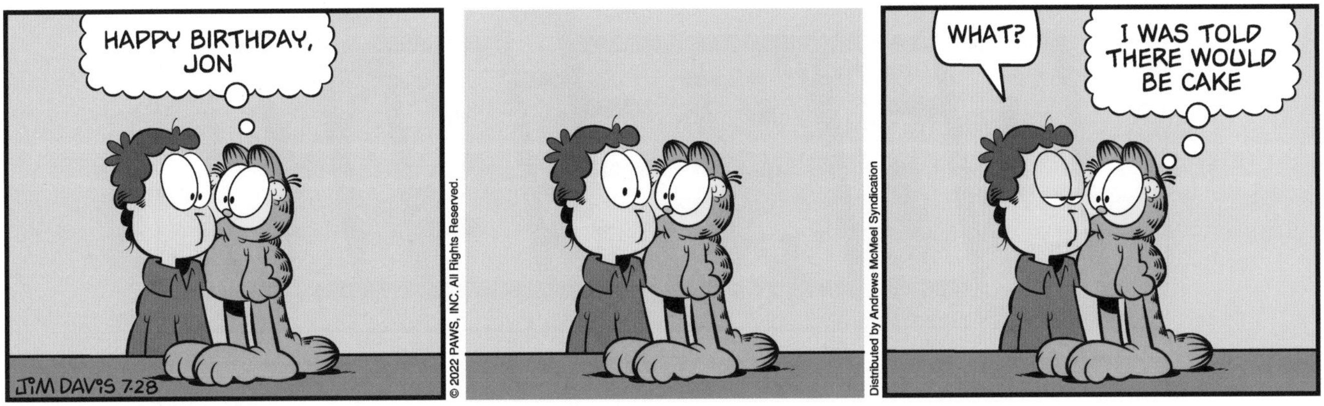
HAPPY BIRTHDAY, JON
JIM DAVIS 7-28
© 2022 PAWS, INC. All Rights Reserved.
Distributed by Andrews McMeel Syndication
WHAT?
I WAS TOLD THERE WOULD BE CAKE

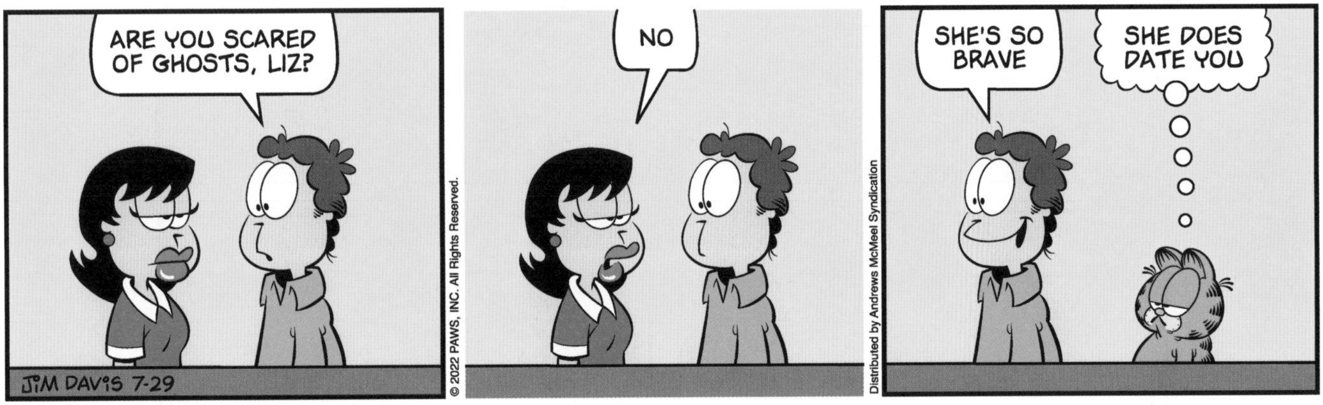
ARE YOU SCARED OF GHOSTS, LIZ?
JIM DAVIS 7-29
© 2022 PAWS, INC. All Rights Reserved.
NO
Distributed by Andrews McMeel Syndication
SHE'S SO BRAVE
SHE DOES DATE YOU

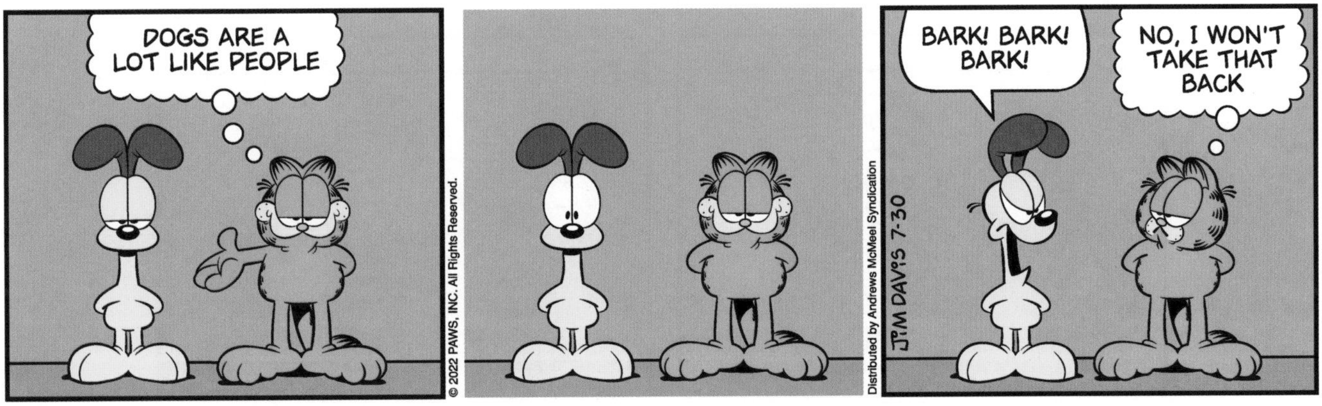
DOGS ARE A LOT LIKE PEOPLE
© 2022 PAWS, INC. All Rights Reserved.
Distributed by Andrews McMeel Syndication
JIM DAVIS 7-30
BARK! BARK! BARK!
NO, I WON'T TAKE THAT BACK

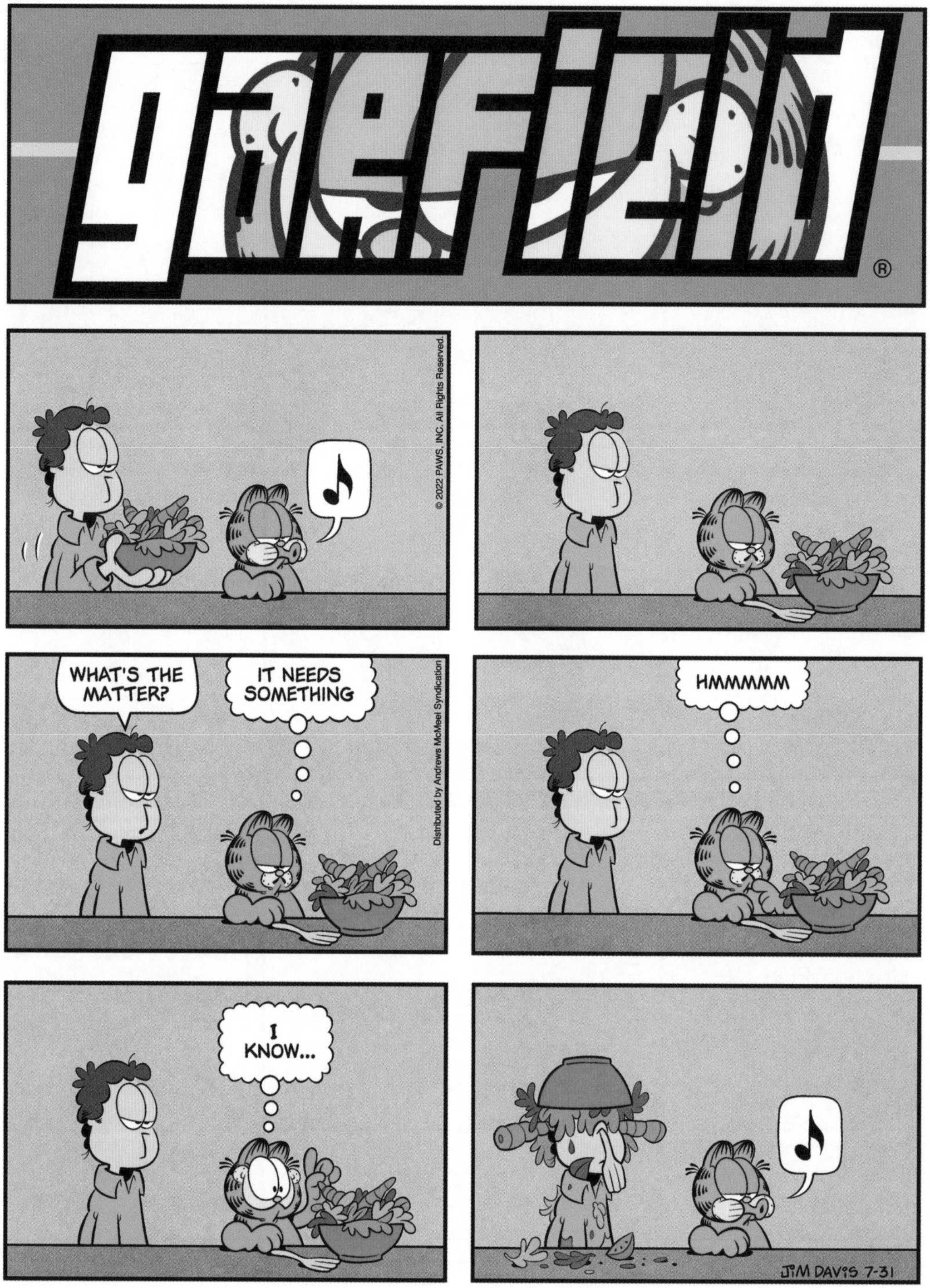
GARFIELD ®
© 2022 PAWS, INC. All Rights Reserved.
♪
WHAT'S THE MATTER?
IT NEEDS SOMETHING
Distributed by Andrews McMeel Syndication
HMMMMM
I KNOW...
♪
JIM DAVIS 7-31

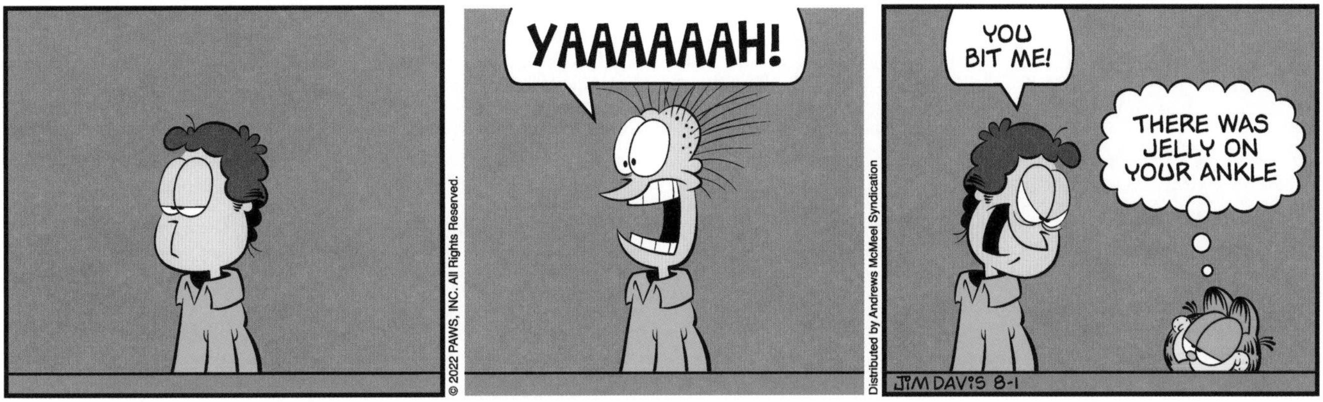
YAAAAAAH!
YOU BIT ME!
THERE WAS JELLY ON YOUR ANKLE
© 2022 PAWS, INC. All Rights Reserved.
Distributed by Andrews McMeel Syndication
JIM DAVIS 8-1

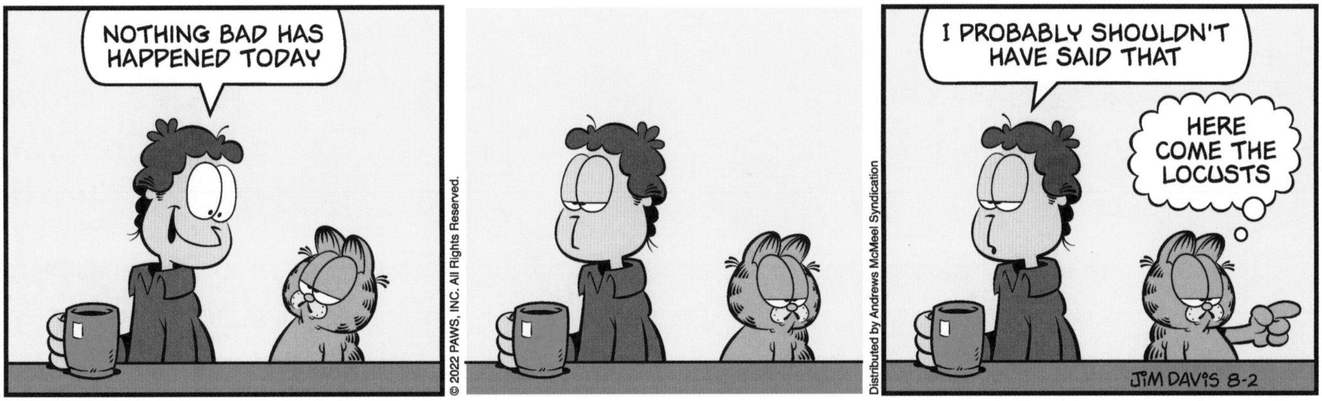
NOTHING BAD HAS HAPPENED TODAY
I PROBABLY SHOULDN'T HAVE SAID THAT
HERE COME THE LOCUSTS
© 2022 PAWS, INC. All Rights Reserved.
Distributed by Andrews McMeel Syndication
JIM DAVIS 8-2

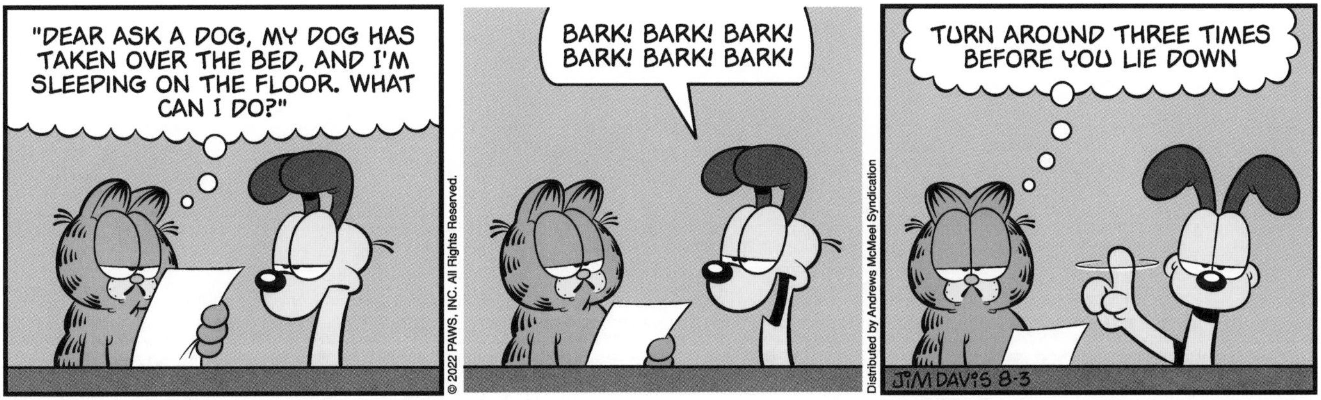
"DEAR ASK A DOG, MY DOG HAS TAKEN OVER THE BED, AND I'M SLEEPING ON THE FLOOR. WHAT CAN I DO?"
BARK! BARK! BARK! BARK! BARK! BARK!
TURN AROUND THREE TIMES BEFORE YOU LIE DOWN
© 2022 PAWS, INC. All Rights Reserved.
Distributed by Andrews McMeel Syndication
JIM DAVIS 8-3

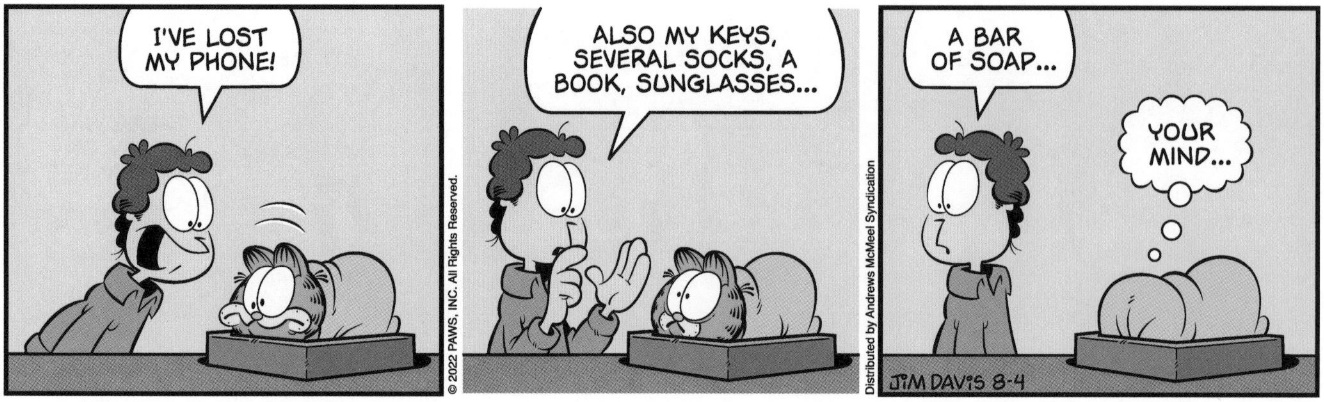
I'VE LOST MY PHONE!
© 2022 PAWS, INC. All Rights Reserved.
ALSO MY KEYS, SEVERAL SOCKS, A BOOK, SUNGLASSES...
Distributed by Andrews McMeel Syndication
A BAR OF SOAP...
YOUR MIND...
JIM DAVIS 8-4

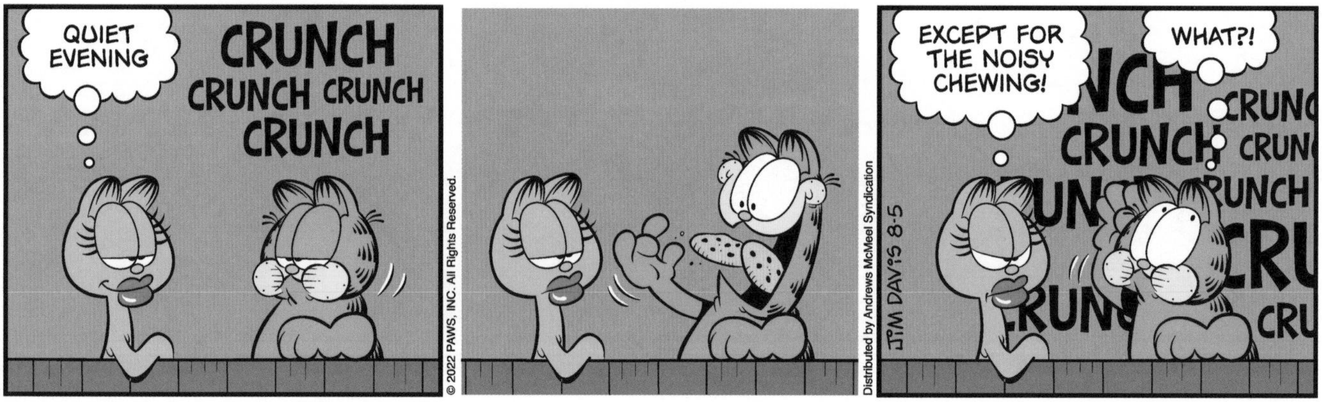
QUIET EVENING
CRUNCH CRUNCH CRUNCH CRUNCH
© 2022 PAWS, INC. All Rights Reserved.
Distributed by Andrews McMeel Syndication
JIM DAVIS 8-5
EXCEPT FOR THE NOISY CHEWING!
WHAT?!

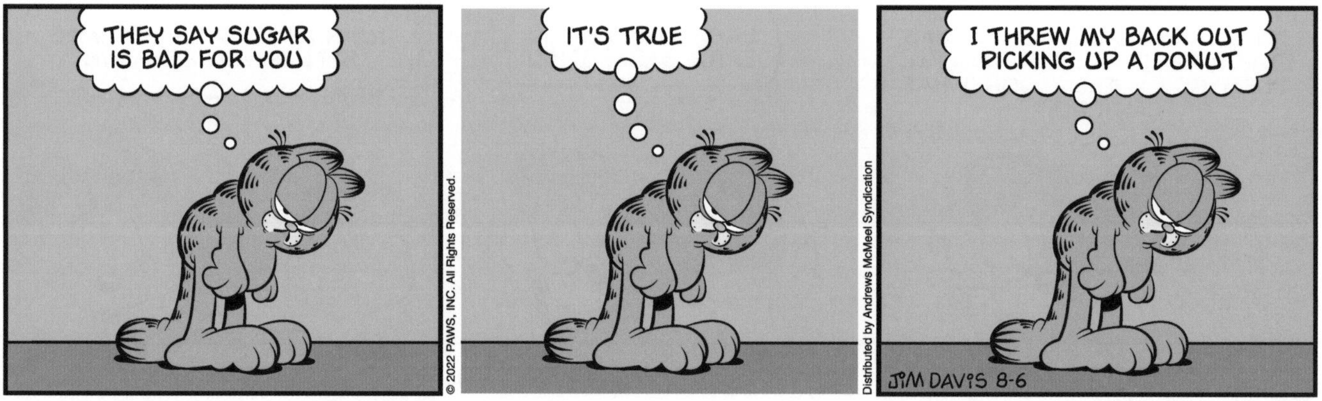
THEY SAY SUGAR IS BAD FOR YOU
© 2022 PAWS, INC. All Rights Reserved.
IT'S TRUE
Distributed by Andrews McMeel Syndication
I THREW MY BACK OUT PICKING UP A DONUT
JIM DAVIS 8-6

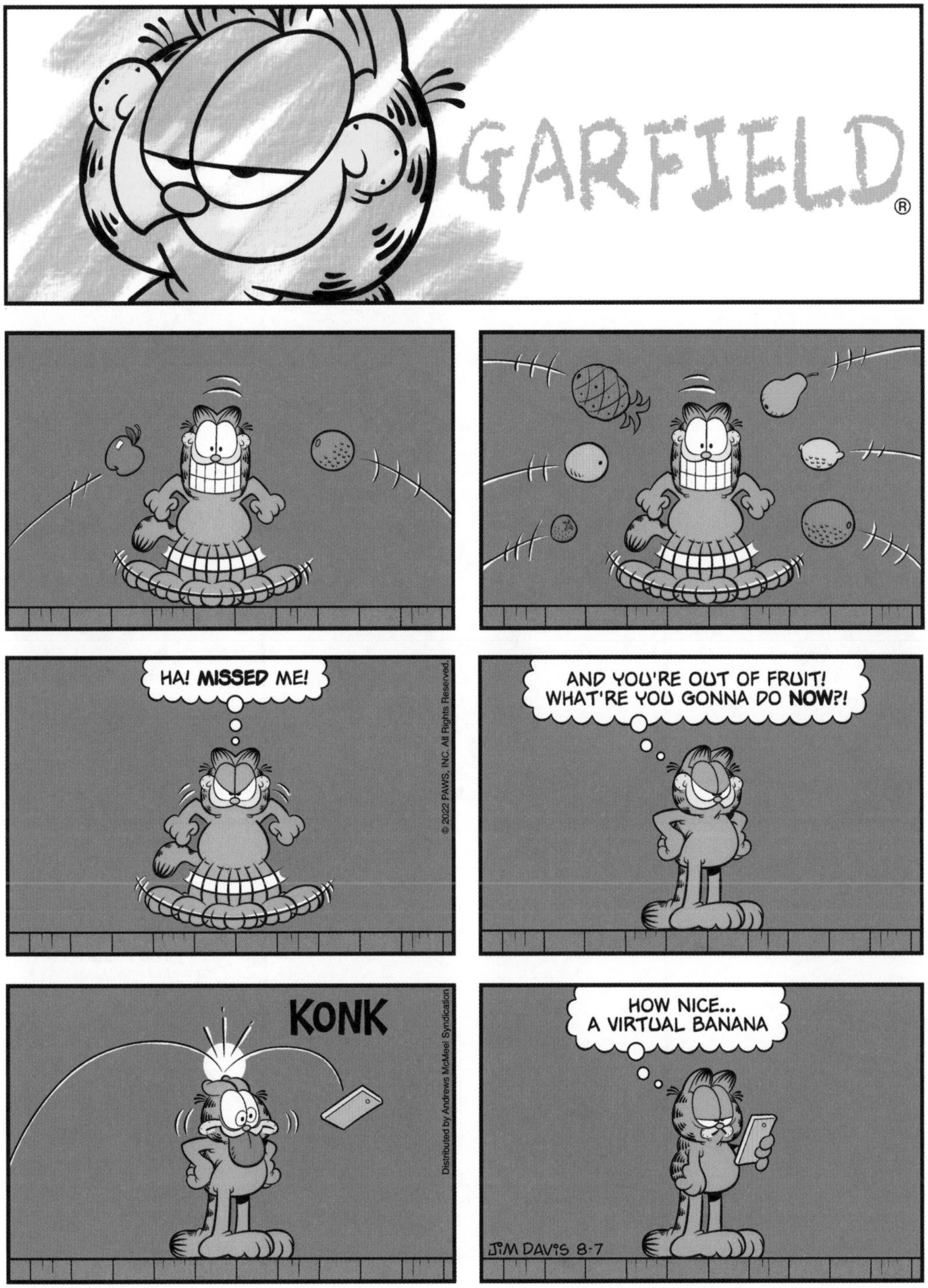
GARFIELD®
HA! MISSED ME!
AND YOU'RE OUT OF FRUIT! WHAT'RE YOU GONNA DO NOW?!
KONK
HOW NICE... A VIRTUAL BANANA
JIM DAVIS 8-7
© 2022 PAWS, INC. All Rights Reserved.
Distributed by Andrews McMeel Syndication

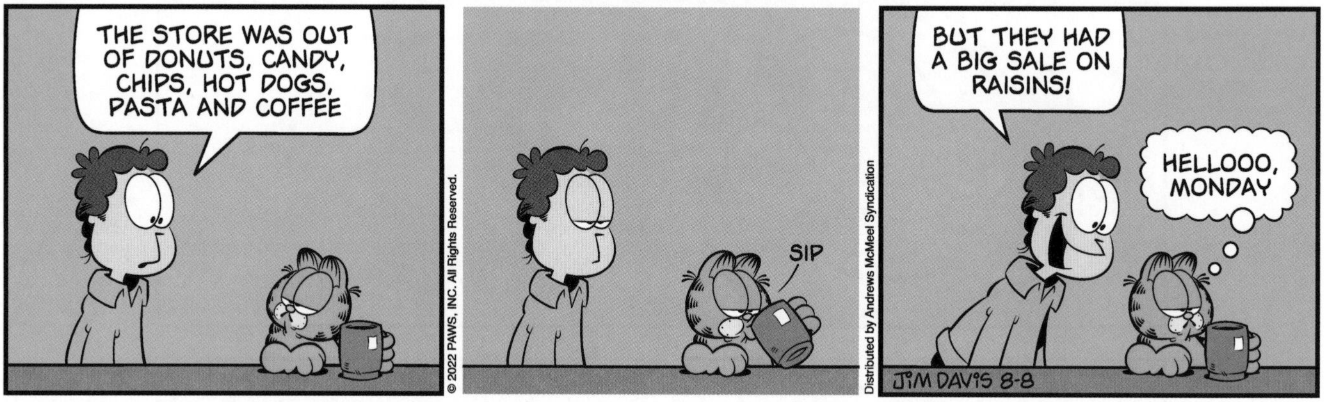
THE STORE WAS OUT OF DONUTS, CANDY, CHIPS, HOT DOGS, PASTA AND COFFEE
SIP
BUT THEY HAD A BIG SALE ON RAISINS!
HELLOOO, MONDAY
© 2022 PAWS, INC. All Rights Reserved.
Distributed by Andrews McMeel Syndication
JIM DAVIS 8-8

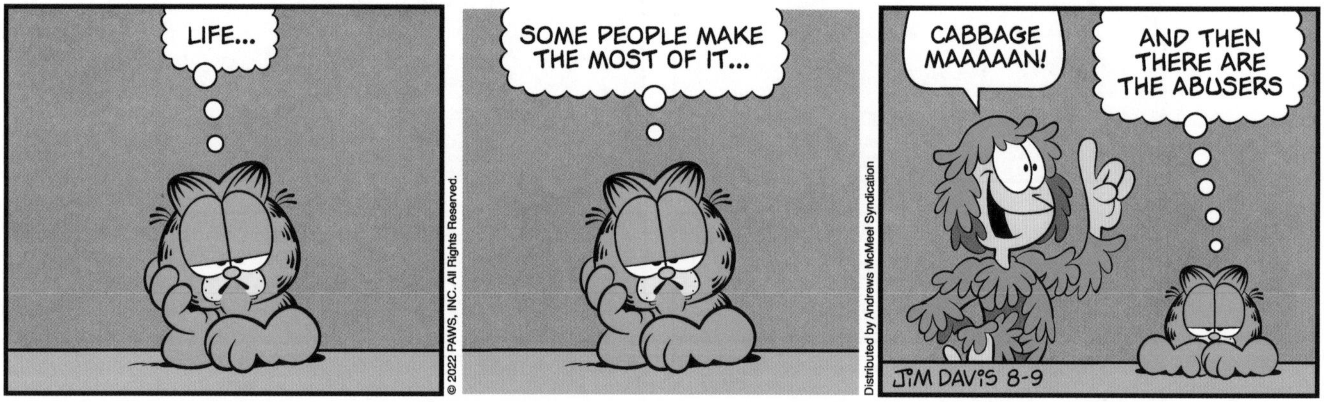
LIFE...
SOME PEOPLE MAKE THE MOST OF IT...
CABBAGE MAAAAAN!
AND THEN THERE ARE THE ABUSERS
© 2022 PAWS, INC. All Rights Reserved.
Distributed by Andrews McMeel Syndication
JIM DAVIS 8-9

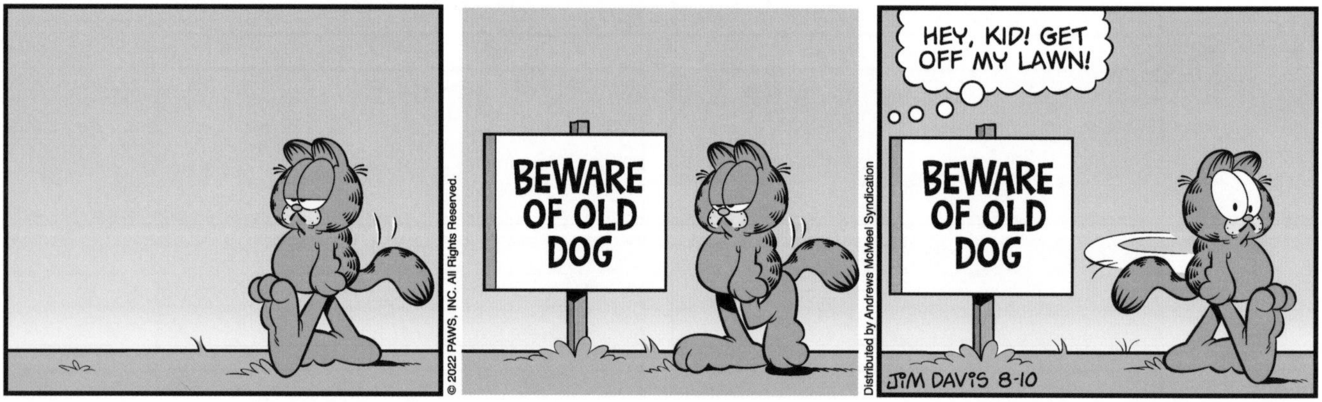
BEWARE OF OLD DOG
HEY, KID! GET OFF MY LAWN!
BEWARE OF OLD DOG
© 2022 PAWS, INC. All Rights Reserved.
Distributed by Andrews McMeel Syndication
JIM DAVIS 8-10

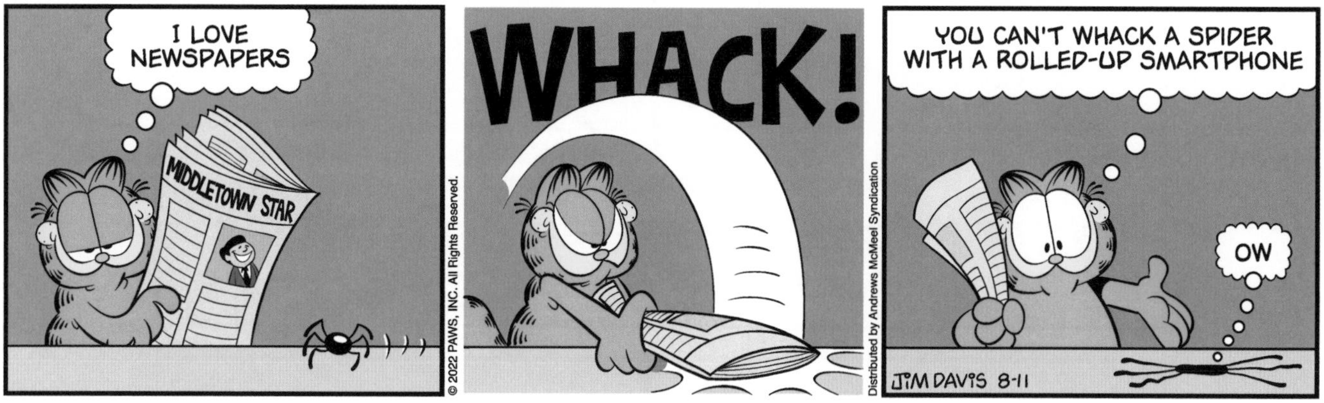
I LOVE NEWSPAPERS
MIDDLETOWN STAR
WHACK!
YOU CAN'T WHACK A SPIDER WITH A ROLLED-UP SMARTPHONE
OW
JIM DAVIS 8-11
© 2022 PAWS, INC. All Rights Reserved.
Distributed by Andrews McMeel Syndication

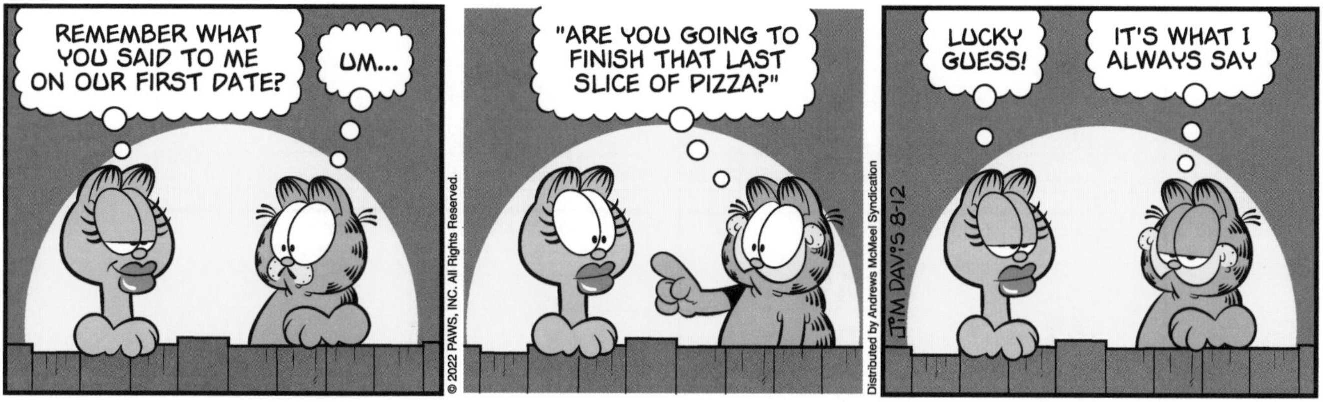
REMEMBER WHAT YOU SAID TO ME ON OUR FIRST DATE?
UM...
"ARE YOU GOING TO FINISH THAT LAST SLICE OF PIZZA?"
LUCKY GUESS!
IT'S WHAT I ALWAYS SAY
JIM DAVIS 8-12
© 2022 PAWS, INC. All Rights Reserved.
Distributed by Andrews McMeel Syndication

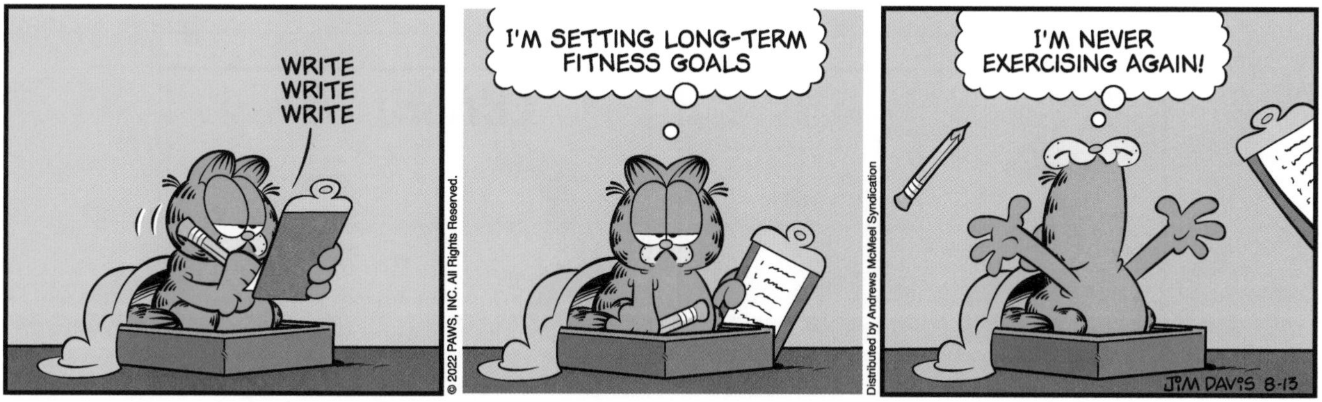
WRITE WRITE WRITE
I'M SETTING LONG-TERM FITNESS GOALS
I'M NEVER EXERCISING AGAIN!
JIM DAVIS 8-13
© 2022 PAWS, INC. All Rights Reserved.
Distributed by Andrews McMeel Syndication

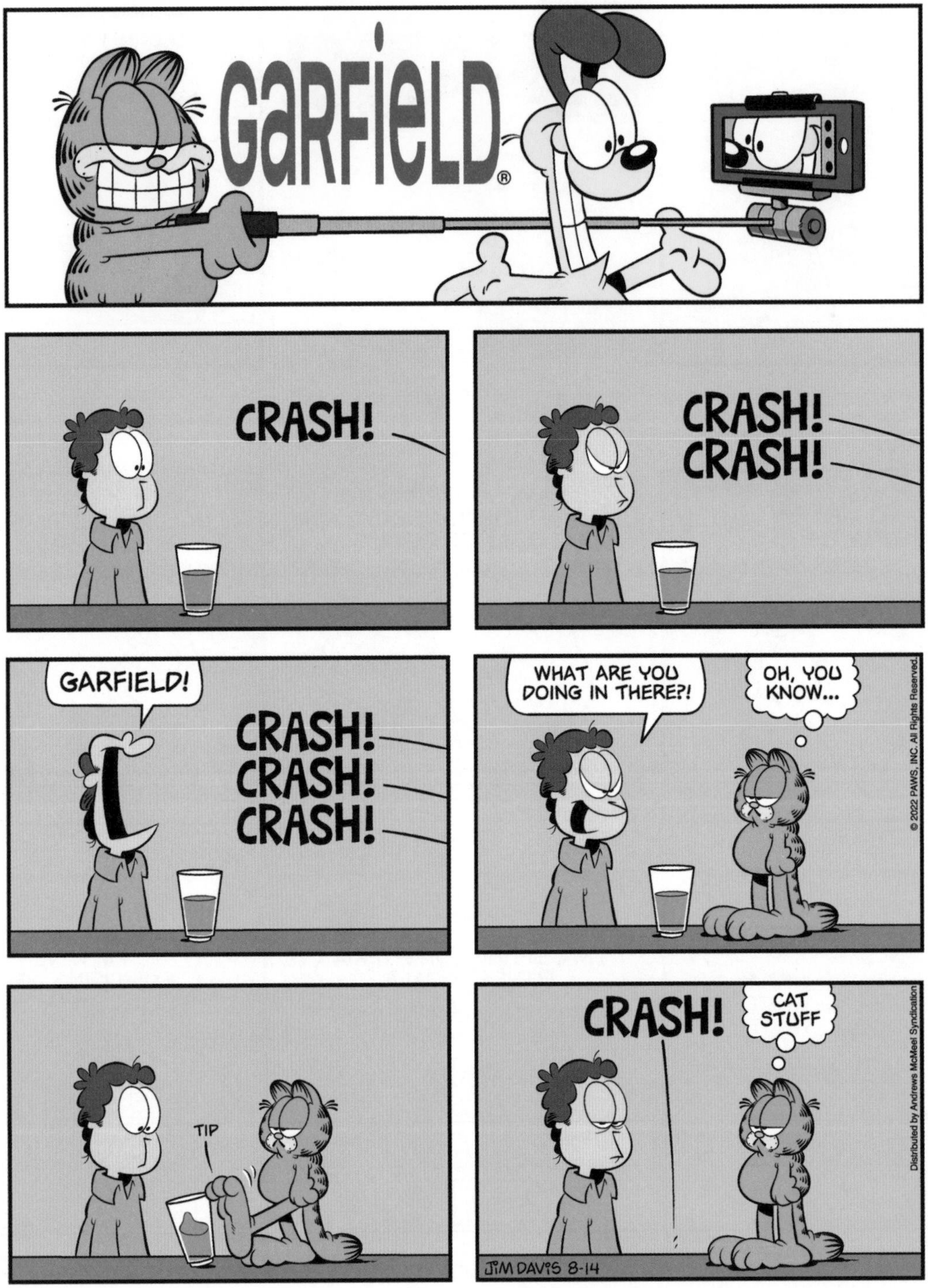
GARFIELD®
CRASH!
CRASH!
CRASH!
GARFIELD!
CRASH!
CRASH!
CRASH!
WHAT ARE YOU DOING IN THERE?!
OH, YOU KNOW...
TIP
CRASH!
CAT STUFF
JIM DAVIS 8-14
© 2022 PAWS, INC. All Rights Reserved.
Distributed by Andrews McMeel Syndication

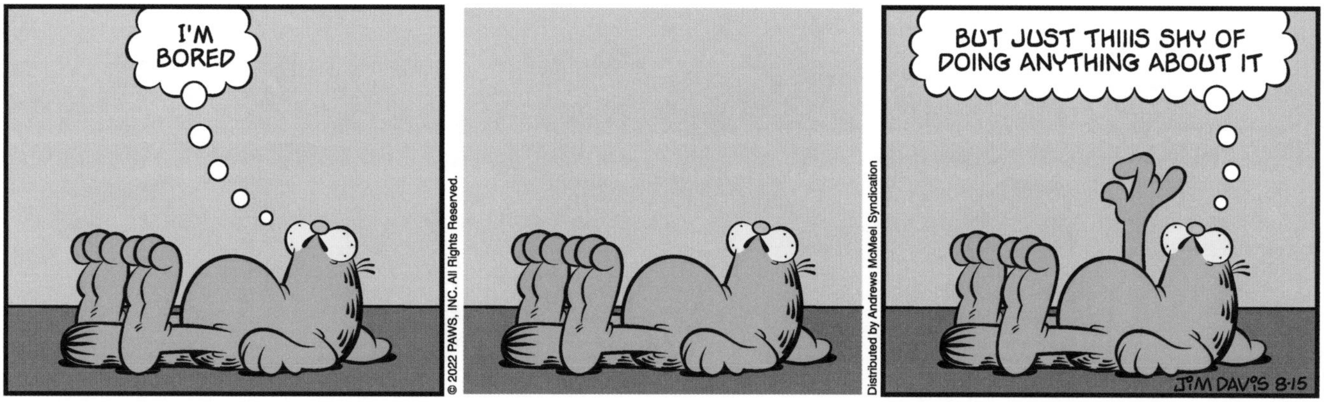
I'M BORED
© 2022 PAWS, INC. All Rights Reserved.
Distributed by Andrews McMeel Syndication
BUT JUST THIIIS SHY OF DOING ANYTHING ABOUT IT
JIM DAVIS 8-15

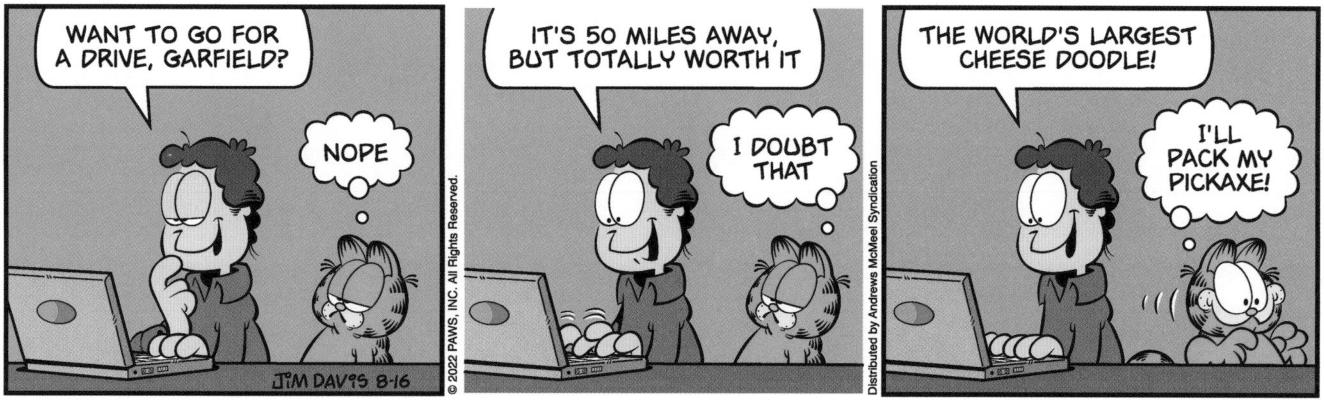
WANT TO GO FOR A DRIVE, GARFIELD?
NOPE
JIM DAVIS 8-16
© 2022 PAWS, INC. All Rights Reserved.
IT'S 50 MILES AWAY, BUT TOTALLY WORTH IT
I DOUBT THAT
Distributed by Andrews McMeel Syndication
THE WORLD'S LARGEST CHEESE DOODLE!
I'LL PACK MY PICKAXE!

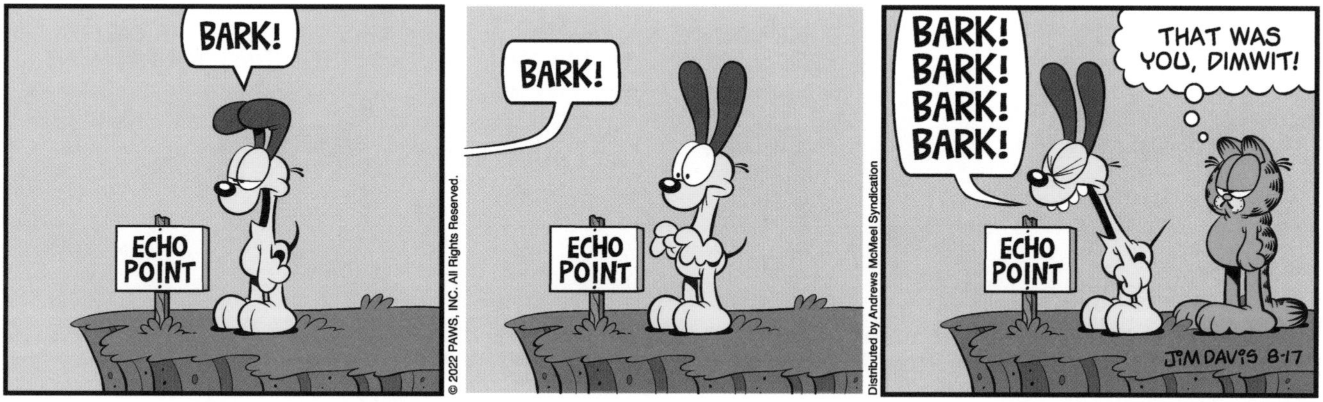
BARK!
ECHO POINT
© 2022 PAWS, INC. All Rights Reserved.
BARK!
ECHO POINT
Distributed by Andrews McMeel Syndication
BARK! BARK! BARK! BARK!
THAT WAS YOU, DIMWIT!
ECHO POINT
JIM DAVIS 8-17

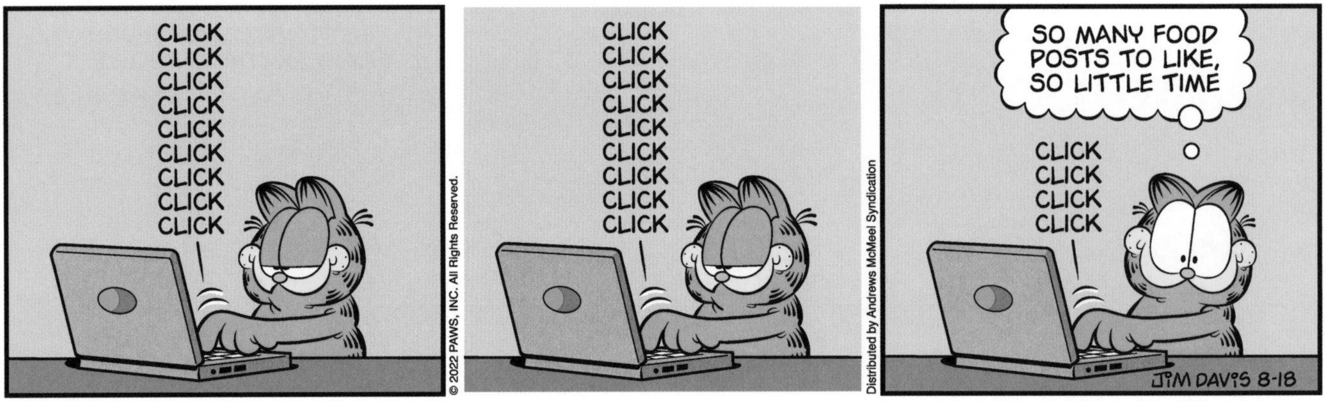
CLICK CLICK CLICK CLICK CLICK CLICK CLICK CLICK CLICK
CLICK CLICK CLICK CLICK CLICK CLICK CLICK CLICK CLICK
SO MANY FOOD POSTS TO LIKE, SO LITTLE TIME
CLICK CLICK CLICK CLICK
JIM DAVIS 8-18
© 2022 PAWS, INC. All Rights Reserved.
Distributed by Andrews McMeel Syndication

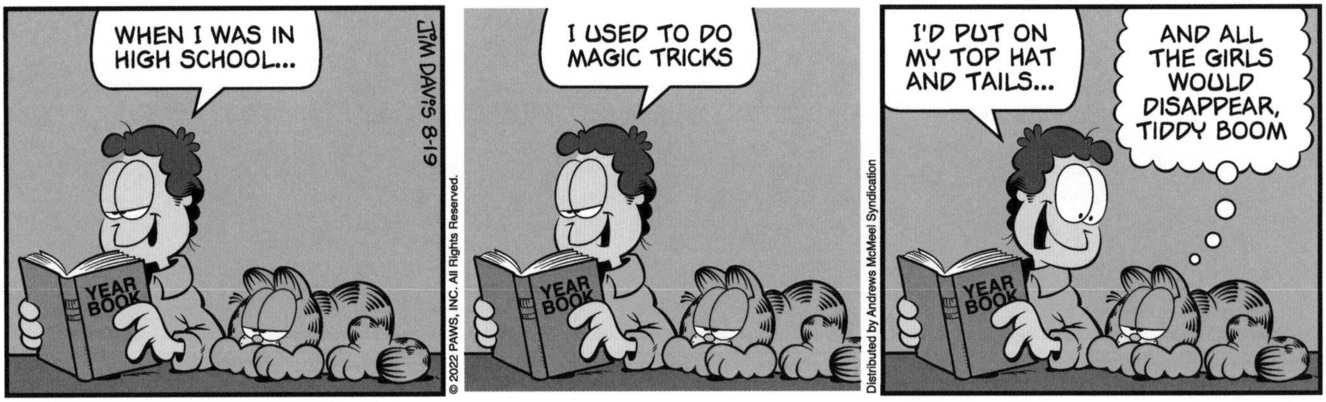
WHEN I WAS IN HIGH SCHOOL...
JIM DAVIS 8-19
YEAR BOOK
I USED TO DO MAGIC TRICKS
I'D PUT ON MY TOP HAT AND TAILS...
AND ALL THE GIRLS WOULD DISAPPEAR, TIDDY BOOM
© 2022 PAWS, INC. All Rights Reserved.
Distributed by Andrews McMeel Syndication

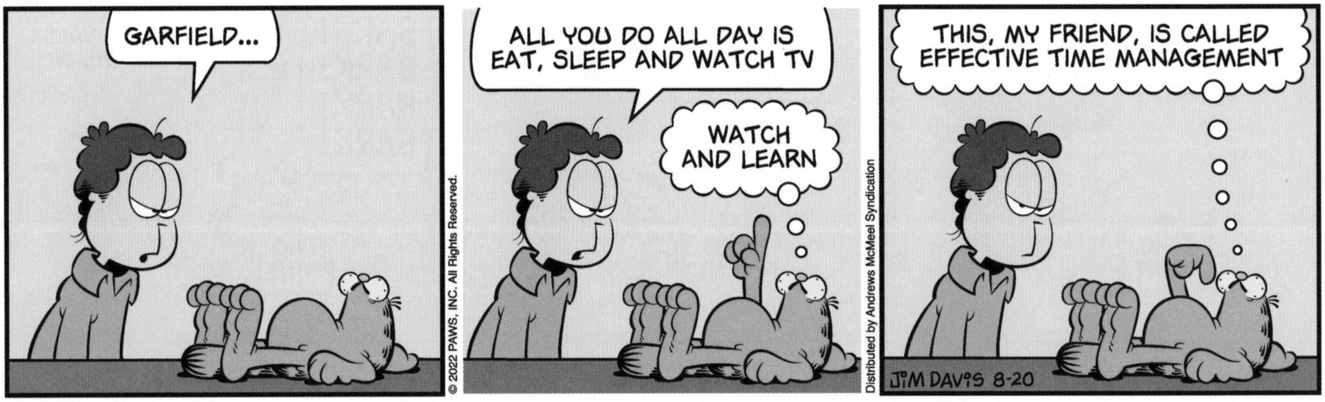
GARFIELD...
ALL YOU DO ALL DAY IS EAT, SLEEP AND WATCH TV
WATCH AND LEARN
THIS, MY FRIEND, IS CALLED EFFECTIVE TIME MANAGEMENT
JIM DAVIS 8-20
© 2022 PAWS, INC. All Rights Reserved.
Distributed by Andrews McMeel Syndication

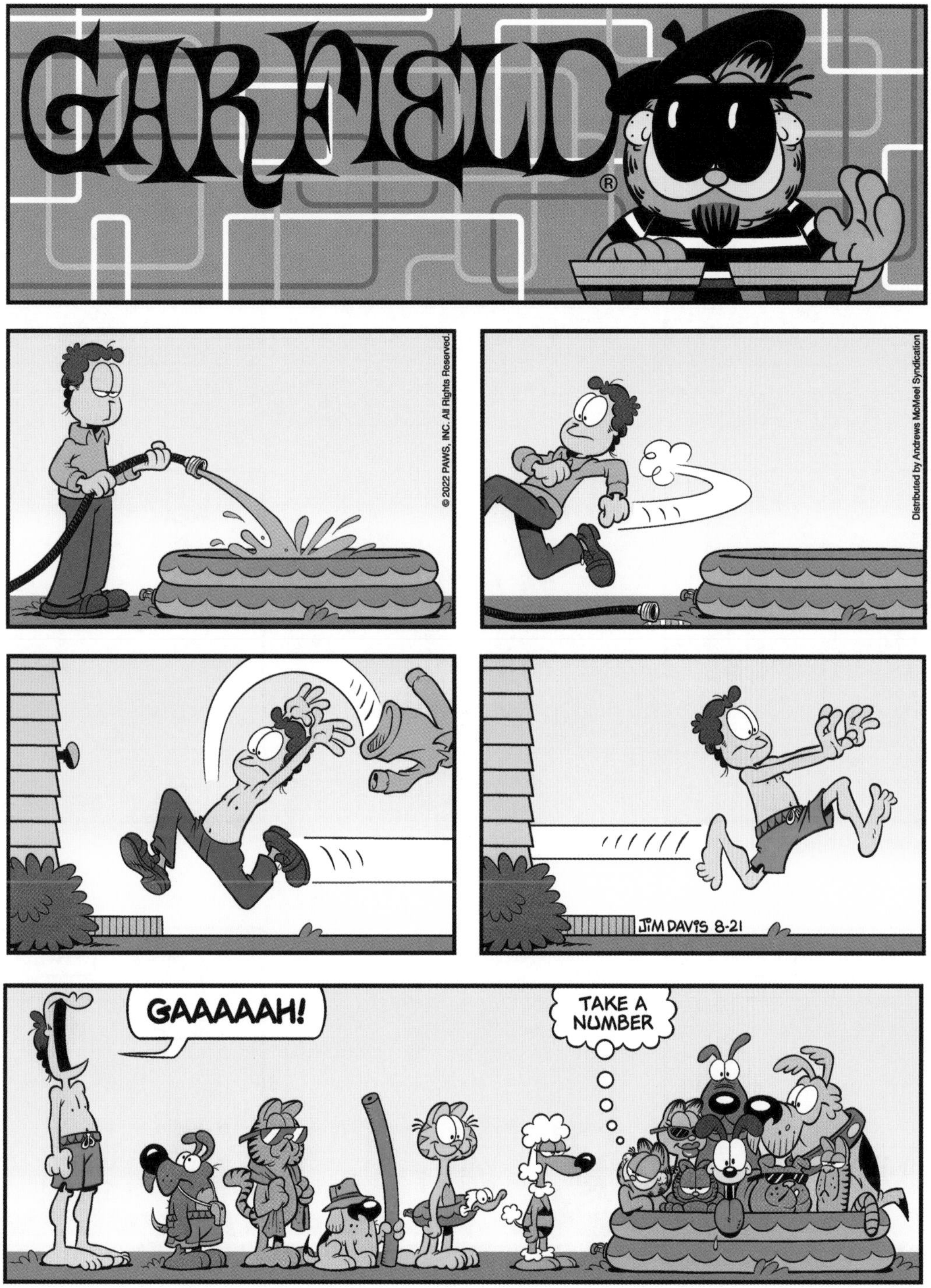

GARFIELD®
© 2022 PAWS, INC. All Rights Reserved.
Distributed by Andrews McMeel Syndication
JIM DAVIS 8-21
GAAAAAH!
TAKE A NUMBER

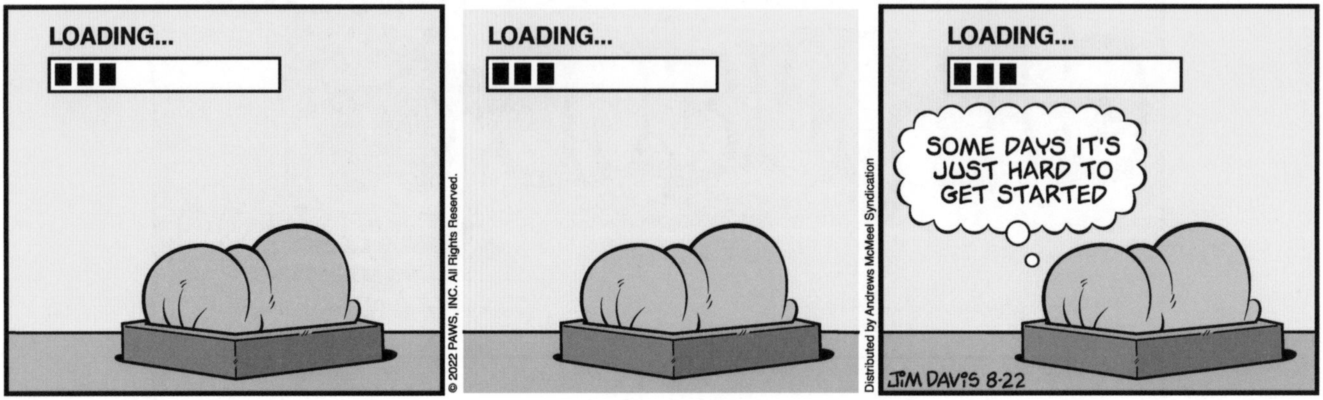
LOADING...
LOADING...
LOADING...
SOME DAYS IT'S JUST HARD TO GET STARTED
JIM DAVIS 8-22
© 2022 PAWS, INC. All Rights Reserved.
Distributed by Andrews McMeel Syndication

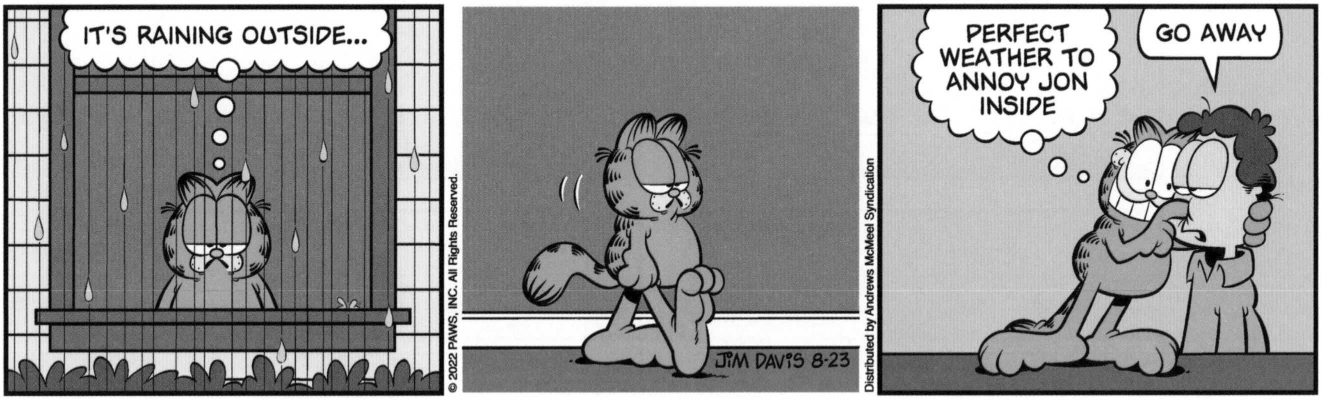
IT'S RAINING OUTSIDE...
JIM DAVIS 8-23
PERFECT WEATHER TO ANNOY JON INSIDE
GO AWAY
© 2022 PAWS, INC. All Rights Reserved.
Distributed by Andrews McMeel Syndication

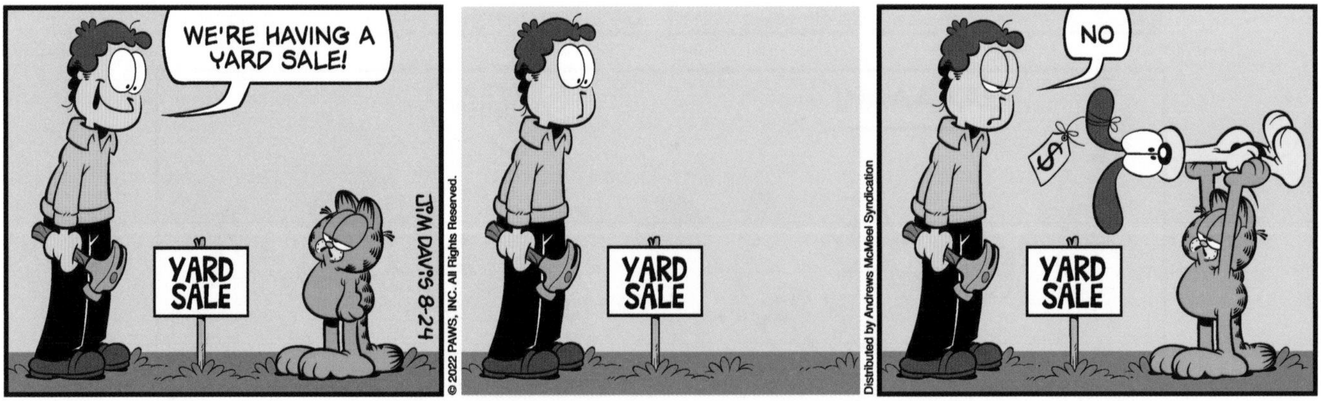
WE'RE HAVING A YARD SALE!
YARD SALE
JIM DAVIS 8-24
YARD SALE
NO
YARD SALE
© 2022 PAWS, INC. All Rights Reserved.
Distributed by Andrews McMeel Syndication

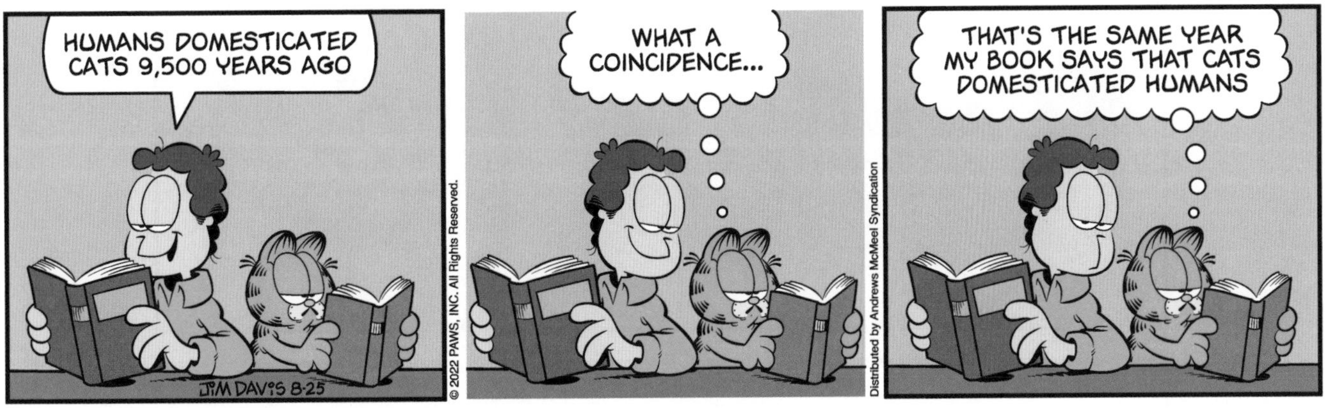
HUMANS DOMESTICATED CATS 9,500 YEARS AGO
JIM DAVIS 8-25
© 2022 PAWS, INC. All Rights Reserved.
WHAT A COINCIDENCE...
Distributed by Andrews McMeel Syndication
THAT'S THE SAME YEAR MY BOOK SAYS THAT CATS DOMESTICATED HUMANS

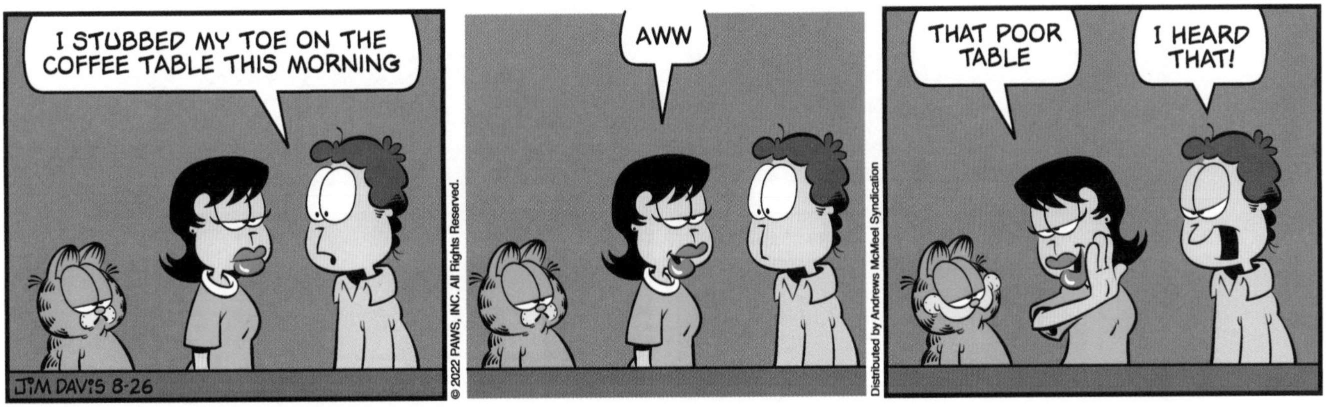
I STUBBED MY TOE ON THE COFFEE TABLE THIS MORNING
JIM DAVIS 8-26
© 2022 PAWS, INC. All Rights Reserved.
AWW
Distributed by Andrews McMeel Syndication
THAT POOR TABLE
I HEARD THAT!

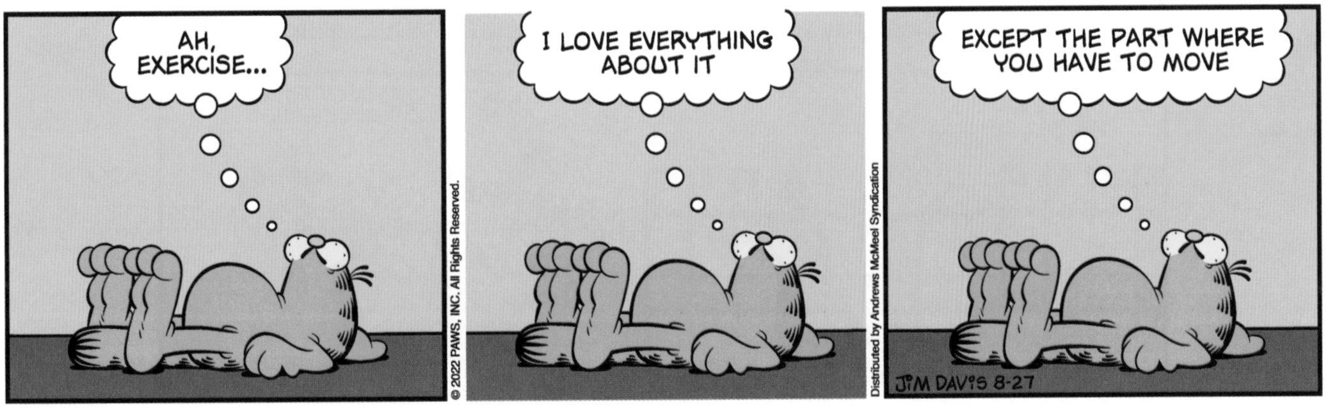
AH, EXERCISE...
© 2022 PAWS, INC. All Rights Reserved.
I LOVE EVERYTHING ABOUT IT
Distributed by Andrews McMeel Syndication
EXCEPT THE PART WHERE YOU HAVE TO MOVE
JIM DAVIS 8-27

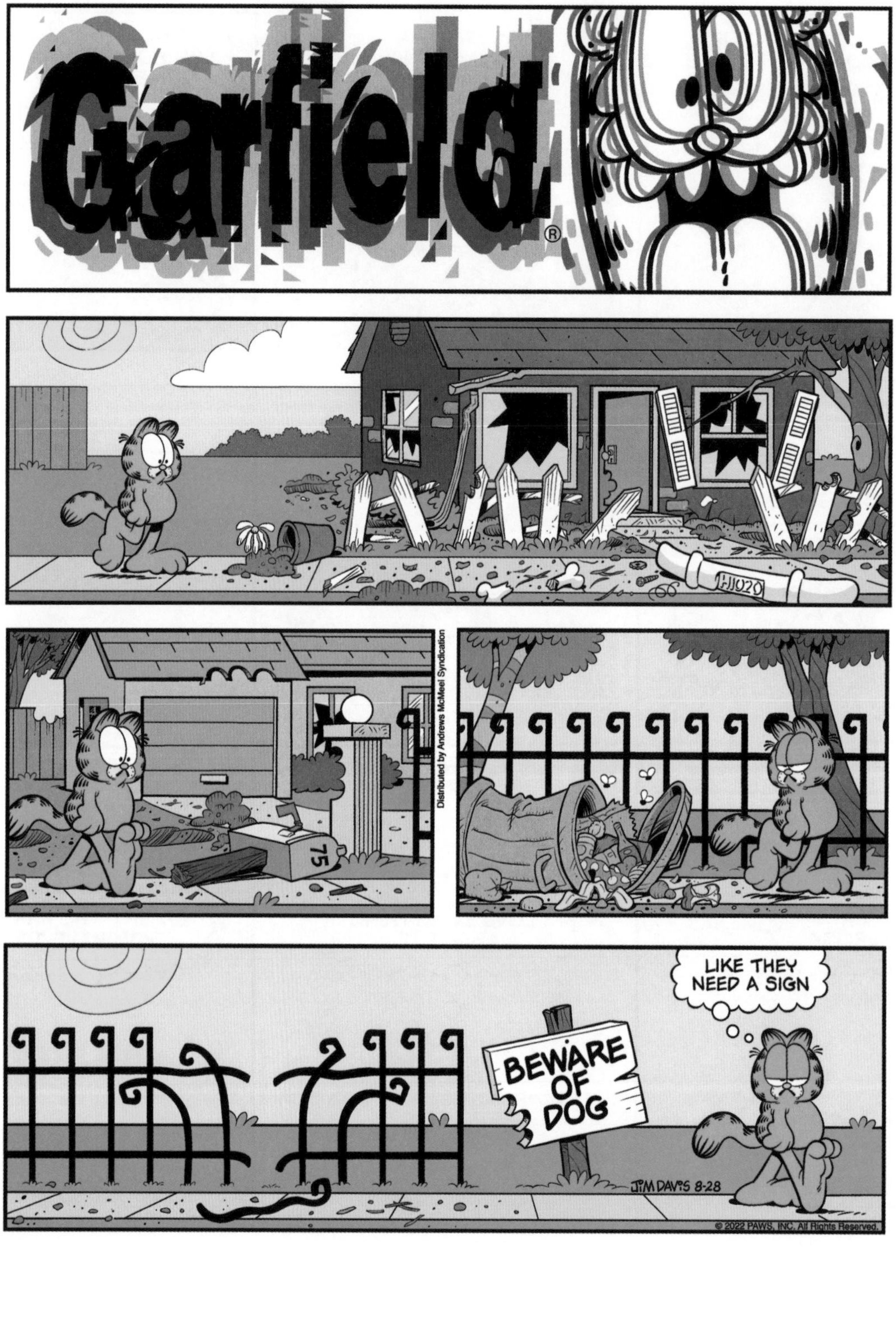
Garfield®
HI020
Distributed by Andrews McMeel Syndication
75
LIKE THEY NEED A SIGN
BEWARE OF DOG
JIM DAVIS 8-28
© 2022 PAWS, INC. All Rights Reserved.

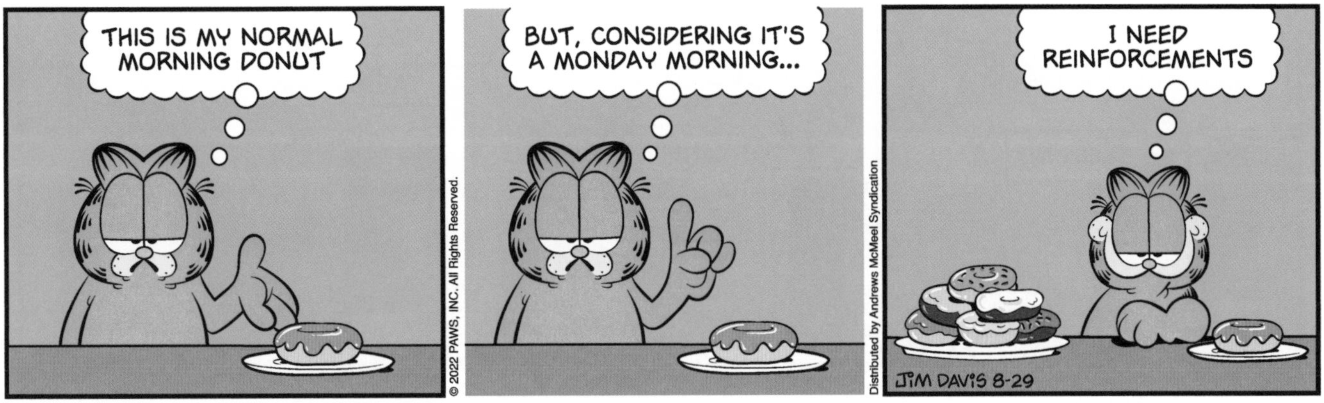
THIS IS MY NORMAL MORNING DONUT
BUT, CONSIDERING IT'S A MONDAY MORNING...
I NEED REINFORCEMENTS
JIM DAVIS 8-29

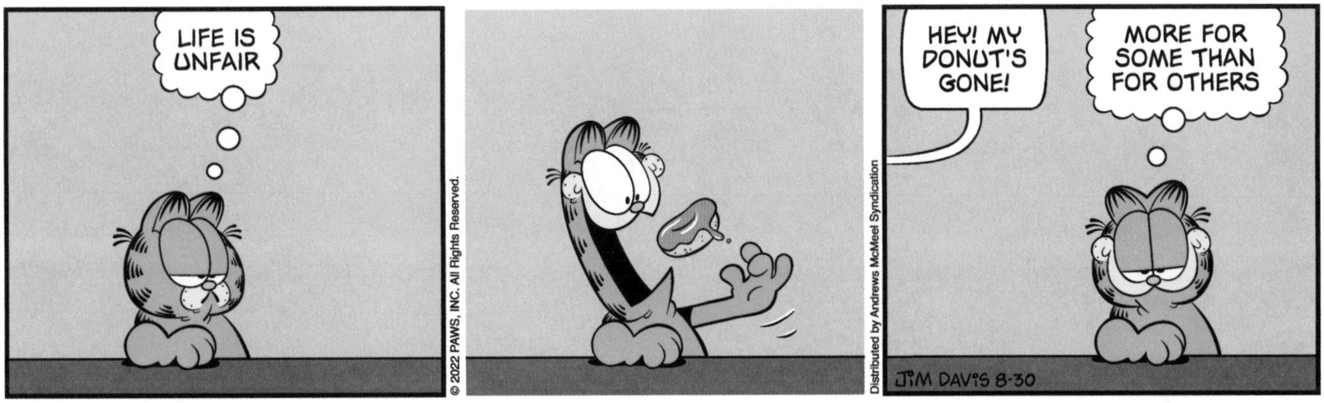
LIFE IS UNFAIR
HEY! MY DONUT'S GONE!
MORE FOR SOME THAN FOR OTHERS
JIM DAVIS 8-30

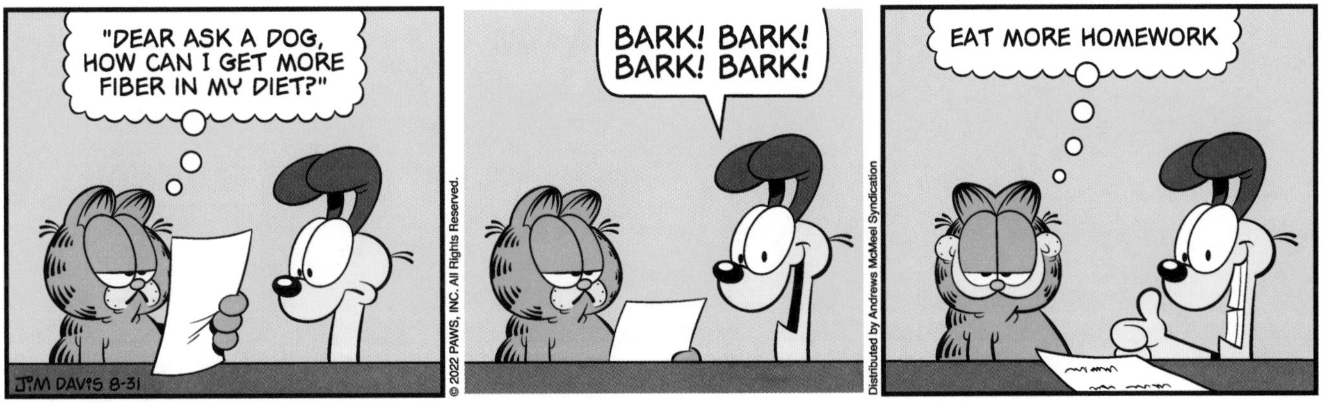
"DEAR ASK A DOG, HOW CAN I GET MORE FIBER IN MY DIET?"
JIM DAVIS 8-31
BARK! BARK! BARK! BARK!
EAT MORE HOMEWORK

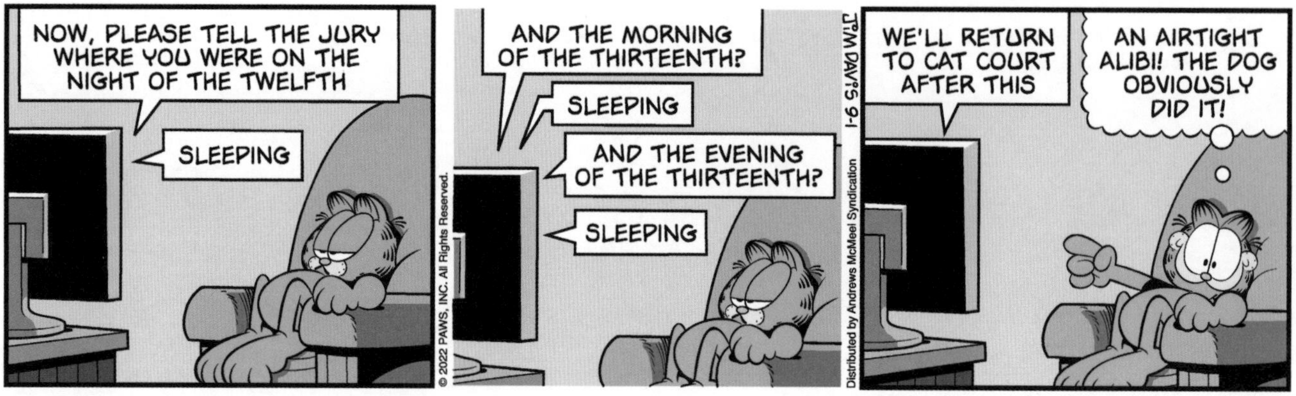
NOW, PLEASE TELL THE JURY WHERE YOU WERE ON THE NIGHT OF THE TWELFTH
SLEEPING
AND THE MORNING OF THE THIRTEENTH?
SLEEPING
AND THE EVENING OF THE THIRTEENTH?
SLEEPING
© 2022 PAWS, INC. All Rights Reserved.
JIM DAVIS 9-1
Distributed by Andrews McMeel Syndication
WE'LL RETURN TO CAT COURT AFTER THIS
AN AIRTIGHT ALIBI! THE DOG OBVIOUSLY DID IT!

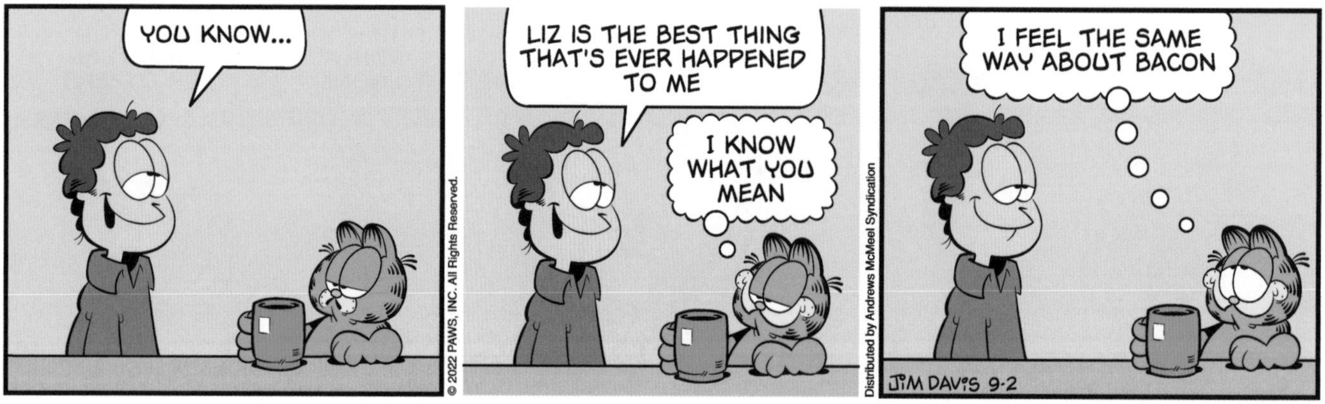
YOU KNOW...
LIZ IS THE BEST THING THAT'S EVER HAPPENED TO ME
I KNOW WHAT YOU MEAN
© 2022 PAWS, INC. All Rights Reserved.
Distributed by Andrews McMeel Syndication
I FEEL THE SAME WAY ABOUT BACON
JIM DAVIS 9-2

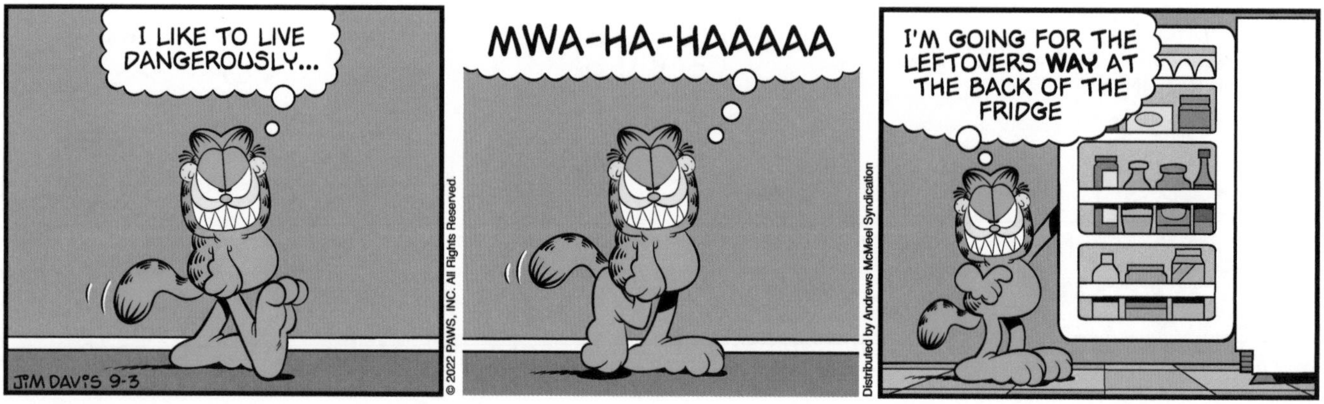
I LIKE TO LIVE DANGEROUSLY...
JIM DAVIS 9-3
MWA-HA-HAAAAA
© 2022 PAWS, INC. All Rights Reserved.
Distributed by Andrews McMeel Syndication
I'M GOING FOR THE LEFTOVERS **WAY** AT THE BACK OF THE FRIDGE

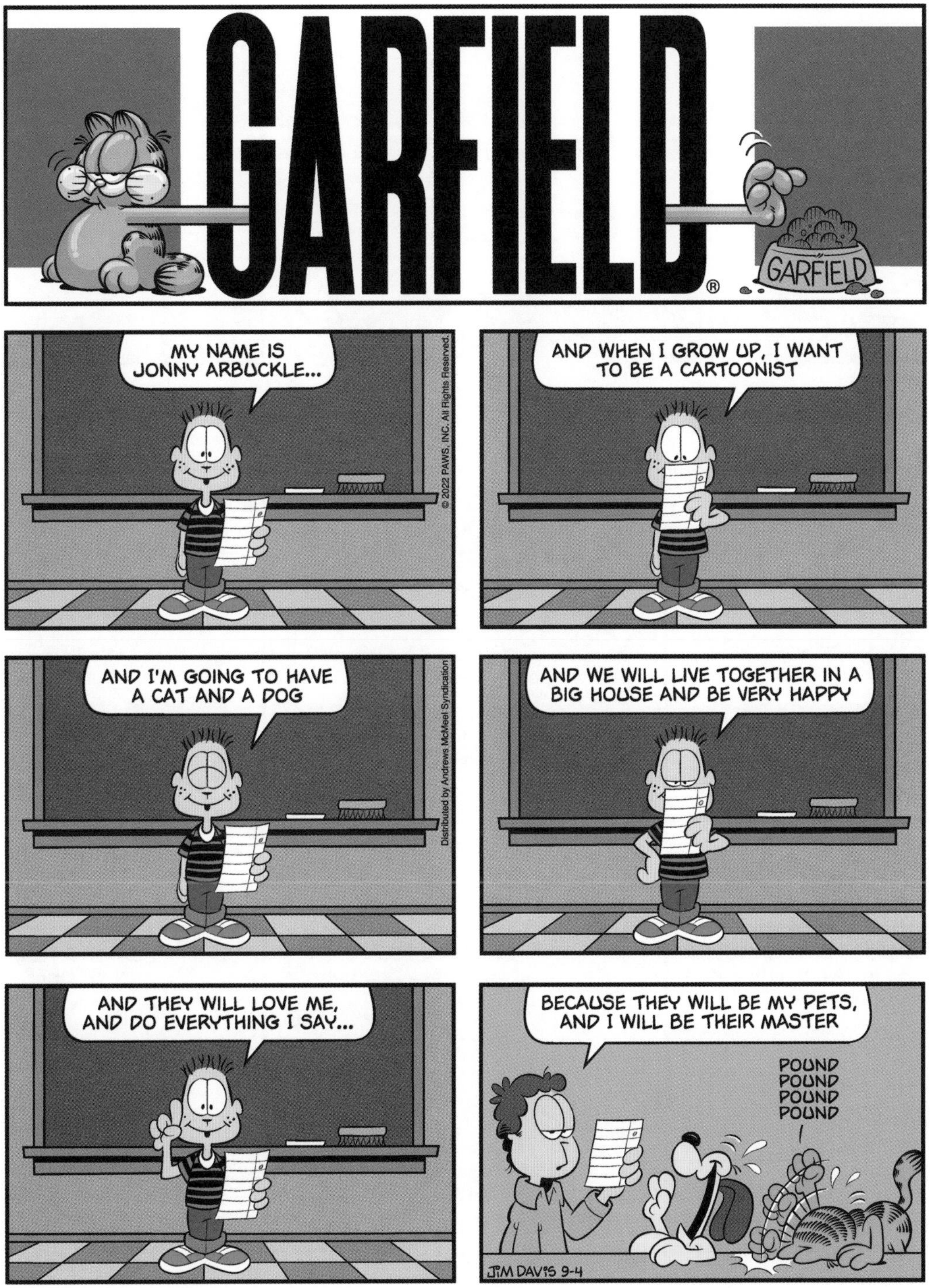
GARFIELD®
GARFIELD
MY NAME IS JONNY ARBUCKLE...
© 2022 PAWS, INC. All Rights Reserved.
AND WHEN I GROW UP, I WANT TO BE A CARTOONIST
AND I'M GOING TO HAVE A CAT AND A DOG
Distributed by Andrews McMeel Syndication
AND WE WILL LIVE TOGETHER IN A BIG HOUSE AND BE VERY HAPPY
AND THEY WILL LOVE ME, AND DO EVERYTHING I SAY...
BECAUSE THEY WILL BE MY PETS, AND I WILL BE THEIR MASTER
POUND POUND POUND POUND
JIM DAVIS 9-4

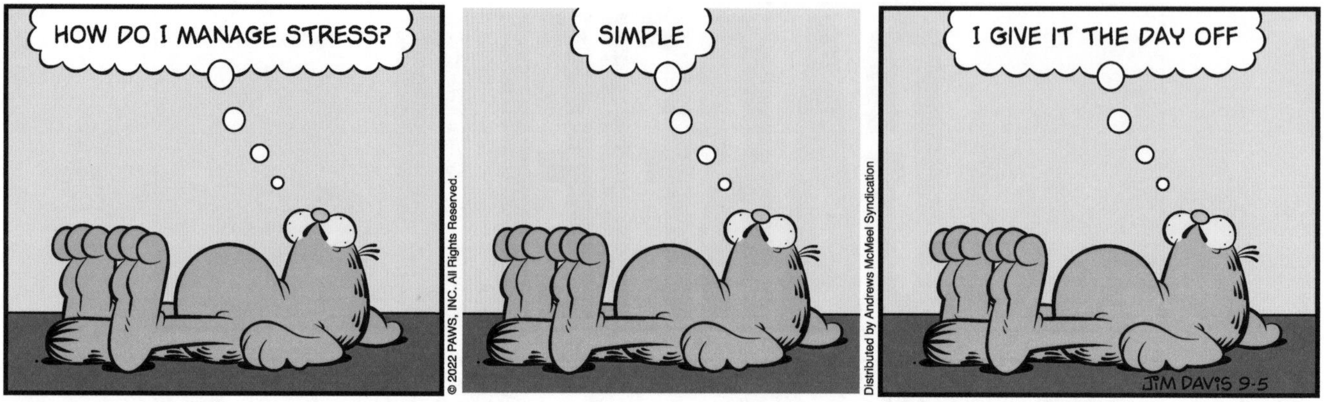
HOW DO I MANAGE STRESS?
SIMPLE
I GIVE IT THE DAY OFF
JIM DAVIS 9-5
© 2022 PAWS, INC. All Rights Reserved.
Distributed by Andrews McMeel Syndication

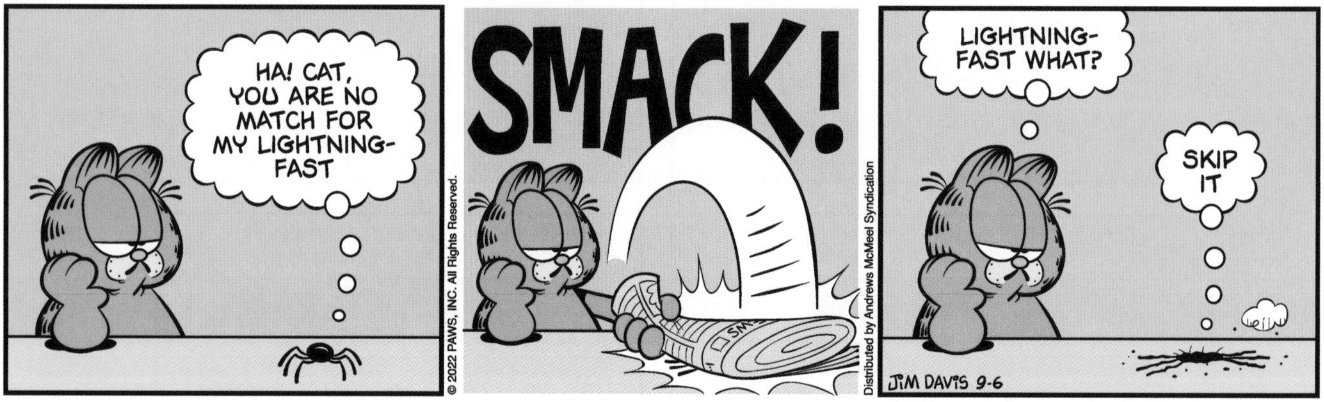
HA! CAT, YOU ARE NO MATCH FOR MY LIGHTNING-FAST
SMACK!
LIGHTNING-FAST WHAT?
SKIP IT
JIM DAVIS 9-6
© 2022 PAWS, INC. All Rights Reserved.
Distributed by Andrews McMeel Syndication

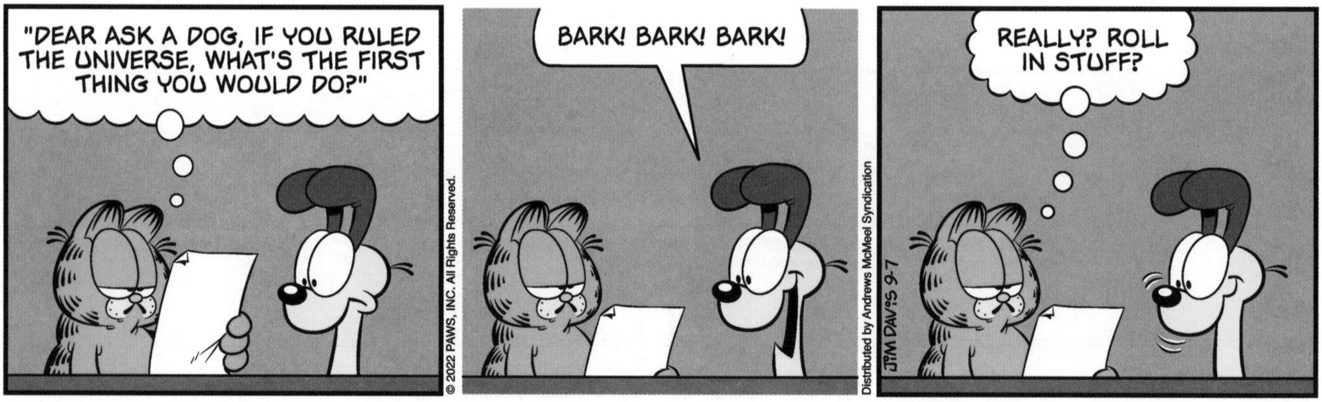
"DEAR ASK A DOG, IF YOU RULED THE UNIVERSE, WHAT'S THE FIRST THING YOU WOULD DO?"
BARK! BARK! BARK!
REALLY? ROLL IN STUFF?
JIM DAVIS 9-7
© 2022 PAWS, INC. All Rights Reserved.
Distributed by Andrews McMeel Syndication

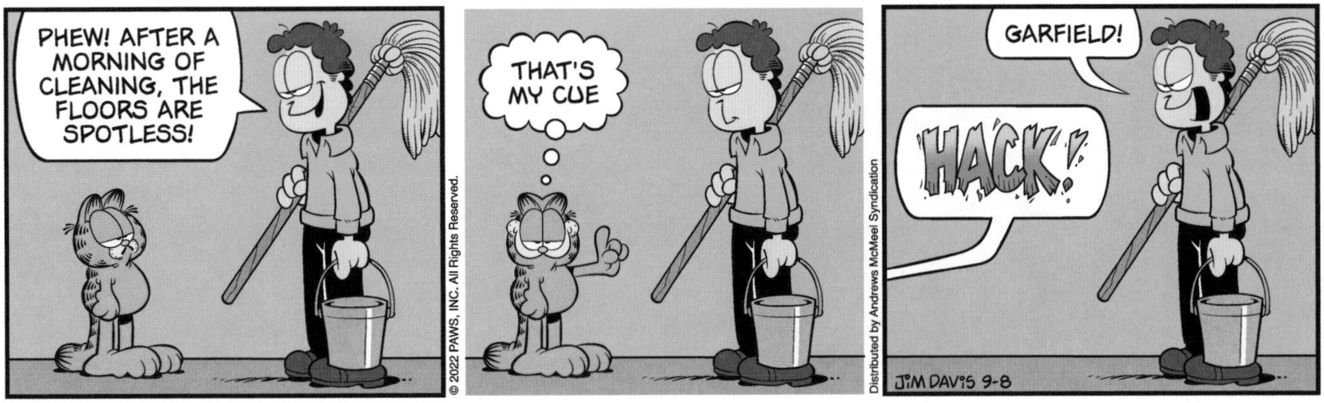
PHEW! AFTER A MORNING OF CLEANING, THE FLOORS ARE SPOTLESS!
THAT'S MY CUE
GARFIELD!
HACK!
© 2022 PAWS, INC. All Rights Reserved.
Distributed by Andrews McMeel Syndication
JIM DAVIS 9-8

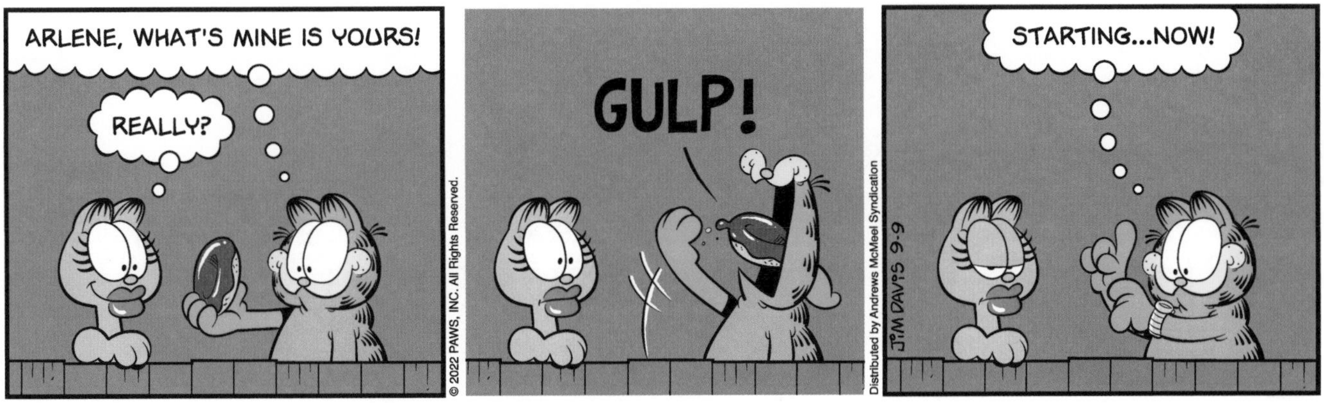
ARLENE, WHAT'S MINE IS YOURS!
REALLY?
GULP!
STARTING...NOW!
© 2022 PAWS, INC. All Rights Reserved.
Distributed by Andrews McMeel Syndication
JIM DAVIS 9-9

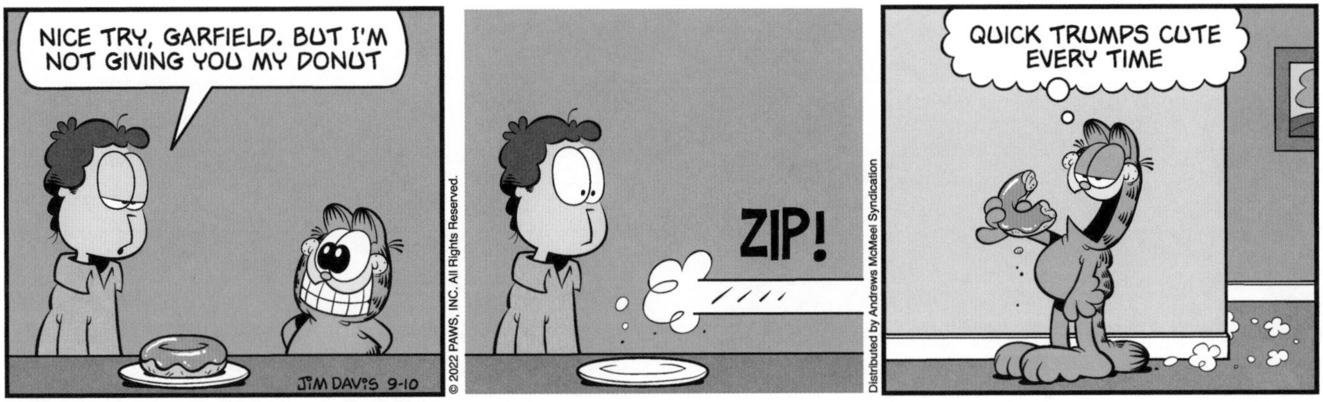
NICE TRY, GARFIELD. BUT I'M NOT GIVING YOU MY DONUT
ZIP!
QUICK TRUMPS CUTE EVERY TIME
© 2022 PAWS, INC. All Rights Reserved.
Distributed by Andrews McMeel Syndication
JIM DAVIS 9-10

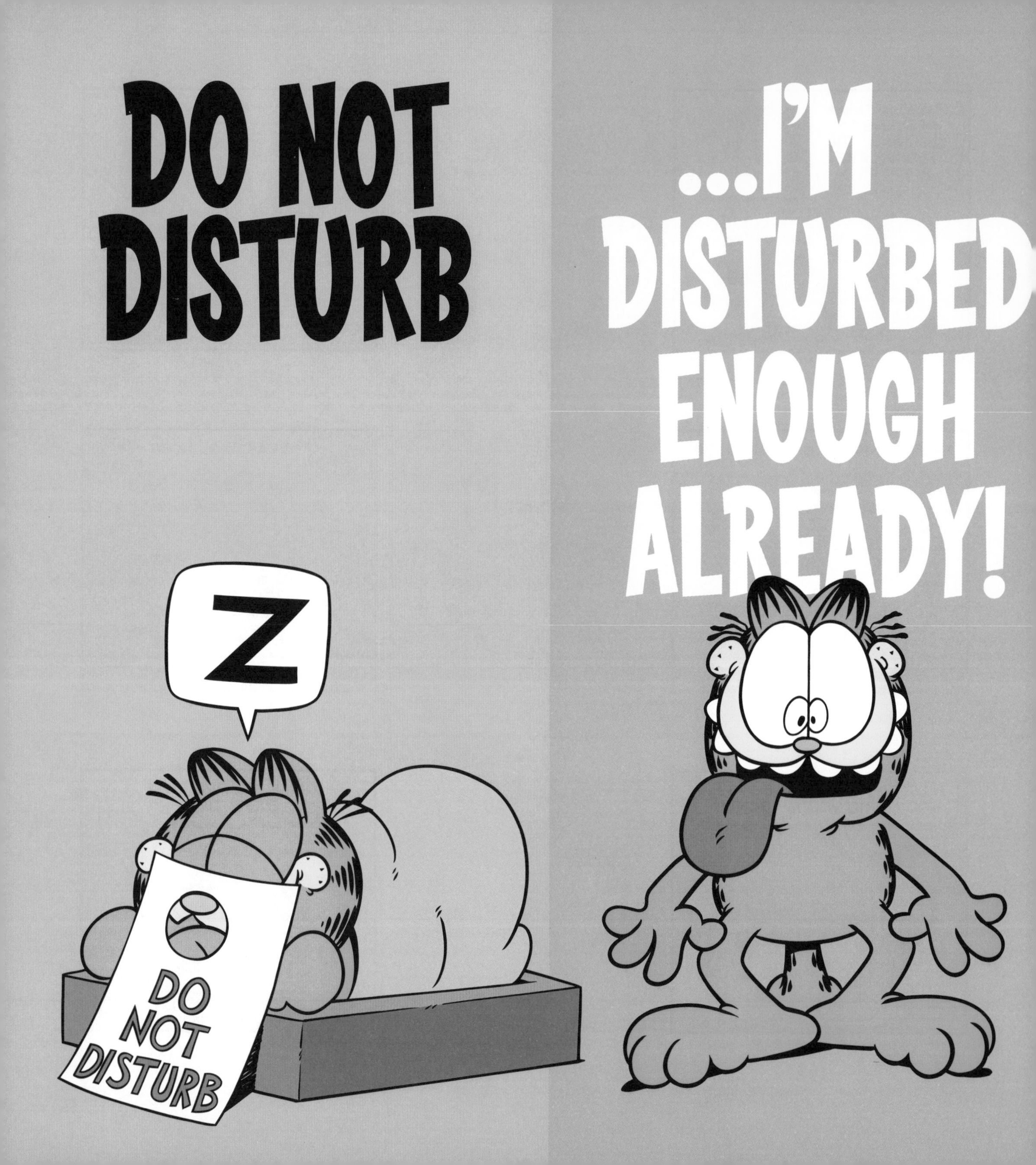
DO NOT DISTURB
Z
DO NOT DISTURB
...I'M DISTURBED ENOUGH ALREADY!